The Energy Edge

The Energy Edge

PAMELA M. SMITH, R.D.

LifeLine
Press

A Regnery Publishing Company • Washington, DC

Library of Congress Cataloging-in-Publication Data

Smith, Pamela M.
    The energy edge / Pamela M. Smith.
        p.   cm.
    ISBN 0–89526-331-9
    1. Health—Popular works.   2. Nutrition—Popular works.
    3. Fatigue—Popular works.   I. Title.
    RA776.S648   1999
    613—dc21   98–52980
                                                                                   CIP

Published in the United States by
LifeLine Press
An Eagle Publishing Company
One Massachusetts Avenue NW
Washington, DC 20001

Distributed to the trade by
National Book Network
4720-A Boston Way
Lanham, MD 20706

Printed on acid-free paper.
Manufactured in the United States of America

BOOK DESIGN BY MARJA WALKER
SET IN BERLING ROMAN

10 9 8 7 6 5 4 3 2 1

Books are available in quantity for promotional or premium use. Write to Director of Special Sales, LifeLine Press, One Massachusetts Avenue, NW, Washington, DC 20001, for information on discounts and terms or call (202) 216-0600.

Dedicated to my husband, Larry
for your love
for your passion to invest in things that count
for your desire to live forever more on the Energy Edge.

Contents

Acknowledgments

I am deeply grateful to so many people who have been my cheerleaders and encouragers—my family and friends are a "treasure of life" for me.

Special thanks to the incredible staff at LifeLine Press—you have given of your creativity and time in phenomenal ways. To Richard Vigilante—thank you for helping to shape my vision for this book, and wanting it to be.

To Jennifer, Marja, Erica, and Duffy—your help has been invaluable… thank you so much!

Special thanks to Traci Mullins for your wonderful touch… and energy!

And special thanks to Debbie Cole, Ned Heath, Jenny Phillips, and Dr. Chris Chappel for allowing me to "sound out" *The Energy Edge*.

PART ONE

The energy crisis

CHAPTER ONE

So tired of being tired

Her day starts early—very early—and she wakes up tired. The alarm goes off at 4:45 AM, and the morning routine gets started: kids out of bed and out the door, lunches packed, and the schedule packed fuller still. "By 8 in the morning, I'm already exhausted and feeling like I've already put in a full day; then I realize I have a full day ahead of me!" forty-two-year-old Sara laments. "By 5 PM, the time I want to be at my best for the people I love, I'm exhausted, cranky, and craving sweets. By 8:30 in the evening, I'm on the couch in a coma. I do sleep at night, but wake up in the morning just as tired. I don't just want energy, I *need* energy. I just don't think I can go on this way!"

Sara, a working mother of two teenagers, is not alone. Her plea for energy may sound like your own.

Or maybe *this* sounds like you: You're waiting for an elevator to get to that meeting that began ten minutes ago. You wait, and wait—the car seems to be forever stopped on the seventh floor. You glance at your watch and make a sudden decision to go for the stairs. After all, you're only going to climb five flights—no big deal. And it *is* no big deal—till you find yourself out of breath by the third landing. By the time you get to the meeting room, you have to stand outside for several more minutes just to get back to normal breathing and the ability for conversation. Yet, you're dripping with perspiration and aware that your face is quite red. Whatever happened to that robust health and boundless energy you took for granted not so long ago? Never mind where it went—*how can you get it back?*

Is Fatigue In Control?

You may be like millions of Americans who unknowingly allow fatigue to control their lives. Sure, you know you're tired and could use more energy, but you don't realize how much the power drain is negatively affecting the quality of your life. Consider the warning signs by asking yourself these questions:

❖ *Am I always tired, even after a full night's rest?*
❖ *Am I irritable at certain times of the day?*
❖ *Do I have trouble thinking clearly and remembering things?*
❖ *Have I gained weight, or had trouble losing it?*
❖ *Does my mind fog when I'm forced to make quick decisions?*
❖ *Do I feel as though I've lost my sense of humor?*
❖ *Am I picking up colds and flus more often?*
❖ *Do I wake up in the middle of the night, unable to get*
  back to restful sleep?
❖ *Do I have difficulty staying consistent with an exercise routine?*
❖ *Do I crave sweets much of the time?*
❖ *Do I struggle with depression?*

Although we may associate the desire to be a couch potato with a lack of energy, we aren't so used to linking mental confusion, short-term memory loss, irritability, lowered immunity, insomnia, mood swings, sweets cravings, even a difficulty with losing weight and staying with an exercise plan, with a lack of energy. Yet this void affects every part of our life—physical, emotional, relational, and spiritual. We have just become accustomed to feeling bad.

In my work as a nutritionist and wellness coach, I see clients from all walks of life—top executives, professional athletes, homemakers, ministers, college students, teachers, retirees—and they all have a similar heartfelt cry: "I am out of energy and out of control of this thing called life!" Living life today is tough, and living an energy-filled life is tougher still. We have innumerable demands, stresses, and obligations placed upon us, yet little supply to meet those demands. Most of us have families, friends, careers, community and church commitments, pets, houses, yards, and hobbies—all demanding time and attention. But that's time—and

> *Energy has become a most precious and rare commodity.*

energy—we just don't have. Polls show again and again that most Americans feel as though they don't have time to do everything that needs to be done, much less fun time to recharge their batteries. Little wonder that the desperate message I hear every day sounds like a tape recording: *"I'm just so tired."*

How about you? Do you feel as if you rarely have enough time or energy to take a bike ride in the country, read a novel, practice that golf swing, try out some new recipes, or cultivate a new relationship? Do you feel as though you barely have the energy to rise up to the demands and needs of life—let alone your wants? The needs most easy to ignore are your own.

The Right Stuff

We *all* need energy that lasts as long as our days last. And most of us desire the side benefits of vibrant living as well: sharpened concentration, enduring memory, high productivity, a bright attitude, a hopeful perspective, stress resiliency. This is the "right stuff" we need for effective, fulfilled lives. Yet I'd have to say most of us just don't have it.

Statistics show it as well. Studies have shown that one out of five people suffers from extreme fatigue. Many more feel like falling asleep on their feet. More still (six out of ten) are chronically tired—forlorn, grouchy, and unable to think creatively. And nine out of ten say they feel very stressed most days and extremely stressed one or two times a week. It is estimated that Americans make 500 million office visits to doctors each year to complain about generalized fatigue.

What is the cause? Sometimes, fatigue stems from elusive factors such as sleep problems, any number of medical conditions, the side effects of medication, or something as simple (yet little known) as not drinking enough water. But more often the likely cause is something predictable: simply a chronic lack of self-care. We are underfed and underfueled and unable to step up to all the tasks and opportunities at hand. We push our bodies through the day without the right food as though we were cars that could run without gasoline. We aren't getting enough rest and are being overcome by the stresses of living life. Yet we are too busy or too tired to do anything about it. And these lifestyle blocks allow our natural energy stores to leak away unused.

Sure, you know you need more rest and that getting in better shape would do you a world of good. But when? How? With what? I hear it everyday: *"Take care of myself? Eat well? Exercise? Relax? Sleep eight hours? Right... I already have too much to do and never enough time to do it all. I surely don't have anything left over for those things!"* And there's some truth in that.

But I don't believe it's the whole truth. *What we're lacking isn't the time, it's the energy.* Sure, most of us are busier than we've ever been. But the problem is that when free time does arise, we're just too exhausted to do anything we'd like to do, or feel called to do. Instead, we fall asleep on the couch, zone out in front of the TV, or take part in activities or conversations that profit us little. Why? Because the things we like to do or dream of doing require a supply of energy that we can't seem to muster up when we need it.

Energy has become a most precious and rare commodity. But it's *not* impossible to recover. An energy level that starts early and ends when your day ends may sound like an elusive butterfly, but I've written this book to give you hope and vision for exactly that—and to equip you with practical strategies to see that energy becomes a reality in your life. The main theme of *The Energy Edge* is very simple: *You have all the energy you need.* You do because you were created with an amazing and efficient energy system already installed!

You see, the human body contains a power plant capable of producing more than enough energy to do just about anything that a person wants to do, and then some. Energy is scripted into every cell in our bodies. We only need to learn how to release—and not hinder—the incredible power within.

Releasing Your Natural Resources

Many factors come into play to determine the release and effectiveness of our energy. A number of chemical factors, hormones, and neurotransmitters, along with lifestyle choices and conditions, all influence how strong and alert we feel at any given moment—and how successfully our energy system is operating. If you are experiencing good levels of energy now, it is because this system is functioning well to keep you energized. With fine tuning, you can further enhance your performance to its peak. However, if you or the people you love are in desperate need of energy, getting this inborn energy system operative and running smoothly is your best bet for achieving a sense of well-being and vitality.

There *is* a way to release a virtual river of energy and stamina from within and use that energy to live a life that is dramatically different. It doesn't take more time to adopt these effective strategies, it just takes a small amount of planning—and the

> *Energy is scripted into every cell in our bodies. We only need to learn how to release— and not hinder—the incredible power within.*

rewards are enormous! And that's what the Energy Edge is all about. In this book you will find a plan for energized living that allows you to tap into the power you need to live life well. We now have years of scientific research to guide us, and I've assembled the latest on how to live better and live longer—and *not* live with fatigue. We will take a look at the foods and beverages you consume and those you don't, your breathing and exercise patterns, the power of your mind and moods, your relationships, and your beliefs. We'll explore specific upgrades you can make in your ways of living that can transform your "I'm so tired" into "I'm bursting with energy!"

The Energy Edge is not meant to be an exhaustive diagnostic guide for illnesses and maladies. Although fatigue is not generally rooted in serious illness, it can be a caution flag, an early warning sign, even a last stage symptom. It is often the symptom that propels a person to seek a thorough physical exam. If you have been experiencing persistent fatigue (for a month or more) the first action step you should take is to see your physician. Get an "all points check" before following the Energy Edge guidelines and principles. Having your doctor's okay will make your efforts much more safe and effective.

I truly believe that you can add years to your life, and life to your years. Decades of research and experience back up this belief. But the real art of living well will remain what it has always been: learning how to bring meaning and vitality to whatever time you have by embracing the life-giving principles of living and loving. As you focus on your energy supply—and win over the forces that neutralize and vandalize it—you can add productive years to your life, empower your thinking processes, maintain a joyful sense of well-being, and energize your life!

I have been living a life committed to wellness for over twenty-five years—eating well, living fit, attempting to meet my needs on all levels—in short, to thrive rather than just survive. Yet, while immersed in the vast body of research and personal stories I gathered for this book, I became aware of how even I had begun to "settle" for less energy. I've let family crises, professional transitions, mid-life issues, a miscarriage, and the resulting hormonal hurricane become *huge* obstacles to my living well—really well. I had let them vandalize the energy I was committed to having. True, I have had little control over many of these factors and events. But I do have the ability to take charge of what I can: my eating, exercise, breathing, sleep, choice of relationships, and many other factors. I can guard against being invaded by the energy vandals.

Through the writing of this book, I have had reaffirmed to myself this truth: *I am capable of being more than I had become.* The challenges I have experienced are real and difficult, but not insurmountable—and not worth giving up my valuable energy. I am now more committed than ever to a lifestyle that supports vibrant living. May you, too, commit yourself to a lifetime of living with the Energy Edge.

CHAPTER TWO

Spinning plates, spinning wheels

feel like a pinball—ringing some bells and buzzers, making some points, but mostly bouncing around and being batted back and forth!" Dale is a successful thirty-six-year-old company president who is intently focused on living a quality life with his family and friends—and having that be a life of significance. But that focus is easily lost in the midst of his very demanding schedule.

"I juggle ten things at once, phone call to phone call, plane trip to taxi ride. I'm constantly in the middle of a crisis in one area while working on a critical acquisition in another." Every day Dale faces a rigorous test of his stamina and ability to respond on his feet. And while he thrives on challenge and opportunity, he says, "My personal demands have never been greater. The pressure just doesn't stop."

Like Dale, you may long for the "good old days," when life was simple and the world moved much more slowly—when e-mail didn't pile up at the office, dinner baked in the oven instead of in the microwave, phones connected you to real people instead of machines, and days at the office ran nine to six instead of six to nine.

The good old days weren't the 1920s or even the 1950s, they were just a few short years ago—1975 or so. Life was less frenzied somehow. But now you're spinning dozens of plates at one time: "Gotta do that report, gotta make that meeting, gotta get the kids, gotta get dinner, gotta buy that gift, gotta phone those people, gotta exercise, gotta pay bills." You may not have set a foot out-side your door in the morning before you've exhausted yourself. Your churning, spinning thoughts are wearing you out—you and just about everyone else to one degree or another. Again, feeling exhausted has taken on a life of its own.

Or maybe you feel a sense of spinning your wheels—racing madly through life, but going nowhere. It's a statement on life in these times, but seems to be an age-old problem. And like an overloaded computer, we begin to work more slowly, break down more frequently, and constantly operate on the verge of crashing. Because we don't have time for any of it, even the time to notice how badly we really feel, we tend to drown out the "I'm so tired" message with aspirin for aches, caffeine for weariness, and sugar for mid-afternoon slumps.

Dale's daily grind forced him to take a close look at his lifestyle. He had been eating too much and at the wrong times, exercising too little, and not taking any time to relax his body or mind. Although he had a meaningful life of faith, he was having a hard time making the time to connect spiritually. His marriage was suf-fering from neglect. He had stopped having fun.

It wasn't the culmination of all of these things going wrong that led Dale to seek out my help—it was a middle-of-the-night visit to the emergency room with crushing chest pains. The diagnosis: classic stress giving a wake-up call. He had no blockages, his heart was clear and seemingly functioned fine; but the stress chemicals running amuck in his body triggered an electrical surge that resulted in muscle spasms. The discharge prescription given by the ER physician was to slow down, relax, and cut out the stress. His stress levels soared just hearing it. Dale wasn't able to just "cut out the stress."

During his first consultation with me, I could clearly see that although the demands on him were great, he did have more abil-ity to take charge of his life than he realized. Yes, there was much in Dale's life that he could not control, and these things were major stressors to him because he felt responsible—and was expected to be. But there was also a great deal that he *could* take charge of: his eating, his exercise, his schedule—and this in turn would bring a new order to his life and enable him to better withstand the challenges.

Health now had Dale's attention, and he attacked the project of upgrading his lifestyle habits like he would a corporate acquisition. He's now eating often and well and has embraced exercise with an iron grip for its stress-reduction powers. He's finding that he is now more productive in less time, and has begun to schedule more time to invest in his family and friends as well as to get away and reflect. Dale is no longer waking up in the middle of the night with anxiety attacks; he's sleeping well most nights and waking up feeling refreshed. He's so positive—and in awe—about the benefits of his new way of life that he's invested in a wellness initiative for his employees. "I want everyone in my company to have the energy I now have," he explains. "I began a wellness program to save my life, but what I've gotten is my life back—better than ever!"

Stress: A Fact Of Life

"If I can just get through this week, it'll get better".... *"If I can just make it through the holidays, things won't be so crazy"*.... *"This is a particularly difficult time, but the schedule will calm down soon"*.... *"It's just been a really tough month, it's not always this frenzied."*

These are the statements of a stressed person who is dreaming that the stress in his or her life will go away—or get better. It doesn't. At least, it hasn't for my clients and it hasn't for me. There's always something new waiting to stress and challenge me. The good news is that the stress doesn't really get worse either— it just gets different. Every day, every week—it's a little different, but it's always there, just as intense.

Stress researchers explain this by naming stress the unavoidable price of modern life. Nearly nine out of ten Americans say they experience stress every day, and high levels several times a week, and one in four complains of high levels every day. This statistic, and our experience, tells us that no one of any age is immune to stress, and that we could certainly use some new perspective in how to overcome its effects.

The problem in treating this human condition is identifying and understanding it. Stress is one of those words that everyone knows the meaning of, but no one can define. What's stressful to one person may not be to another. Our reactions to life events vary from person to person; what frazzles me may challenge and inspire you.

Any change that requires you to adjust your way of doing things can be a cause of stress. It can be good or bad, as major as retirement or the death of a loved one; or as minor as a traffic jam, a missing set of keys, or a surprise visit from a friend. Research shows time and time again that it's not the amount of stresses in life that affects health and well-being, but one's response to the situations that causes the negative results.

Many of us refer to upsetting life events as stress, when in fact those are *stressors*. Like a coffee cup, we all have a certain capacity. Just as whether the coffee spills over the top when poured depends on the cup's size, people who have a seemingly large capacity to deal with challenge may not "overflow" under stress.

I don't know what causes overflow in your life, but my stressors always have something in common. The situations and life events that are most stressful for me are always about *control*; my unhealthy stress response always arises when I try to control what is beyond my control: people, events, situations, choices of others. The stress levels run particularly high when I'm in a position of responsibility—with others depending on me—but I can't control all of the factors. And my personal tension rises higher still when my demands rise higher than my resources. For example, when the demand to complete a project by Friday outweighs my perception of my level of energy and creativity, or if giving a presentation to a professional group requires a level of knowledge I don't believe I possess, the result is a crushing feeling of stress.

Our physical bodies were designed to survive the stresses we encounter in life. We were created with a "stress tracking system" that is intricately programmed to seek and find stress signals. This "stress sensor" (the pituitary gland in our brain) is much like radar equipment, and is constantly on the lookout for what appears to be danger to our survival. When this master gland picks up stress signals, it sends a hormone messenger to our body's adrenal system (located near the kidneys) to prepare us to *fight* the present danger, or *flee* to escape. These chemical messages set in motion the symptoms of stress. They cause a shifting of the chemical balance deep within our system, triggering chemical reactions that slow down the metabolism and other bodily functions (such as digestion), as well as causing blood to pool in our muscles and fluid to gather in the extremities, and priming the body for action with spurts of the stress hormones adrenaline and cortisol.

The body's functions radically modify to meet the stress demands. The heart beats faster, blood pressure rises, the rate of breathing increases, and muscles tense up. Proteins are converted into sugar, which causes insulin levels to surge and the blood sugar to fluctuate wildly. The roller coaster ride your blood sugar takes in response to stress affects your mood, concentration, appetite, and of course, energy level.

The "fight-or-flight" response was intended to "kick in" as a response to a threat. This surge of chemical reactions may have ensured our early ancestors' survival when facing grizzly bears, but it can wear us down when it results from ever-present dangers we try to "grin and bear." Our bodies read traffic jams, deadlines, financial pressures, or relationship struggles all as our modern-day grizzlies. Adjusting to new situations, new rules, new roles, and new expectations—all trigger the stress response.

Sometimes, we may react to stress in a different way than the classic fight-or-flight response. Instead, we may "play possum" and withdraw. Just as a possum rolls over and plays dead when threatened, a person may "roll over" into hopelessness, depression, and feelings of being out of control. Physiological reactions include a decreased heart rate and muscle tone. When chronic, this kind of "play dead" reaction may actually invite life-threatening illness by deadening the immune system's response, dulling the mind, and causing the organ systems to function less efficiently.

The key word with any kind of negative stress is *chronic*. All of the adaptive mechanisms for the stress response were intended as a short-term alert/alarm to prepare us for fight or flight and to help us recover once we escape the danger. But today's bodies— exposed to chronic, unresolved stress—never have a chance to recover and break out of the fight-or-flight mode. Instead, they stay stuck in the stress response mode.

When the body is exposed to the same stress again and again, and there is no stress release, the body stores are depleted and the body systems are put to extraordinary demand. The body begins to show signs of damage—with fatigue being a cardinal symptom. Being stuck in stress causes chemical surges which can also result in headaches, backaches, sleep disturbances, anxiety, depression, arthritic pain, asthma, gastrointestinal upsets, skin disorders, and weight and eating problems. In fact, the American Institute of Stress reports that 75 to 90 percent of all doctor visits involve stress-related complaints. Over time, severe and chronic stress can suppress the immune system and greatly tax the brain, bringing problems with attention, concentration, and memory, not to mention fatigue. Fatigue is the message your body sends to you when it's stressed and spinning—when you need to slow down, take a break, or take it easy.

The truth is we all have the power to shape and maintain our energy levels, more than we realize. But most of us just don't recognize the factors that deplete our precious energy, nor do we recognize the stepping stones to longevity and peak performance.

Dale didn't when I began helping him assess his lifestyle and find solutions to his energy crisis. The goals and action steps I developed for him are the core message of the Energy Edge: *In order to achieve a harmonious balance within our body and soul and tap into the reservoir of energy within, we must begin by righting the wrongs in our bodies and get them working for us, not against us.*

Living On The Energy Edge

Many people reach for a drug or a drink when they want to boost their mood; a vitamin, herb, or energy brew when they need more pep. This is not only unhealthy, it is unnecessary. Regardless of how you've been living life and the level of vitality you've experienced up till now, you can receive phenomenal benefits from *the energizers*—power points for a life filled with energy. From strategic eating and exercise, to attitudes and thinking patterns, to relaxation and play, the energizers are concepts and tools that will equip you to thrive. Some of these power points for energy will give you a boost immediately, with a single meal or specific activity. Others require consistent behavior, but even with these the results can come quickly.

When you incorporate the energizers into your life, you'll begin to experience an energy level that is up and even, and a clarity of thinking and creativity that will enhance your performance in any setting—in family discussions, at business meetings, in negotiations, under deadline pressures, in sports. And the great news about energy is this: *energy begets energy.* People who have and put out tremendous energy are energized by their very activity. Physical activity oxygenates all parts of the body, including the brain. It enhances circulation and increases the metabolism. The result? Energy. Similarly, having the energy to love, reflect, or create produces pleasure chemicals in the brain, which in turn lift up mood and energy. The more energy you have, the greater your desire to give of yourself and, in turn, the more energetic you feel.

Adopting the energizers will definitely introduce wonderful

changes into your life, yet they can only take you so far. Before you can experience the full measure of the energy you were created with, you must recognize and correct the habits, activities, attitudes, and chemical imbalances—the *energy neutralizers* and *energy vandalizers*—that steal your vitality.

Although I'll talk a lot more about these energy enemies in Parts 3 and 4, let me now briefly state that energy *neutralizers* are states of body and mind that cause your energy to leak away, unused. Energy is neutralized by lack of self-care (not getting enough sleep, not eating the right foods) combined with states of imbalance (negative stress, worry, hormone fluctuations, depression, and illness).

The Energizing Top Ten Power Points for the Energy Edge

1. **Breathe!**
2. **Drink Plenty of Water**
3. **Eat Strategically**
4. **Sleep Well**
5. **Get Moving**
6. **Nourish Your Brain**
7. **Manage Your Moods**
8. **Energize Your Domain**
9. **Take Time-outs**
10. **Boost Your Immune System**

The energy *vandalizers* are specific lifestyle choices that operate as agents of fatigue. They often come wrapped as "friendly energy" (sweets, fast food, caffeine, alcohol, tobacco) but wreak havoc and leave you at a deficit.

To break out of the exhaustive fatigue cycle, you just have to start somewhere. You may find that simply drinking water in the amounts you need will be an amazing energizer. Fueling your energy will give you the motivation and the resources to exercise. Eating well and exercising will promote more restful sleep. You'll start to feel good enough to notice when you feel bad—reminding you to slow down and take a breather. The stress reduction you enjoy will lead to greater productivity and free more time to invest in the quality relationships and activities in your life.

Many of the energizing power points have several components, but they all represent a change in your attitude or lifestyle that will release more energy. It is not important to enact the lifestyle upgrades in any certain order, or to completely master one before you learn about the others. However, I have put these principles into a logical progression, beginning with meeting your physical needs.

As previously stated we'll investigate each of the energizers in detail in the next section, but here's a quick overview of the primary strategies for infusing your life with energy.

1. BREATHE TO RECHARGE. There's a big difference between breathing to live and breathing to recharge. Actually, the way you breathe can either boost or drain your energy. Many of us breathe shallowly and through our mouths which sends the body into the fight-or-flight response—quickening pulse, pumping adrenaline—a chronic state of stress that saps energy. However, proper breathing can quiet our stress responses, enhance our energy, sharpen our awareness, and even diminish pain. Well-oxygenated blood is better able to deliver energy-providing oxygen to your body tissues and carry away waste products. So, breathe deeply and easily!

2. DRINK WATER TO ENERGIZE. Thirsting for energy? You may be—more than you know! Dehydration is the number one factor for fatigue, yet people constantly run low on fluids. We drink soda, coffee, tea, juice—everything but the beverage that energizes best: water.

3. EAT FOR ENERGY. Looking for the next best thing to a youth potion? Try eating strategically, with a focus on timing, balance, and variety. When it comes to having all the energy you want and need, eating the right foods at the right time is one of the most powerful—and longest lasting—energy impacting choices.

4. SLEEP TO RECHARGE. Aside from food, one of the body's main sources of fuel is sleep. Rejuvenating rest is as valuable a spoke in the wheel of wellness as nutrition and exercise. Yet many of us are chronically sleep-deprived, and it's taking a toll on our health and productivity.

To "seal up" the energy cracks and live vitalized lives, it's crucial to have restful sleep to recharge our physical, emotional, and mental batteries.

5. EXERCISE TO RELEASE ENERGY. The *fastest* way to feel energized is to exercise—it is a powerful tool for the release of energy. Much more than a weight loss measure or a cardiovascular strengthener, it's an active, take-charge step for cutting away at the stress response and boosting your immune system. Just thirty minutes of aerobic activity will boost your energy, mood, and alertness because it causes the release of beta-endorphins, the naturally occurring opiates that help you feel happy, less stressed, and more vital. For a quick boost, just get moving—even a short walk around the room will do!

6. MIND YOUR MIND FOR ENERGY. Brain fatigue may deplete your ability to think young and act young. Your brain may be in need of certain nutrients found in everyday foods to help sharpen your mind and bring clarity and alertness to your thinking abilities. Once you learn ways to properly fuel your brain, you can keep it fit and ready for action.

7. LIFT YOUR MOOD TO LIFT YOUR ENERGY. The key to sealing up the energy leaks caused by mood swings is to learn techniques to short-circuit the negative emotions and downward swings. Learn to manage your moods by stabilizing your brain's neurochemistry, and become more aware of your changing moods so you can match activities with your energy levels.

8. ENERGIZE YOUR DOMAIN. You might be surprised to learn that what you're surrounded with in your living space and workplace can make all the difference in your energy response. Light, color, noise, and smells all have the power to both exhaust and energize you. Simple changes—such as changing the light bulbs, stopping for fresh flowers, soaking in the sun, or turning on some foot-tapping music—can stop the energy drain of your day and power boost you out of fatigue ditches.

9. TAKE TIME-OUTS TO RE-ENERGIZE. To really enjoy life physically, emotionally, relationally, and spiritually, you must take the time to recharge and renew your body, mind, and spirit. Otherwise, you'll get depleted, tired, and sick. The gift of renewal is one you need and deserve, and it *is* possible to fit reenergizing time-outs into your busy schedule.

10. BOOST YOUR IMMUNE SYSTEM TO BOOST YOUR ENERGY. A strong immune system not only better protects us from infections and diseases, but also helps to keep us feeling good, looking great, thinking clearly, and brimming with energy. We can't be healthy or even *feel* healthy without an immune system that's in good working order.

These ten energizers, the power points for the Energy Edge, are the best tools I know to defuse stress in the physical arena of your life. Meeting your body's needs in these ways makes all the difference in your ability to "ride the wave" of stress, rather than drowning in its undertow.

So, are you ready to live on the Energy Edge so you can keep pace with your life and enjoy its blessings? If so, turn the page. It's time to learn how to use the energizers to tap into all the energy you need.

PART TWO

The energizers

CHAPTER THREE

Breathe!

Ever breathe a sigh of relief? Gasp in shock or pain? Feel the need to vent at someone? These are all sublingual expressions of the recognized close connection between the way we breathe and how we feel.

The pressure of a deadline can leave us wiped out for the afternoon. Fear makes us tense our muscles, which leads to fatigue, just as if we were working out. Fear can also make us hold our breath, depriving us of oxygen. This too can lead to fatigue.

Breathing isn't something we normally have to think about—we inhale and exhale at a fairly steady pace, without much thought or worry over how we're doing. But people with breathing problems, for instance those who tend to hyperventilate, have much to be gained from learning how to breathe *correctly*.

Deep, slow, oxygenating breaths are one of the simplest things you can do to relieve stress, energize yourself, and keep control of yourself in any situation. Healthy breathing can help you overcome

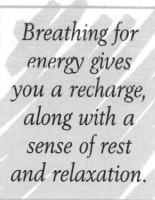

Breathing for energy gives you a recharge, along with a sense of rest and relaxation.

the low energy and high stress levels that result from rapid, shallow, or deep, heaving breaths. But because breathing seems so simple, so automatic, it's difficult to think that energy can be boosted just from taking a breath of air. And it certainly is automatic, but so is eating. And how many people do that right?

Back To Basics

Getting the right amount of oxygen into the bloodstream depends on a balance of carbon dioxide and oxygen in the blood. When you breathe in a panicked way, each breath throws that balance off. But you can actually train yourself to breathe in a way that energizes you.

When you're relaxed, you breathe slowly and deeply, inhaling vital, energy-producing oxygen. When you're tense, you tend to breathe lightly and rapidly, delivering less oxygen to your body's cells. Stress can be considered suffocation to your blood cells. When you're tense, the brain increases its demand for oxygen, yet the shallow breathing that accompanies stress decreases the oxygen intake and transfer. Shallow breathing impairs circulation and depletes energy.

Breathe To Energize

Studies suggest that 80 percent of us don't know how to breathe in an energizing way; we put our emphasis on inhalation, but the energy and stress release is found in exhalation.

Freeze for a moment, holding your body in its exact position. Notice that your shoulders may be shrugged or tense. Correct your posture; imagine being suspended from above with your head erect, light and alert. Next, exhale slowly, draining your lungs—concentrating on the stress being blown out of your body. Now, slowly fill your chest with air. Expand your diaphragm (the cone-shaped muscle that forms the floor of your chest cavity) by pushing your stomach down and out. Then breathe again… in and out… fully. In and out… in and out. When you inhale, picture breathing in life. Stress out, life in. Repeat this kind of "in and out" breathing—fully, at least ten times—whenever you feel tired or stressed. Your body and mind will soon feel refreshed.

When you feel tense, you may be breathing from your chest rather than your diaphragm. To test your breathing, place one hand on your upper chest and one hand on your abdomen. If the hand on your chest rises when you inhale and contracts when you exhale, you're chest breathing. This type of breathing brings in huge amounts of air at one time, and activates the fight-or-flight alarm reaction. This is good in a life-threatening emergency, but not in daily living. Chest breathing keeps your body in a state of chronic stress.

In contrast, breathing from your diaphragm tells the body: "Everything is okay... you are in control." So, before the pressures of life attack again, take two minutes to practice this type of breathing. Place one hand on your upper stomach, just below your chest. Inhale while you imagine you're filling a small balloon inside. Fill it in all directions—top, bottom, forward, backward. Breathe in until you feel comfortably full, but not too full. Your stomach should gently rise and then fall as you exhale. Make the exhalation a little bit longer than you think you should. Hold it for a half-second before you inhale again. Your upper chest should stay flat throughout. Once you're breathing from the right spot, focus on making your breathing as even and steady as possible. You'll find that your tension dissipates.

Ready to blow a gasket because your computer just froze *again*? Put your hands flat on your desk and take about fifteen slow, deep breaths. Breathe in, breathe out. You'll feel calmer, and you'll unwind all the energy-depleting tension before it has a chance to overtake you. Practice this energizing and relaxing deep breathing so that you can do it automatically when under stress. Try it at any time the tension builds, or when you know the potential is there—in meetings, at your desk, during a crisis, or when you feel tired, unfocused, confused, mad, scared, anxious, or bored.

Two/One Breathing

You can further expand your stress-busting expertise by learning how to manipulate the way you exhale. Since exhaling slows the pulse, a technique called two/one breathing—in which you exhale for twice as long as you inhale—uses this phenomenon to work diaphragmatic breathing even more effectively.

To practice the two/one breathing technique, follow these steps:

1. Sit quietly and do diaphragmatic breathing.
2. When your breathing becomes balanced and even (it will take a few minutes), gently slow your rate of exhalation until you are breathing out for about twice as long as you breathe in. The easiest technique: count to six when you exhale, three when you inhale—or eight and four. You shouldn't end up doing deep breathing; you want to alter the rhythmic motion of your lungs, not fill or empty them completely.
3. Once you've established your rhythm of breathing, stop the mental counting and focus on the smoothness and evenness of your breath flow.

Hyperventilation

Many people suffering from fatigue simply have poor breathing patterns, or chronic hyperventilation syndrome (HVS). Their stress response is the expression of each cell in the body choking for air, and producing less and less energy.

If you have HVS, you breathe shallowly and rapidly (more than eighteen times per minute), leading to an excessive loss of carbon dioxide. The loss of carbon dioxide affects the blood's hemoglobin, making it less able to carry oxygen throughout the body. So even though you are breathing quickly, you are getting less air. Along with other symptoms fatigue results in anxiety, frequent sighing or yawning, and a tingling, coldness, or numbness in the fingers. Many of these symptoms are due to holding your breath to make up for the carbon dioxide lost in hyperventilating. In addition, you have to work harder to breathe, which in and of itself is tiring.

How to overcome hyperventilation problems? First, sit or stand up straight—correct your posture. Keeping your tummy firmly tucked in when you stand or sit up straight will relax your diaphragm muscles and improve their movement during breathing. Second, if you breathe from your nose, keep your mouth closed. Your nasal passages are too narrow to allow for hyperventilation. Third, the standard treatment: breathe into a closed paper bag held tight against your face. With this bag-breathing, carbon dioxide is trapped into the bag where it is recirculated, preventing carbon dioxide levels from falling. Finally, learn the art of breathing for energy.

You receive more than air through proper breathing—you invite regeneration into your body. Breathing for energy gives you a recharge, along with a sense of rest and relaxation. So take a nice long, slow breath. Now, take another one. Feel better?

CHAPTER FOUR

Drink plenty of water

I t may be hard to believe, but the number one factor for fatigue is dehydration—pure and simple. If you do nothing else in your quest for energy but begin to drink water each day—and drink a lot of it—you will experience a phenomenal boost in your energy and sense of well-being. Few of my clients think of water as their most important energy enhancer, yet many of the symptoms of fatigue that we blame on too much stress and too little sleep are simply the result of thirst.

At the end of a long workday, when you feel rotten and headachy, with your body in a strange zone between sore and numb, your body is crying out to be hydrated. Chances are you've only drunk enough water to wash down a few aspirin, and have had little else since that coffee or diet soda this morning. You've been breathing dry, air-conditioned or heated air at the office, and the chronic stress in your routine has caused some moments of intense perspiration. And of course, you've been losing fluids through the day through normal body functions—fluids that haven't been replaced. You're parched!

The right amount of water can be the difference between success and failure, both in a workout or in the workplace. Water is important for energy production for several reasons. Consider that your body is comprised primarily of water (it's 92 percent of your blood plasma, 80 percent of your muscle mass, 60 percent of your red blood cells, and 50 percent of everything else in your body). Every cell in your body relies on water to dilute biochemicals, vitamins, and minerals to just the right concentrations. The body also depends on the bloodstream to transport nutrients and other substances from one part to another, and this too depends on optimal fluid concentration. Blood volume actually decreases and "thickens" when you are dehydrated, meaning that the heart has to work harder to supply your body with needed oxygen. And remember, oxygenated blood is energy for your body.

Water is vital for maintaining proper muscle tone, allowing muscles to contract naturally, which prevents dehydration. When dehydrated, the muscles are more injury-prone and will not work to optimal performance. In fact, dehydrated muscles will work only to 30 or 35 percent of their capacity. This spells mediocre performance for athletes and tiredness, achiness, and headaches for you.

Drink Yourself Well

The idea that water is an important ingredient to good health is a simple truth to understand. But drinking more water is a challenge for most of us. Most Americans have grown up drinking just about anything but water. We list our favorite beverages as soda, coffee, tea, juice—with water being good only for washing down pills, washing away dirt, and brushing our teeth. Although we often hear that we should drink water, it's easier to reach for something else. And we pay a price: we miss out on water's benefits.

Water is an essential nutrient. Without food, a person can survive (although not well!) for days, even months. But without water, the human body can survive only three to five days.

Again, water is an energy booster because it is a critical component of functions that are essential to your body's health. First, along with proper protein and salt intake, water works to release excess stores of fluid, much like priming a pump. It is *the* natural diuretic. No other beverage works like water to prevent the body from holding excess fluids. Second, water transports the energy nutrients throughout your body and is essential for maintaining your body temperature. Third, water helps you digest food and maintains proper bowel function and waste elimination. Being a mild laxative, water actually activates the fiber you eat, allowing it to form a bulky mass that passes through the gastrointestinal tract easily and quickly. Without proper water, fiber becomes a difficult-to-pass "glue" in your colon!

Water is the only liquid we consume that doesn't require the body to work to metabolize or excrete it. Even fresh juices do not provide the solid benefits of pure, wonderful water, since they require your body to process the substances they contain.

With soft drinks, your body has to work overtime to process and excrete the chemicals and colorings. Although based on water, they are "polluted" water. Many other beverages, particularly those that contain caffeine, actually remove more water than contained in the beverage itself. Coffee, tea, and some sodas contain tannic acid, a product that interferes with iron and calcium absorption, and com-

> *The right amount of water can be the difference between success and failure, both in a workout or in the workplace.*

petes for excretion with other bodily waste products such as uric acid. When not properly excreted, this uric acid can build up in the body and crystallize around the joints. This build-up leads to joint pain in elbows, shoulders, knees, and feet, especially former injury spots, and is a type of gouty arthritis. Men are particularly prone to uric acid excesses. This is one reason why a cup of tea or coffee, although fluid based, just doesn't do the job. Furthermore, water works to lubricate joints.

If you're still not convinced about the wonders of water, consider this: Water also works to keep the skin healthy, resilient, and wrinkle-resistant. It could honestly be labeled an "anti-aging" ingredient!

How Much Do I Need?

My answer is always the same: eight to ten eight-ounce glasses each day—more when you exercise, travel by plane, or live at high altitudes. Sound overwhelming? Never thirsty? You're not alone. The water prescription brings out cries of anguish from many who hear it.

You need that much because you lose that much every day. Your body continually loses water as it performs necessary functions. Even breathing uses up your fluid stores; every time you exhale you blow off body water—a total of about two cups per day. Water evaporates from your skin to cool your body, even when you aren't aware of sweating. These losses, along with that lost in regular urination and bowel movements, total up to ten cups per day. When perspiring heavily, the amount lost can double or triple.

Take heart! As you begin to meet this need by drinking more water, your natural thirst will increase. You may find water drinking habit-forming; the more you drink, the more you want.

Start increasing your intake any way you can: through a straw, in a sports sipper, from a silver pitcher. Add fresh lemon or lime, drink sparkling water, or buy bottled water—just drink it! Try filling a two-quart container with water each morning, and then make sure it's all gone before you go to bed. I also encourage a habit of drinking a twelve- to sixteen-ounce glass of water right after each meal and snack through the day. If you are eating as often as you should, every three hours or so, this will provide a large proportion of the fluid you need.

Once you feel thirsty, you've already lost a significant amount of fluid. As your fluid level decreases, you'll start to notice a decline in physical performance, along with other early warning signs of dehydration: impatience, slight nausea, flushed skin, dizziness, headaches, and weakness. You may have never related these energy-taxing symptoms to a lack of water.

Mild dehydration can easily result from skipping a meal, working in dryer air, changing climates, air travel, or drinking too much caffeine or alcohol. You may say—normal life! And if you are exercising (whether digging dandelions in the back yard or training for a triathlon) you are losing water and dehydrating at even a faster rate. If you continue to lose water and fail to take in adequate liquids, dehydration can quickly progress to the dangerous extreme of heat exhaustion. In this condition, you can experience blurred vision, hearing problems, swallowing difficulties, lack of saliva production, rapid pulse, shortness of breath, soaring temperatures, and an unsteady gait. Dehydration such as this occurs much too often in athletes, hikers, and bikers unprepared for hot weather. It can be fatal, so it's not to be ignored.

Water works to keep the skin healthy, resilient, and wrinkle-resistant—it could be labeled an "anti-aging" ingredient!

Remember: Do not rely on your thirst mechanism. It will prompt you to replace only 35 to 40 percent of your body's hydration needs. Also, don't rely on your intake of other fluids; no other liquid works like water to hydrate your tissues. Soda, even juice, lingers in your stomach instead of heading directly for your cells as water does. If you do not take in adequate water, your body fluids will be thrown off balance, and you may experience fluid retention, constipation, unexplained weight gain, and a malfunction in your natural thirst mechanism.

Tips For Staying Hydrated

❖ Start your day with eight to sixteen ounces of water. While the coffee or tea are brewing, drink a cup or two of water. You wake up with a water deficit, so drinking water soon after awakening will gently restore hydration. Many of my clients swear by a cup of warm water with a squeeze of lemon first thing in the morning to gently jump start their digestive system. They declare it the answer to their "regularity" problems.

❖ Get your eight-a-day. This isn't a diet principle; it's just how your body is wired. Take water breaks routinely, at least every thirty-five to forty-five minutes, even more frequently when the air is dry or hot. Another tip is to drink twelve to sixteen ounces after each meal and snack. Try to drink little or nothing with your meal (sip water if you must), because washing food down with water dilutes the digestive function.

❖ Get more when you need it. As already mentioned, you may not automatically know when you need more, but look for the subtle signs of dehydration—dry eyes, nose or mouth, and mild fatigue. Expect it when it's hotter or dryer than normal, if you're more stressed than normal, and when you exercise.

Not to make you obsessive, but it's a good idea to glance at your urine occasionally. Other than first thing in the morning, a dark yellow color is a sign your kidneys are having to concentrate the waste in too small a volume of liquid. Pale-colored urine gets a smiley-face—indicating good hydration status.

❖ Don't wait until you're thirsty to drink. It's already too late. Again, your body's thirst mechanism doesn't kick in until you're already on your way to dehydration. Instead, drink on a schedule.

❖ Keep water where you are. You're more apt to keep up with water needs if you keep drinking water close at hand. Freeze large bottles of water overnight and pull them out in the morning. The water thaws through the day, but still is chilled. Keep a glass or a pitcher of water at your desk, and refill it often. At home, keep a pitcher or large bottle of water in the refrigerator, with a glass on the counter to serve as a reminder.

❖ Avoid dehydrating food and drinks. Caffeine-containing beverages like coffee, tea, some sodas, and alcoholic beverages act as dehydrators, further increasing, and never replacing, your fluid needs. As a matter of fact, each cup of coffee or tea adds an extra cup of water to the eight-to-ten a day requirement. Who has room—or time? And if you're a beer drinker, don't go for a brew when you're trying to hydrate. As thirst-quenching as it may seem, it's really working against you.

❖ Fill up before you work out. Drink sixteen ounces of water fifteen to thirty minutes before your workout. Avoid starting to exercise when you're already thirsty; you're guaranteed a substandard performance if you are low on water before you even begin to move.

❖ Continue to fill up while you're working out. Drink six to eight ounces of water every twenty minutes during your workout or training. This may seem like a lot, but even this doesn't begin to keep up with typical sweat losses. When possible, drink cool water—it is absorbed into the system more quickly. No need for a sports drink to replenish electrolytes unless you're exercising longer than ninety minutes.

❖ Practice air travel smarts. Drink as if you're going into an exercise workout: sixteen ounces before your flight, then at least eight more every hour aloft. Stick with water or juices—avoid dehydrating caffeine or alcohol-containing beverages.

❖ If you start craving salt, go for water. Once your fluid stores drop below a certain level, your thirst mechanism cuts off all together. (Possibly to preserve your sanity if you're lost in the desert?) What turns on is a desire for salt—or salty foods. It's one of those magnificent things the body does: Because extra sodium holds more fluids in the body, the salt craving is a survival mechanism to slow life-threatening dehydration. Notice a craving for hot dogs and nachos at the beach? Look for a water bottle instead.

Is Tap Water Okay?

Be sure not to let the bottled versus tap versus treated water controversy get in the way of your health. Many people do; they don't trust their tap water, so they drink no water at all. Public water systems today are well monitored for safety, and bottled water companies are now beginning to fall under similar standards. You can assure yourself of the purity and safety of your local drinking water by checking with your local EPA or health department, or by contacting EPA's Safe Drinking Water Hotline at 1-800-426-4791. If you lack confidence in the answers you receive, you can also have your water tested privately. The agencies mentioned above can give you the names of testing laboratories.

If you drink bottled water, choose brands from bottlers who bottle their water in glass or clear plastic containers and are able and willing to provide an analysis or certification of purity. And buy only spring or purified water—a bottle labeled "drinking water" may just come from your municipal water system. You would do just as well turning on your faucet.

The biggest concern with tap water is that it is treated with chlorine to remove contaminants. As important as chlorine is for purifying our water, there have been concerns raised about its contribution to the risk of heart disease, its impact on miscarriage, and long-term effects on the immune system. I encourage my clients to attempt to avoid water that has an obvious taste or smell of chlorine. When you travel, order bottled water.

You may want to get information on a water purifying system for your home, if you don't already have one. Steam distillation is the most reliable, and most expensive, form of filtration. The next best is reverse osmosis, which forces the water through a cellophane-like, semipermeable membrane that acts as a barrier to contaminants like asbestos, copper, lead, mercury, and even some minute organisms like *Cryptosporidium*. Reverse osmosis systems require a good bit of water pressure to function, and are often difficult to access for filter changes. The replacement filters also can be quite expensive.

Activated carbon filters use granules, precoat (a fine powder), or solid block to remove unpleasant odors, colors, and off-tastes from drinking water, and do a very good job in removing chlorine and some contaminants. If all you're after is good taste and less chlorine odor, and you aren't concerned about microorganisms or other contaminants, a simple table-top pitcher with a carbon filter (such as Brita) will suffice. If you drink tap water, the taste may improve after refrigerating it for twenty-four hours (the chlorine will dissipate). This can be a low-cost way to get the more refreshing taste of bottled water without the cost.

Your choice of which water to drink comes down to taste, cost, and availability. Regardless, the bottom line is this: drink eight to ten glasses of water a day, and more if you exercise heavily. Don't allow anything to become a substitute for the beverage your body likes best: water, the beverage of champions!

CHAPTER FIVE

Eat strategically

Multi-million dollar basketball superstar Shaquille O'Neal steps up to the free-throw line. Not known for his foul shot percentages, every stress mechanism within Shaq's powerful 7'1", 325 lb. body goes into operation as his performance anxiety builds.

The entire basketball arena is filled with fans yelling "Get it!" or "Miss it!"—depending on where the team is playing. He is surrounded by players from the opposing team "talking trash" and by his own teammates, on edge, depending on his bucket. The coaches are on the sideline, desperately wanting the point.

Adrenaline spurts through Shaq's body. His muscles tense, his heart races. Blood rushes to his extremities, his body temperature control goes awry, his concentration fades. The ball is released, and, in a worst-case scenario, it hits the rim and bounces off—a miss. Dejected, Shaq has to shake it off and get back into the game. Or, maybe he makes the shot. Either way, he has to overcome the moment of anxiety and keep playing, keep performing at his peak.

I worked as Shaq's "food coach" for the years he played for the Orlando Magic. I planned his menus, had a team of chefs going to the market and preparing his meals; I even ordered his room service for "away" games. He desperately needed my advice for eating well to stay well—and not catch every cold and flu he was exposed to. (He had been very prone to respiratory infections prior to our working together.)

Shaq needed expert planning for staying fit and fueled on and off the court. He had to be pumping with energy. But when he needed guidance the most was when he was most in need—to withstand the stress of taking a shot he was more apt to miss than get. Because he had always been an outstanding player with an awesome presence, he had been able to "get by" with eating whatever, whenever. It had certainly gotten him a multi-million dollar contract in the NBA. How bad could his diet be?

Shaq had been created with an incredible body, and blessed with incredible gifts. But his careless eating was blocking the free-flow of those gifts and preventing his learned skills from coming through consistently. To stay the course, and stay a champion, it was going to take a new strategy for living life—a strategy for living on the Energy Edge.

My energy work with elite athletes like Shaq easily transfers into the lives of everyday people who similarly need to be operative from a point of strength. The same principles for a life that's filled with energy and the ability to think clearly and focus—to be our very best—are very similar to the principles I work with in the lives of Shaquille O'Neal, or Mark Price, a professional golfer. All are people who want to be their best in terms of peak performance.

Most of us are not elite athletes, nor do we bring in Shaquille O'Neal's dollars and fame. Nevertheless, we all have an individual "court of life" on which we are expected to perform day by day with perfection, endurance, and stamina. We too have daily "fouls" committed against us, and we are continually stepping up to the "line"—surrounded by encouraging team players and critical opposing forces alike. We are charging full steam ahead in life with too much to do and too few resources from which to pull. It's a stressful way to live, and we require a different level of fueling and fitness to rise up to the new levels of stress.

That's where eating strategically comes in, with a focus on timing, balance, and variety. When it comes to having all the energy you want and need, eating the right foods at the right time is as basic as getting enough sleep. What you *don't* eat will rob you of energy just as much as what you do eat. There are a number of dietary upgrades that you can make to boost your energy level throughout the day.

Eating for the Energy Edge isn't about what you *shouldn't* be eating; it's not about how bad potato chips or ice cream or red meat may be for you. Instead, it's about the food and lifestyle choices that power you with high-octane energy fuel. The food you eat shapes the optimal performance and effectiveness of all your body mechanisms.

Nutritional Literacy

Many of my clients are health-conscious eaters, well-educated nutritionally and committed to smart food choices. By understanding the physiological changes behind fatigue and other physical symptoms and how to manage them, my patients are able to stabilize their body chemistries and grab hold of an energy level they thought impossible.

But not all of my patients are quite so "nutritionally correct." Take Kathleen, as an example. Kathleen had always been naturally thin, the kind of person that others envy. She struggled to keep weight *on*, and was used to hearing people say, "You're so lucky, you can eat all the garbage you want!" And garbage she did eat—whatever and whenever she felt like.

Kathleen's days are familiar to many. She awakens with a blaring alarm, and struggles to get up in the morning. She's not hungry for breakfast and, she reports, "Busy people can't take time for that anyway." A diet soda and doughnut midmorning carry her until lunch, when she has a quick burger or personal pizza on the run. If Kathleen is feeling particularly healthy, she may opt for a big salad, and feel smug about it, even if she did pour on the dressing. Then, around three in the afternoon, she starts to look for a candy bar... or chips... or soda... or something, feeling like she just won't make it through the day without it. But her personal slump hour would be the beginning of a night filled with nonstop eating. Because weight was no problem, Kathleen had never—up to now—considered her overeating to be a problem.

However, she was starting to suspect that eating couldn't be so thoughtless. She was turning forty in the spring and had decided to compete in a triathlon before that momentous birthday. It was a life goal of Kathleen's, and she was serious about it. But one practice run brought her soberly to my office, looking for guidance on how to jump from a life filled with Twinkies, fries, and hit-and-miss eating, to one that she considered to be monk-like, overwhelming... and very confusing.

An information-overloaded Kathleen sat before me saying, "Pam, consider me 'nutritionally illiterate.' I know there's been a lot of information out there about how to eat right, but I just never bothered with it. Now I'm in terrible shape, thin but exhausted, and I'm almost forty. I *know* that I have to eat better. I'm tired and I *need* to eat better, and I *want* to meet the needs of my body the best way I can. I just don't have a clue how."

Kathleen needed a lot more than counseling—she needed a crash course in nutrition. There was no natural instinct that was going to draw her to a good diet and keep her from an unhealthy one. She needed some firm directions for a new way of living her daily life.

Eating To Get Well

Living an energy-filled life requires a nutrition plan that goes far beyond traditional or fad dieting. It was only a decade ago that the world of nutrition began to go beyond dieting for weight loss alone and instead focused on living life well each day—and preventing the diseases of tomorrow. The focus turned toward learning to *eat well to live well*—using food for its inherent healing powers, as a fuel we need to get us well and keep us well.

Most of us underestimate the effect of our eating on our

energy. We don't connect morning sluggishness or afternoon sleepiness to when and what we eat. We know that food is our body's fuel, but most of us resist an even flow. As our schedules get full, it's easy for a consistent eating routine to go awry. Eating falls into an erratic, catch-as-catch-can affair that can't supply our energy needs. Yet when life is most stressful—when it seems we have the least amount of time to eat well—we have the most to gain from it.

Taking charge of the physical you is one thing that you can control, even in the midst of a situation that feels very out of control. Paying attention to how you eat is a small-time investment with a tremendous payback of increased resiliency in the midst of stress.

Edible Energy

Most Americans, particularly women, have been trained practically since birth to consider food and calories the enemy—and restrict them maniacally, other times schizophrenically. But the truth about food and the calories it brings to your body is simple: food is just good-tasting units of energy.

The primary operating mechanism for this energy system is simple: it takes food to make energy. As we all learned in grade school science, the food we eat gets converted to glucose, which is the brain's and lungs' only energy source and the most efficient and common form for the remaining body cells. A single molecule of glucose can trigger the production of nearly thirty-eight molecules of ATP, the energy molecule that fuels the cells. Without ATP, the cells go on a hunger strike and muscles stiffen, refusing to function. Our moment by moment personal energy, at the most basic level, is all about how much ATP our body is producing. Food—and calories—give us the power to breathe, think, move, crack a joke, make love. Taken in appropriate amounts at the proper times, they are a *very* good thing.

It's not just the energy consumed—it's the energy *burned* that counts. Our stressful lifestyles have slowed our metabolic rate to a

How Much Is Enough?

To calculate if you are getting enough fuel, use this formula: multiply your current weight by 16 if you're active, by 12 if you weight train by lifting the remote control. This gives you the approximate number of calories you typically burn in a day—and the amount that will give optimal energy. An active 125-pound woman needs roughly 2,000 calories, a sedentary one needs only 1,750. An active 175-pound man needs 2,800 calories, a sedentary one needs only 2,100. To gain one pound per week, 500 calories should be added daily; to lose one pound per week, 500 calories should be cut daily.

Eating less than 1,500 calories a day can slow your metabolic rate by 30 percent and leave you deficient of energy-releasing nutrients. Your memory, concentration, and judgment can be impaired. Since weight loss efforts means cutting back on those valuable energy-giving calories, it requires upping the ante of quality and timing of eating.

snail's pace, resulting in fats being stored rather than burned for energy. Our body is designed to slow itself as a protective response to such energy deficits. As a result, erratic eating patterns keep our metabolism stuck in low gear, storing away every meal as if it were our last. But what is stored isn't being used for energy—which is why overweight doesn't mean over-energized. If the available energy was the only factor for living an energized life, we could live on sugar (which is almost pure energy) and overweight people would have the most energy of any of us (each pound of stored fat is actually 3,500 calories of stored energy).

But to burn those calories—metabolize them into energy—nutrients are required. These vital nutrients are the vitamins and minerals found in foods. Certain nutrients are considered the energizers because they act as catalysts for calorie burning. The B-complex vitamins, magnesium, and zinc are important examples. (We'll talk more about them in Chapter 17.) Also important is chromium, which helps to transport glucose (blood sugar) through the cell membranes so that it can be burned for energy. Iron is also vital, because it delivers oxygen to inside the cells, "fanning the flame" of calorie burning.

Many people may be getting plenty of calories, but they are not getting enough of the nutrients to help metabolize those calories to realize the energy. Or, their metabolisms may be so slowed in response to the chronic stress in their lives that they cannot burn the calories effectively. Either way, there's a present-day energy crisis!

Regardless of the number of calories consumed when we do eat, the body can use only a small amount of energy quickly. The rest is thrown off as waste or stored as fat. And because the majority of us eat most of our calories overloaded into just a few concentrated hours in the evening, our bodies are robbed of precious energy fuel for the remaining twenty hours, until the next feeding frenzy. We not only go wrong in how much we eat or what we eat; we also eat entirely too much at the wrong time. The vast majority of us get most of our energy in after six in the evening—which is just *too much too late*.

Eating For The Energy Edge

What if we stopped trying not to eat, or not to cheat, and started planning how best to charge up our internal motor? Then we'd be eating for energy—to feel great all day, relax and play all evening, and rise to almost any occasion.

To activate our metabolisms and get our bodies working for us—and with us—we need to go for the Energy Edge's eat-right prescription: small meals of high-energy, whole grain carbohydrates and power-building, low-fat proteins complemented by brightly colored fruits and vegetables, at least every three hours. This means:

EAT EARLY—start every day with breakfast.
EAT OFTEN—energize with power meals and snacks every 2 1/2 to 3 hours.
EAT BALANCED—have both carbohydrates and proteins at each mini-meal.
EAT LEAN—choose low-fat sources of protein and avoid fatty foods.
EAT BRIGHT—include lots of brightly colored fruits and vegetables.

Eat Early

Although it may not seem like news, breakfast is still the most important meal of your day—don't leave home without it! If you want to start your day with a boundless energy level, your metabolism in high gear, and proteins actively building your body, then never skip breakfast! View eating breakfast as a primary performance booster.

Breakfast is important—it "breaks the fast" your body has been in during the hours of night rest. Think of your body as a campfire that dies down during the night and in the morning needs to be "stoked up" with wood to begin burning vigorously again. Without stoking, the fire will die down for lack of sparks. Your body is very similar; it awakens in a slowed, fasting state, and needs breakfast to rev it into high gear.

If you choose not to eat breakfast, your body not only stays slowed down, but, as in the case of a campfire, your metabolism will die down even more, conserving itself for functioning in this disabled, starved state. Continuing to starve your body will leave it dragging through the day at a slowed-down metabolic state, unable to work efficiently. When the evening "gorge" begins, much of the food you eat will be wasted or stored as fat. All that food can't possibly be used up because your body isn't burning energy at a fast rate—the fire has already gone out. It's like dumping an armful of firewood on a dead fire!

Don't think for a minute that you are cutting calories by skipping breakfast. The truth is, those calories would be burned by your body's higher metabolic rate. You are only robbing your body of performance fuel. Research shows that missing breakfast can undercut reading skills, memory, and the ability to concentrate. A recent breakfast study showed a full letter grade differential in children who had breakfast compared with those who did not. Not only that, the study reported a poorer attitude and behavior problems among the children who missed breakfast.

But Breakfast Just Makes Me Hungry!

A common reason for skipping breakfast is that it seems to start a vicious appetite machine, making you hungry every few hours. It's true—and it's a good thing! It's all about your body working correctly. When you starve your body in the morning, waste products are released into your system, temporarily depressing your appetite and allowing you to starve without feeling hungry for many hours. In addition, you've let your body go into a slowed metabolic state, and you're setting yourself up for a gorge. (As soon as you begin to eat, your appetite is really turned on!) Not only will you overeat because your blood sugar level has fallen so low, but, like the campfire, your body will not be able to burn those calories well. Remember—your body just cannot handle such a large intake of food at one time; your needs go on twenty-four hours a day.

Eat breakfast soon after you get up (within the first half-hour of rising), and have three different foods for breakfast—a quick, energy-starting simple carbohydrate (fruit or "soft" juice), a long-lasting complex carbohydrate (grains, cereals, bread, or muffins) and a power-building protein (dairy, egg, or meats). This good-for-you balance will allow a slow and steady release of glucose into your bloodstream to feed your brain and muscles with vital energy. Selecting whole foods, rather than a Danish and fruit punch, also gives your body the vitamins and minerals it needs to transform the energy nutrients into usable fuel.

Go light and easy if time is a push; try some eat-and-go meals like fresh fruit and skim-milk shakes, cheese-toast and fruit, or freshly fruited yogurt with a muffin. Or try the breakfast recipes on page 246—meals designed to give you the perfect start to an energy-filled day.

Eat Often

Once you get your day started with breakfast, keep your energy high and even by eating often throughout the day. One of the more powerful influences on our performance and well-being is our blood sugar level. When our blood sugars are up and even— but not too high—we are brimming with energy and vitality. When the levels are bouncing widely and wildly, our energy, mood, memory, clarity of thought—overall peak performance—is apt to rise and fall right with them.

Blood sugar levels normally crest and fall every three to four hours. As sugars fall, so will your well-being, concentration, and ability to handle stress. Your body will need about half an hour to convert what you eat to energy—so don't wait until you're cranky and starving to eat. If you've starved all day, the drop in sugars will be a "free fall," leaving you weak, sleepy, and dizzy, with an

Power Snacks

❖ **Whole grain crackers or Raisin Squares cereal and low-fat cheese** (like string cheese, part skim mozzarella, or Laughing Cow Lite Cheese Wedges)

❖ **Fresh fruit or small box of raisins and low-fat cheese**

❖ **Half of a lean turkey or chicken sandwich**

❖ **Plain, nonfat yogurt blended with fruit or all fruit jam, or Stonyfield Farms yogurt**

❖ **Whole grain cereal with skim milk**

❖ **Wasa bread with light cream cheese and all fruit jam**

❖ **Baked low-fat tortilla chips with fat-free bean bean dip and salsa**

❖ **Health Valley graham crackers or rice cakes with natural peanut butter**

❖ **Popcorn sprinkled with parmesan cheese**

❖ **Homemade low-fat bran muffin with low-fat or skim milk**

❖ **Crisp bread with sliced turkey and Dijon mustard**

❖ **Small pop-top can of water-packed tuna or chicken, with whole grain crackers**

❖ **Half of a small, whole wheat bagel or English muffin with 2 tbsp. light cream cheese**

❖ **Dill tortilla rolls: whole wheat tortilla spread with Dill Cream Cheese Spread (light cream cheese, lemon juice, pepper, and dill)**

❖ **Fruit shake: skim milk blended with frozen fruit and vanilla**

❖ **Trail mix: 1 cup unsalted dry roasted peanuts, 1 cup unsalted dry roasted shelled sunflower seeds, and 2 cups raisins.** (Make it in abundance and bag up into 1/4 cup portions for a whole snack.)

appetite raging out of control. There's one thing that doesn't fall with blood sugars, and that's your appetite. As the blood sugars crash, the body responds by sending a chemical signal to the brain's appetite control center, demanding to be fed. And your cells are screaming for a quick energy source—not broccoli or cauliflower, but *chocolate* or *chips!*

Remember, eating smaller meals every few hours will prevent your appetite and cravings from swinging out of control, as well as control the sleepiness brought on by large meals. A blitz of too much makes you drowsy by diverting blood from the brain to the stomach. For example, overeating at lunch has been shown to result in a sluggish performance in mid-afternoon. Studies show that scores on mental acuity tests were lower in subjects who ate large lunches. Instead, keep your energy and concentration *up* and cravings *down* throughout your day by eating small amounts more often.

But I thought I wasn't supposed to eat between meals, you may be thinking. Wrong! Healthy and wise snacking is like throwing wood on a fire throughout the day to keep it burning well. It will result in more energy, a vibrant metabolism, and a constant, usable source of nutrients. This means your eating day should consist of three meals with at least two healthy snacks. Ideally, eat 25 percent of your day's calories at breakfast, 25 percent at lunch, 25 percent at dinner, and the other 25 percent in healthy snacks.

When most people think of snacks, they picture potato chips, candy, and sodas. These types of snacks are "empty calories," providing high amounts of fats, sugars, salt and calories, but little or no vitamins or minerals. A healthy snack, on the other hand, provides you with real nutrition and will keep your blood sugar levels from dropping too low. It will keep your metabolism burning high, with your needs satisfied, and still not load you down with unwanted, unneeded fat, salt, sugar, and calories. It will also invigorate your mind. Tests have shown that a snack eaten fifteen minutes before skill tests of memory, alertness, reading, or problem solving greatly increased performance in test subjects, while those individuals who had eaten breakfast and lunch, but no snack, scored lower.

"Power snacking"—eating the right amounts of the right foods at regular intervals—is an important component of maintaining the Energy Edge. (see power snack ideas on page 50.) The savvy snacker should go for a combination of carbohydrates and protein. Carbs metabolize quickly and provide a quick boost in blood sugar levels, while proteins digest more slowly and keep your energy up over a longer period. Eating strategically is essentially a balancing act, achieved by giving your body the right foods at the right time put together in effective ways. This means having both carbohydrates and proteins at every meal and snack.

Eat Balanced

Balancing your intake of carbs and proteins is vital to utilizing nutrients optimally. Carbohydrates are 100 percent pure energy; they are your body's fuel, designed to burn fast, clean, and pure. Carbohydrates should be eaten *with* a protein to protect this building nutrient from being wasted as a less efficient source of energy. This allows protein to be used for its most important functions: building new cells, boosting your metabolism, building body muscle, keeping body fluids in balance, healing and fighting infections, and making beautiful skin, hair, and nails. Always remember: carbohydrates *burn* and proteins *build*. You need them both!

Energy-Boosting Carbohydrates

Carbohydrates are found in plant foods (wheat, corn, oats, rice, barley, fruits, and vegetables), and are nutrition heavyweights themselves. They are packed with fiber, vitamins, and minerals that allow your body to stay operative from a point of strength.

Carbohydrates are considered the ideal fuel choice because they are easily converted into glucose, the type of sugar that is your body's main energy supply.

Carbohydrates for Energy

SIMPLE CARBOHYDRATES

Fruits

All fruits and fruit juices, apples, apricots, bananas, berries, cherries, dates, grapefruit, grapes, kiwis, lemons, limes, melons, nectarines, oranges, peaches, pears, pineapples, plums, raisins.

(Generally one serving of simple carbohydrate is obtained from 1/2 cup fruit, 1/2 cup fruit juice, or 1/8 cup dried fruit. This gives 10 grams of carbohydrate.)

Nonstarchy Vegetables

Asparagus, beets, broccoli, Brussels sprouts, cabbage, carrots, cauliflower, celery, green beans, green leafy vegetables, kale, mushrooms, okra, onions, snow peas, sugar snaps, summer squash, tomatoes, zucchini.

(Generally one serving of simple carbohydrate is obtained from 1/2 cup cooked vegetables or 1 cup raw vegetables or juice. This gives 10 grams of simple carbohydrate.)

COMPLEX CARBOHYDRATES

Grains

The following amounts provide one serving of complex carbohydrate, giving 15 grams:

Barley, bulgur, couscous, grits, kasha, millet, or polenta, cooked ...1/2 cup	Crackers or mini-rice cakes 5
	Crispbread or rice cakes 2
Bread ....1 slice	Oats, uncooked ....1/2 cup
Cereals.....................1 oz.	Fat-free tortillas 1
(1/4 cup of concentrated cereal such as Grape-Nuts or granola, 1/2 to 3/4 cup flaked cereals, and 1 cup puffed cereal)	Wheat germ ....1/4 cup

Starchy Vegetables

Black-eyed peas, corn, green peas, lima beans, rutabagas, turnips, potatoes (white and sweet), winter squash.

(Generally one serving of complex carbohydrate is obtained from 1/2 cup cooked starchy vegetables, giving 15 grams.)

Some carbohydrates are digested and absorbed quite simply, allowing them to be quick-burning forms of energy. These are the simple carbohydrates, found in fruits, unsweetened juices, and crunchy vegetables. Complex carbohydrates, found in grains, root vegetables, and legumes, require more time to convert into a usable form of energy; they are digested more slowly and absorbed more evenly into the system as fuel.

When choosing carbohydrates, go for the most "whole" form possible and thus benefit from the all the fiber, nutrients, and natural chemicals they were created with. This means eating fruits and vegetables with well-washed skins on, and choosing fruit rather than fruit juice. When it comes to grains, look for the word *whole* as the first ingredient. Choose whole grains when you can, such as brown rice and whole-grain breads, crackers, pastas, and cereals. They supply much-needed vitamin B6, chromium, selenium, and magnesium, all nutrients that are critical for activating energy production and release. Whole-grain carbohydrates are particularly valuable because they have not had the outer layers of grain removed; they contain many more vitamins, minerals, and fiber than the refined, white products. It's true that refined grains such as white flour are often enriched with added thiamine, niacin, riboflavin, and iron. But many of the original nutrients remain missing in these foods, including the B-complex vitamins and the minerals involved in carbohydrate metabolism.

Consider this story: A man walking down the street was approached by a robber who, at gunpoint, forced the man to turn over his valuables, including all that he was wearing. After the man stripped, the thief exclaimed, "You sir, have just been refined." Then he returned only four items: the man's watch, one shoe, his undershirt, and his necktie. The thief now proclaimed, "I have just enriched you!"

Returning four nutrients and leaving out twenty-one is what this enrichment caper is all about. When a whole wheatberry is refined, every nutrient is affected (twenty-one are completely lost), and all of its protective fiber is stripped away. In the enrichment process, only four are added back. Don't be fooled by manufacturers and advertisements. White, refined carbohydrates, even though enriched, are never as good nutritionally as whole grains.

Refined grains, including white rice and pasta, are also missing fiber, the dietary component that serves as a "time-release" sub-stance, allowing your body to absorb food's carbohydrates more slowly and evenly. This is why certain carbohydrates have such a high "glycemic" index, meaning they get into your bloodstream as sugar almost as quickly as sugar itself. These quick bursts of energy can ultimately cause fatigue by creating a drop in blood sugar due to insulin surges.

Sugar can be a quick pick-me-up. It's broken down quickly, so within minutes of eating, blood sugar is already on its way to your muscles and brain to energize them for performance. And that's the problem—what comes up quickly will come down quickly. Too much sugar will be a drain on anyone's energy metabolism, and a serious one for people with sensitive blood sugar responses.

Many people without functional, or disease-oriented, hypo-glycemia nonetheless are very sensitive to the rises and falls in blood sugars. Once a person with a tendency toward *reactive* hypoglycemia has eaten, their blood sugar rises quickly—very quickly if they've consumed a refined carbohydrate with a high glycemic potential. Their insulin levels rise in response to the higher blood glucose level to move the sugar into the cell to be processed. These high insulin levels outlast the sugar burst, taking more and more sugar into the cells, dramatically dropping the blood sugar levels to a less-than-desirable level. The result is that the person soon feels spacey, unable to concentrate, weak, sleepy, anxious, sweaty, or dizzy.

The quick drop in blood sugar will also trigger a craving for more carbohydrates—the essence of what is termed "sugar addiction." In addition, the higher levels of circulating insulin stimulate the stor-age of fat in the body, and inhibit the burning of fat as energy. This is why eating evenly and wisely will keep the body burning fat and releasing optimal energy. (If you suspect you may be strongly reac-tive to sugar level swings, read more in "Are You Seduced By Sugar?" on page 175.)

The key is to get plenty of carbohydrates, but make them whole and don't overload. If you eat lunches that are high in carbohydrates but low in protein, you may find yourself feeling tired in the afternoon. That's because carbohydrates trigger the insulin surge described above along with an increase in the brain's production of the calming chemical serotonin—the brain's feel-good drug. Protein on the other hand can offset carbohydrate-induced sleepiness—and much more.

Power Proteins

Your need for protein is not to be ignored—it is the "new you" and it becomes the building blocks for your entire body. Protein works to replace worn-out cells and to regulate your body functions, including the stabilization of your energy levels.

Many of the diets of our time have promoted protein as *the* food to eat for weight loss. The truth is that an all-protein, no-carbohydrate diet so imbalances the body that you *do* lose weight; it's just the wrong kind of weight loss—mostly water and muscle mass, and little fat. Instead, a balanced intake of both carbohydrate *and* protein at every meal and snack allows the most attractive, healthy, and most permanent weight loss. (Read more about healthy weight loss in chapter 25.)

Anything that comes from an animal (poultry, fish, meat, eggs, cheese, milk, and yogurt) gives you complete protein, supplying all the essential amino acids that your body can't make or store. The only plant source of quality protein, a miraculous one, is the legume family (dried beans and peanuts). Their pods absorb nitrogen from the soil and become an excellent high-fiber, low-fat protein source. Yet, because they lack sufficient amounts of one or more of the essential amino acids, they are considered "incomplete" proteins. They are best eaten with a grain (a corn, wheat, rice, or oat product) or a seed (sunflower, sesame, pumpkin) to be complete. Examples of high-quality dynamic duos are: peanut butter on bread, black beans over rice, beans and tortillas or cornbread, or a peanut and sunflower seed trail mix. Generally, 1/2 cup of cooked beans serves as two ounces of protein when mixed with an appropriate grain or seed, and 3/4 cup equals three ounces of protein.

Women generally need at least 50 to 55 grams of protein, and men generally need 65 to 70 grams—needs that are based on their percentage of lean body mass. More protein is needed in times of stress, or when actively working to build muscle or to maintain muscle mass while losing fat weight. Generally, one ounce of meat contains about 7 grams of protein, meaning women need a minimum of 7 to 8 ounces per day and men need a minimum of 9 to 10 ounces per day.

But, the *amount* of protein eaten is not the only secret to abundant energy and wellness; equally important is the need to take in protein in smaller, evenly distributed amounts throughout the day. Protein is not stored, so it must be replenished frequently throughout the day, each and every day. And this is where people go wrong. Never, never believe anybody or anything that tells you that you don't need protein, or to eat it only once a day. You are robbing your body of protein's healing and building power all day long.

Protein for Power

Each serving equals 1 ounce of protein (7 grams)

Nonfat milk or nonfat plain yogurt . . . . 6 oz.

Low-fat cheeses . . . . 1 oz. (or 1/4 cup grated)

1% low-fat or nonfat cottage cheese, or part-skim or fat-free ricotta . . 1/4 cup

Eggs (particularly, use egg whites) 1

Flaked fish (i.e. tuna, salmon) . . . . 1 oz.

Seafood (crab, lobster) . . . . 1/4 cup

Seafood (clams, shrimp, oysters, scallops) . . . . 5 pieces

Poultry . . . . 1 oz. (or 1/4 cup chopped)

Beef, pork, lamb, veal (lean, trimmed) . . . . 1 oz.

Legumes (black beans, garbanzo beans, Great Northern beans, kidney beans, lentils, navy beans, peanuts, red beans, split peas, soybeans, and soy products such as tofu and soy milk) . . . . 1/4 cup

Natural peanut butter . . . . 2 tbsp.

Generally, your power snacks should include at least 1 to 2 ounces of protein, and your meals should provide 2 to 3 ounces after cooking. If possible, get a food scale and periodically weigh your protein portion to be sure you are getting enough. Getting *enough* protein at the right time is a vital ingredient for an energized life.

Choose your proteins wisely—make them low-fat; studies are showing that as fat goes down, immune and metabolic power goes up, as does energy. It has been theorized that overeating fat causes an increase in the viscosity—or thickness—of the blood, causing a decrease in your blood's oxygen-carrying capacity. This results in a decrease in energy metabolism. In contrast, eating a balanced diet low in fat, yet high in whole grains, fruits, and vegetables, gives us higher levels of energy and alertness, better stress management, and even improved memory and sleep.

Eat Lean

One of the drawbacks to eating protein more often is that many popular choices are also high in fat. While fat is an essential nutrient needed in limited amounts to lubricate your body, transport fat-soluble vitamins, and produce hormones, eating fat-laden foods to excess is also the major dietary risk factor in many killer diseases.

Most experts recommend limiting dietary fat intake to 25 to 30 percent of calories, yet Americans take in approximately 40 percent of their daily calories from fat. Chances are you may be eating more than you even realize. A typical adult eats the fat equivalent of one stick of butter a day! And there's nothing like fat to make us fat!

Even if you have been blessed with a metabolism that burns ever brightly, allowing you to maintain your weight easily, excess fat intake can cause problems nonetheless. You may not be *seeing* the problem, on the scale or on your waistline, but fat sludge in your bloodstream vandalizes your energy stores.

When counseling even the thinnest of the elite athletes I've worked with, I develop a meal plan that, though high in calories and focused in protein, is nonetheless very low in fat. Penny Hardaway is a lean basketball playing machine who has a difficult time keeping weight on. One summer, while I was working with the Orlando Magic, we needed him to gain seventeen pounds of muscle mass. This required almost 9,000 calories a day, but very little fat.

High-fat eating doesn't add up to healthy, muscle-mass weight gain for an athlete, and it doesn't work to increase performance and stabilize energy for you. By choosing the low-fat versions of protein foods, you will get all of their goodness without the risk.

Eat Bright

Brightly colored fruits and vegetables such as carrots, sweet potatoes, tomatoes, broccoli, spinach, romaine lettuce, strawberries, etc., are loaded with antioxidants like beta-carotene and vitamin A, folic acid and other B vitamins, along with vitamin C. These nutrients are vital to wellness as they neutralize chemicals believed to damage body processes, and they serve to boost energy potential by boosting the immune system.

Generally, the more vivid the color of the fruit or veggie, the higher in nutrients it will be. The bright color is the sign that these are treasure chests of protection, and triggers for releasing energy and immunities. That deep orange-red color of carrots, sweet potatoes, apricots, cantaloupe, and straw-

Tips to Retain Nutrients

❖ Buy vegetables that are as fresh as possible; frozen is the next best choice. Avoid those frozen with butter or sauces.

❖ Use well washed peelings and outer leaves of vegetables whenever possible—they have a high concentration of nutrients.

❖ Store vegetables in airtight containers in the refrigerator.

❖ Do not store vegetables in water. Too many vitamins are lost.

❖ Cook vegetables on the highest heat possible, in the least amount of water possible, and for the shortest time possible. Steaming, microwaving and stir-frying are great cooking methods.

❖ Cook vegetables until tender crisp, not mushy. Overcooked vegetables lose flavor along with vitamins.

berries is a sign of their vitamin A content. Dark green leafy vegetables like greens, spinach, romaine lettuce, broccoli, and
Brussels sprouts, are also loaded with an extra bonus of being *the*
source of folic acid, a "must have" for health and wellness.

Five servings a day of brightly colored fruits and vegetables will
help to keep the doctor away... and ten servings will allow you to
thrive, especially if complemented with other antioxidant-rich
foods such as garlic, green tea, and soy.

Without trying to calculate every milligram of this vitamin and
that mineral in the foods you eat, the very best way to assure your
vitamin intake is optimal is to go for whole-grain carbohydrates
whenever possible, and choose meals full of a variety of brightly
colored fruits and vegetables.

Combatting Cravings

Sarah has a chocolate fit every month just before she gets her
period. After a tough day at the office, Jim covets tortilla chips.
Debbie suddenly can't resist pasta with rich, creamy sauce—one
reason she's slowly regaining the forty pounds she's just lost.

Most of us have experienced a strong, nearly uncontrollable urge
for a certain type of food. And while we've struggled to keep ourselves from the refrigerator, we may have wondered why we long
so intensely for a particular food. Why do we have cravings? Are we
born to crave?

Most people don't sell their soul for a stalk of celery. They are
driven toward sugar and salt (inborn preferences for infants to drink
breast milk) and fat (inborn preferences for children to sustain
growth). The problem is that even though children outgrow their
biological needs, their tastes persist because of the foods that are cul-
tural and family favorites. They develop passions for peanut butter
and jelly, macaroni and cheese, cheeseburgers, and milkshakes. For
the more sophisticated palates of adults, it's Rocky Road ice cream,
fettucine alfredo, creamy chocolate mousse, and nachos.

The cravings get fueled by diet deficiencies. Fluctuating blood sugars—enhanced by hormone and stress chemicals—stimulate the driving desire for sweets; fluid imbalances drive the desire for salty foods; sustained inadequate intake of calories (lack of supply to meet demand) fuels the desire for fats. This is the physical side of the craving, driving us in a general direction.

Our emotions help determine the exact food we arrive at. The body sends out the "I *need*" signal, the emotions send out the "I *want*" signal—sending us directly toward the comfort food of choice, particularly when comfort is being called for. Our generation's battle cry is "relief is just a swallow away," and for many of us that spells food. The refrigerator light becomes the light of our life.

Mango Apple Chutney

1 Granny Smith apple, thinly julienned
1/2 ripe mango, cut in strips
2 tbsp. hot mango chutney
1/2 red bell pepper, cut into strips
1/4 cup orange juice
juice of 1/2 lime
1 tbsp. chopped fresh cilantro
1/2 tsp. creole seasoning
1 tbsp. low-sodium soy sauce

Mix all ingredients. Refrigerate to blend flavors. Makes 6 servings, 1/3 cup each. Serve with baked tortilla chips and salsa.

A question I'm frequently asked is, "Should I ever just give into my cravings?" The answer depends on how frequently cravings occur! Once a month, sure. But if they hit you often, they take on a life of their own, start robbing from your health and well-being, and suffocate you with guilt!

When cravings do occur, try to make the most of them. If you crave ice cream, choose sorbet and yogurt and top it with fresh fruit. If you crave chips, get the baked version and serve with a fat-free bean dip or top with melted low-fat cheese. Try some taste bud tricks like a baked tortilla chip plate served with Mango Apple Chutney (above) and salsa. The chips are crunchy and salty yet low-fat; the fruit chutney is an uncanny blend of crisp, smooth, sweet, tart, and salty.

Once you've stabilized your body chemistry with the eat-right prescription, you'll find that your body becomes more finely tuned for restful sleep: you can sleep more soundly and wake up feeling more refreshed. Restful sleep is a powerful energizer.

CHAPTER SIX

Sleep well

n all of creation, the principle of rest is modeled for us. The soil of the earth needs a rest from time to time, allowing it to become more productive. Bears hibernate, fish sleep with their eyes open, the most beautiful plants have a period of dormancy. Our needs as creatures are no different. Physiologically, sleep is the repair shop of the body and brain, the process that most thoroughly restores our psychological and physiological vitality after the strain and exertion of life. Along with the building and repair of our muscle tissues, bones, cells, and immune system, restful sleep allows the release of important hormones such as the human growth hormone, which is critical for vitality.

Restful sleeping can become a part of your energized lifestyle prescription; the productivity it gives back to your day is well worth the hours invested. Block in sleep as a priority part of your schedule. By doing this you are making an advance decision that sleep is important because being your very best is important.

If it's a little harder for you to shut off the business of your mind than it is to shut off the light, you may need some tips for sweet sleep. Before you endure one more sleepless night or another morning dragging yourself out of bed, use these tips to keep your body programmed for restful sleep.

ABCs Of Good Zzzs
Be Clock-Driven
When it comes to catching up on lost sleep, timing is everything. Your body's internal time clock is daily reset by getting up at the same time each day. "Sleeping in," even for an hour, can disrupt your biological clock and end up making you feel even more fatigued. This is why research shows that getting to bed earlier in the evening offers an advantage over sleeping late the next morning: getting to sleep an hour earlier can provide the extra rest without upsetting the rhythm. Stick with it; people who are just starting to make up lost sleep can take six weeks to recover fully.

I know this is hard, but try to get up at the same time every day, regardless of when you fall asleep. Set your alarm clock—then put it out of sight. You want to be clock-driven, not clock-obsessed.

Check Your Medicines
Ask your pharmacist or physician if any of your prescription or over-the-counter medications are insomnia triggers. The most common troublemakers are some blood pressure medications, diet pills, diuretics, antidepressants, cold and allergy remedies, and asthma medications.

Also speak with your pharmacist or physician about any chronic use of over-the-counter sleeping aids such as Nytol or Sominex. They contain antihistamines to induce sleepiness and can serve to calm the desperate feelings associated with not getting to sleep; but they also can bring side effects, and like prescription sleep medications, will stop working after a period of nightly use.

Regulate Your Hormones
A female approaching menopause cannot, and should not, ignore the hormone issue. Let the alleviation of troublesome hot flashes and night sweats be your motivator to consider hormone replacement therapy. You will gain many more healthy benefits as well: protection from diseases including heart disease and osteoporosis,

a possible decrease in the risk of Alzheimer's, a brighter perspective and clearer thinking, along with enhanced libido and greater sexual enjoyment.

Cut Out the Caffeine by Midday

North Americans drink 400 million cups of coffee each day, and get extra doses of caffeine in tea or cola-type sodas, cocoa, and chocolate. Recognize that the stimulant activity is still at work five to seven hours after you've ingested it. It can prevent your body from falling into deep sleep, and may awaken you prematurely by disrupting sleep patterns.

Choose Night-Time Snacks Wisely

Overeating, or high-fat, high-sugar snacks after dinner, can result in such an overload to your body that it will resist either getting to sleep or staying asleep. The classic pattern is being awakened at 2:30 to 3 AM, eyes open, heart racing, unable to get restfully back to sleep. It may be the bathroom calling, but it's usually fluctuating blood sugars that brings you to such a light state of sleep that it awakens you. Eating too much too late has put your body into chemical gymnastics. Going to bed hungry can be a sleep-robbing culprit as well. When you're hungry your brain will try to keep you alert until you eat.

A great bedtime snack is a small bowl of whole grain cereal with low fat milk or half a turkey sandwich or a banana with skim milk. All keep the body chemistries undergirded through the night, allowing you to awaken rested and refreshed.

Skip the Nightcap and Night Smoke

Alcohol in the bloodstream makes staying asleep more difficult. In addition, it suppresses dreaming, so it deprives your body of its normal, refreshing sleep cycle. Nicotine is also a stimulant that keeps your body from easily falling asleep. One more reason to kick the habit!

Work Your Body During the Day

With its ability to physically process the stressors of our day, exercise allows for sweeter sleep; it's nature's best tranquilizer! There's no need to run marathons to get its benefits; just a walk, a bike ride, or swim can work wonders with your body, and your sleep. People who work out for thirty to forty minutes, four times a week, fall asleep faster and sleep longer than non-exercisers. Just avoid exercising less than an hour before bedtime—the rise in your body temperature can keep you awake.

Keep It Cool, Dark, and Quiet

People sleep best in rooms that are between 60 and 65 degrees, pitch-black, and silent. If that's a far cry from your bedroom, put up heavy drapes or a light-blocking shade. To drown out traffic noises or a snoring spouse, try wearing ear plugs, or adding "white noise" like a fan or air conditioner.

Sleep on Your Side

This position promotes easier breathing and reduces snoring, which can wake you up. One of the often overlooked causes of daytime fatigue is nighttime posture. Sleeping on your stomach can cause a strain on your back that might be just painful enough to keep you from getting a good night's sleep. For the most restful repose night after night, follow the example of a model sleeper:

❖ A pillow under the knees comfortably flexes your lower spine, making it say "Ahhhh...."

❖ To avoid neck and shoulder aches, use a pillow that's low enough to support your head without flexing your neck. Down pillows work best; foam ones are often too springy.

❖ Be sure you're warm enough. If you have to say curled up all night to keep warm, your back is likely to get sore.

❖ You need enough room to maneuver. This prevents your joints from staying in one position for too long and getting stiff overnight.

Develop a Sleep Ritual

Remember the power of the bedtime story for helping to calm you down as a child? A bedtime routine gives your brain strong cues that it's time to slow down and prepare for sleep. It can be as simple or as elaborate as you like—a warm bath, lighting a candle (particularly a calming lavender one), putting a "brow pillow" on your forehead, snuggling up with your loved one, or listening to classical music. (Just ten minutes of Mozart has been shown to rein in the racing mind—both for sleep and performance. Subjects' IQ scores increased after listening to Mozart but showed no improvement listening to New Age music.)

Some people are avid journal keepers before bed, particularly when their mind is racing. Writing down what you're thinking and feeling helps to "drain the brain" for restful sleep. I have more than a few clients who lay down for five minutes, then get up and make a to-do list, writing down everything that needs to be attended to the next day. Then they set it aside, and make time the next day to deal with their list.

Don't force the sleep issue. If you're still awake thirty minutes after going to bed, get up and do something calming, such as reading, until you're groggy enough to fall asleep. Try to stay awake until your eyes close involuntarily. This works best if you don't keep track of time. Again, set the alarm clock, then set the clock out of sight.

Sleep is the repair shop of the body and brain, the process that most thoroughly restores our vitality after the strain and exertion of life.

Let Bed Be Bed

Don't let it be an office, a place to pay bills, or a home theater. Make your bed restful by using it only for sleeping and romance.

A Snooze You Can Use

Come late afternoon, there are legions of people who'd love to succumb to a quick, restorative rest—and would probably benefit from it. Yet for years, there has been a decidedly undignified aura surrounding the subject of napping.

Bonafide nappers appear to be a selective breed. Scarlett O'Hara was *not* one of them, making the point abundantly clear when she lamented "Why do I have to take a nap? I'm not tired!" Despite her apparent worldliness she didn't know why she *should* nap. It seems to be a secret that nappers know how to get more done and have more fun!

Nappers generally fall into three categories: 1) replacement nappers, who nap because of lack of sleep; 2) preparative nappers, who nap to store up for a planned deficit (also called party napping to the social set); and 3) appetitive nappers, who are napping connoisseurs.

Research shows that 60 percent of adults nap at least once per week. They nap from fifteen minutes to two hours—at their desks, on the subway, while watching TV. Only college students and retired persons are likely to nap easily; they are perceived to have more time on their hands. But that may be changing; more and more progressive corporations are focusing on the power of the nap for enhancing, not robbing, productivity. Some companies, like ice cream's Ben and Jerry's, have initiated napping privileges because of the well-documented scientific studies showing that naps can have a positive effect on both mood and performance. Because of NASA research showing that pilots who take forty-minute sleep breaks on long flights fare better on vigilance tests, several European airlines (such as Swissair) now require their pilots to take naps. It is one of those rare instances where science says that something we like is actually good for us!

God napped on the seventh day. Brahms napped on the piano while he composed the most famous lullaby. Napoleon napped yards from battle, DaVinci napped, Edison napped. Churchill maintained that he *had* to nap during the day in order to cope with his wartime responsibilities, writing, "Nature had not intended man to work from eight in the morning until midnight, without the refreshment of blessed oblivion, which, even if it lasts only twenty minutes, is sufficient to renew all vital forces....You must sleep sometime between lunch and dinner, and no half-way measures.... Don't think you will be doing less work because you sleep during the day....You will be able to accomplish more."

Yet Americans, among the world's most work-driven and guilt-ridden people, have historically looked down their noses at napping. *Real* adults work all day, they *don't* slough off. Breathers, breaks, and naps have been given a bad rap.

Research, however, is giving a wake-up call on napping. Countless studies show the regenerative properties of a twenty-minute nap, and new research is even showing the *protective* properties of a mid-afternoon snooze. A study conducted by the University of Athens Medical School found that Greek men who napped at least thirty minutes a day were 30 percent less likely to have heart problems than those that didn't nap.

The health benefits of napping appear to be related to the human body's tendency to follow its own natural, or circadian, rhythms rather than society's clocks. These circadian rhythms are nature's neural timekeepers in the brain that regulate everything from our hormone levels to our waking and sleeping times.

When researchers had volunteers spend time in an underground room with no clocks or clues as to day or night, and let them sleep whenever they wanted, they found that the subjects slept in two cycles: a longer session at night and a shorter period (a nap!) during the day. Humans have a huge need to sleep at night, and again around 2 to 4 in the afternoon.

It's your mental energy that gets a sudden jolt from a nap—your ability to focus, make decisions, and solve problems. Afternoon shut-eye helps the brain "regroup," thus reducing stress, inattention, and errors. After a short snooze, studies show that subjects who napped score better on tests that measure logical reasoning and reaction time.

Power Napping 101

A catnap can be very refreshing—relaxing your body, boosting your energy levels, improving your mood, clearing the mind, and offering a needed break from the stressful pace of life. Studies show that you don't really even need to sleep to get the rejuvenation you need—just the laying down produces more alertness and clearheadedness, and less anxiety, confusion, and fatigue in the hours that follow. Power Napping may be the best no-cost, no-sweat way to physical and emotional energy.

Here are some Power Napping tips:

MAKE NAPS SHORT AND SWEET. Don't tell toddlers this, but a fifteen-to twenty-minute nap seems to be the ideal nap length for the maximum energy boost. You can stretch it a few extra minutes, but don't go over two hours. Too long a nap can be counterproductive; long naps can allow you to enter into the deeper delta-type sleep, thus causing, not curing, a groggy, disoriented state at wake-up that takes a long time to snap out of. If you seem to need more than an hour's nap in the afternoon, you're probably not getting enough nighttime sleep.

TIME IT SMART. Try not to nap after 4 PM—you'll be more apt to stay groggy afterward and disturb your nighttime sleep. This means you should avoid falling asleep in front of the TV at night. If you're sleepy, turn the TV off and go to bed for the night.

BREAK FOR A NAP, NOT CAPPUCCINO. The ideal nap time is about eight hours after waking up—somewhere around 3 PM. When your afternoon slump begins to take hold, take a fifteen-minute break to recharge. Close the door, turn off the lights. Sit with your eyes closed and be replenished for the time you still have ahead in the afternoon. Then get up and have your afternoon power snack.

TAKE YOUR NAP SERIOUSLY. Close the door to your office, or find a quiet, dim area to snooze. Hold your calls or unplug the phone. Stretch out like you mean it. Instead of dozing off in your chair, take your nap on the couch, in bed—even on the floor. This reclining pose allows you to reach a deeper stage of sleep and awaken with the feeling that you slept much longer than your actual nap time. At least put your feet up.

PLAN AHEAD. Definitely nap in the afternoon if you know you're facing a short night with fewer-than-usual hours allotted for sleep. It has been shown to be much more effective than trying to catch up on your sleep the next morning.

REORIENT YOURSELF. Upon arising from your nap, stretch or take a quick walk.

Napping is an important part of self-care, making a statement that "you deserve a break today." It's a vital time-out for rest—and smart because time-outs are major energizers. The bottom line: rest more and sleep more. Both "seal up the cracks" that leak precious energy from your reserves.

CHAPTER SEVEN

Get moving

The *fastest* way to feel energized is to exercise. And it doesn't take much to bring an energy boost; just a ten-minute walk brings an increase in energy and decreases tension and fatigue *for as long as two hours!* Much more dynamic than a weight loss measure or a cardiovascular strengthener, moving your body is an active, take-charge step for cutting away at the stress mechanism and boosting your energy level.

But everyone seems to know that exercise is good for them and is a vital part of healthful living. Most of us know that regular exercise will help to right the wrongs of our over-stressed bodies. It can gear up a sluggish metabolism, thereby providing help for weight and cholesterol control. It improves muscle tone, helps to reduce blood pressure, boosts the immune system, and puts the brakes on mild depression and stress. And because of what we know, many of us begin exercise programs on a regular basis. Some of us begin them every January 2; others start every Monday morning. However, knowing that exercise is good for us doesn't seem to be enough to compel us to stick with it. As many as 80 percent of those starting an exercise routine drop out soon after starting. Only 40 percent of Americans exercise regularly, and only 20 percent reap aerobic benefits.

Why *don't* people exercise? I believe the answer is simple: It's the viscous cycle of exhaustion people many of us are stuck in. We know we need to exercise, but we are simply too done in to get it done. It's like beating a dead horse! That's why I usually develop a phased energy plan for my clients, first getting them eating well for about three weeks, then encouraging exercise as a result of the overflow of energy. With this dynamic duo, the exercise adds significantly to their energy level.

Aerobic exercise, in particular, is an energy enhancer because it boosts the oxygen-carrying capacity of the bloodstream. During aerobic exercise, your heart pumps more blood, your lungs take in more oxygen, and your blood carries more oxygen and fuel to your muscles. The glucose from your food combines with oxygen in your cells and produces—and releases—the energy molecules you need. This means exercise gives you more energy-boosting oxygen where you need it, faster and more efficiently. And by making your heart more efficient in its function, aerobic exercise improves brain circulation and function as well.

Exercise also helps you think with greater clarity and creativity. It ignites your ability to creatively solve problems, thrive under pressure, and perform at peak levels of effectiveness. As you dramatically increase your oxygen uptake, as well as the production of the red corpuscles that carry oxygen to your brain, the influx of blood oxygen enhances the functioning of every organ in your body. Your thinking power receives a forceful boost, because 25 percent of your blood is in your brain at any one time during exercise.

In addition, the right side of your brain—that area specializing in creative thought and problem solving—becomes more active when you exercise. More than one major problem in corporations has been overcome by savvy decision-makers who choose to exercise to release their creative flow.

Keep reminding yourself that *the fastest way to feel energized is to exercise*. Thirty minutes of aerobic activity—all at once or in three ten-minute spurts—will boost your energy, mood, and alertness. Beta-endorphins—the powerful morphine-like chemicals that promote a sense of well-being—are also released in your brain during exercise. And the good news is that moderate regular exercise brings both a short- and long-term energy boost; it can create a change in biochemistry that launches you into a state of confidence and exhilaration. The overall effect of consistent exercise is to provide you better fuel to work with and a better engine to put it in.

Even if you're slender as a stalk, a sedentary lifestyle can endanger your health. A study at the Cooper Institute for Aerobics Research in Dallas found that thin people who weren't physically active were nearly three times more likely to die young than heavy people who exercised regularly. In fact, it may be that many of the medical risks of inactivity have been mistaken for obesity-related risks. This research is compelling enough to put forth the opinion that it may be better to be overweight and active, than thin and sedentary. Another major study recently showed that chronic inactivity predisposes people to approximately the same risk of early death as smoking!

In addition to being the absolute best energizer, regular aerobic activity reduces the incidence of heart disease and hypertension. It lowers cholesterol, but also is the factor that increases your body's production of the good, protective HDL cholesterol. Exercise enhances your immune system, and generally improves the functioning of almost every organ and system in your body. One study found that those who walked briskly for forty-five minutes a day, five times a week, had half as many colds and bouts with the flu as non-exercisers.

Not exercising, on the other hand, is associated with an increased rate of illness and disease of nearly every type, from the common cold and flu to heart disease and stroke. And because of the interconnected nature of the muscular system, brain, and other processes of the body, being sedentary also depresses your mood, your thinking, and your ability to work productively.

Just Get Moving

That "I'm too tired to work out" feeling will get out of your head once you start moving. You just have to override the message of your stressed-out brain and do something—anything—physical when you're in an energy slump.

When you get home feeling totally beat, push yourself a bit: change into sneakers and go out for a brisk walk. You'll feel a burst of energy afterward. Then the next time you're feeling too pooped to exercise, you'll remember that "buzz" and be quicker to get off the couch. You may even be inclined to expand your workout into a more ambitious run or bike ride, or even a visit to the gym. Soon you'll be healthfully hooked on the buzz of working out and won't even hear those "I'm just too tired" messages from your brain.

If you don't like exercising for the sake of exercise, just do fun things that get you active. Do anything that gets you moving: take the dog out for a walk, chase a football with the neighborhood kids, jog, swim, bike, dance, get your toddler out for a power stroll. Even gardening and mowing the lawn count! Alternate among two or three activities to work a greater range of muscles—and avoid boredom. The notion of "no pain, no gain" is an exercise lie. If you hurt, you'll stop exercising or get hurt—and the benefits of activity will come screeching to a halt.

The best way to begin an exercise program is to get a fitness physical, which can be performed by your doctor or wellness professional. An ideal fitness physical is an "all points check" testing the following: cholesterol, EKG stress test, VO_2 max, fat:lean body composition, blood pressure, and resting heart rate. This test allows you to evaluate if there are any potential risk factors in your planned exercise program, and to set realistic goals. It's a terrific benchmark, and can be very motivating. It is critical to do if you're past the age of thirty-five and/or if you have been sedentary for three months or longer.

The "Jump Start Your Energy" Prescription

You don't have to take up the latest exercise craze in order to become fit. Instead you can forge your own path, at your own pace, and in your own direction. The frequency, intensity, and duration of your workouts will influence the extent of the health benefits you reap. The type and time of exercise you choose will determine whether you stick with it. Consider this exercise guide to be F.I.T.T.:

FREQUENCY—Four to six days a week. Exercising *less* will produce some benefit, but not enough. Exercising *more* may be useful for athletic training, but can lead to injury.

INTENSITY—At a level where you feel slightly out of breath, *without gasping*. Exercise should not hurt. If something hurts, stop and rest. If the pain persists, check with your doctor.

TIME—Thirty to sixty minutes, at a time of day when you feel good and your schedule allows routine to be built.

TYPE—Whatever type of aerobic exercise you enjoy (or could enjoy) and can do regularly.

Choose a time of day to exercise that best suits your schedule. Is it early morning? This is a great choice to beat the heat, and you won't be interrupted by schedule surprises as easily as you might be later in the day. Research has shown that those who begin exercising in the morning are more likely to be at it a year later. If you do exercise first thing, grab a glass of energy-boosting juice first (4 to 6 ounces of apple, white grape, or unsweetened cranberry juice is great), then eat breakfast right after your workout.

If you choose midday as your exercise time, find an indoor activity to protect you from the heat. Exercising in over 90-degree weather is not a wise move. And remember, anytime you are active in the heat, be sure you are drinking lots and lots of water to replenish the fluids you are losing to perspiration.

Is early evening best for you? Although this is a difficult time to stay consistent (easy to just say no after a hectic day!), it's a tremendous time to take advantage of exercise's stress-busting, energizing power. By diverting from your day's activities, you can downshift from stress to relaxation. It's a good time to review the day's events—the good, the bad, and the ugly—and get a pulse on how you feel about the events that occurred.

If you exercise after dinner, make it a half-hour afterward so you won't be doing battle with your natural digestion process. Guard against exercising within half an hour of bedtime, though—your exercised, geared-up metabolism can interfere with restful sleep.

A Well-Rounded Workout

Basically, four types of exercise are needed to provide the best workout and to work all the muscles of your body: warm-up/cool-down, aerobic exercise, conditioning/strength exercise, and stretching for flexibility.

The best energy-boosting exercise for morning or midday workouts is aerobic—jumping rope, jogging, cycling, stepping, and other cardiovascular activities that get your heart pumping and leave you energized. Aerobic workouts are best for maximizing energy, reducing tension, and enhancing physical and mental performance. Cross training and interval training can energize your performance even more. Anaerobic work, such as conditioning and strength training, may tire you out and is best saved for later in the day.

Warming Up/Cooling Down

Use warm-up exercises, such as light side-to-side movements, to limber up your muscles and prevent injuries from the other types of exercise. Never skip the warm-up—it prepares your muscles for the workout (muscles work best when they're warmer than normal body temperature). A warm-up also allows your oxygen supply to ready itself for what is to come, alerting your body to oncoming shock or stress.

You can warm up with stretching, jumping jacks, skipping rope, or jogging in place. You can also warm up with stretching and then beginning a less intense version of your exercise activity—for example, walking before jogging. An adequate warm-up time is three to five minutes.

At the end of your exercise time, also spend three to five minutes cooling down. This allows your body's cardiovascular system to return to normal gradually, preferably over a ten- to fifteen-minute period. This can be considered a "warm-up in reverse" because it consists of the same types of exercises as your warm-up.

Warm-up and cool-down are just as important as the main event. Both can prevent many of the common injuries that take you "out of the race."

Aerobic Exercise

Exercises that work the heart and the circulatory system are by far the most crucial ones for overall body wellness, and particularly for energy-boosting and mood-enhancing. Walking, running, jumping rope, cycling, swimming, and aerobic dancing use major muscle groups, burn fat, and help keep the body working efficiently. Any of these exercises are terrific energy boosters as long as you get your heart rate up consistently for twenty to sixty minutes. It's the *continuous* activity that is most energizing, not the stop-stand-start type that you do in tennis, softball, volleyball, or golf. And it's the routine of exercise that builds a conditioned body—one that adapts much more resiliently to stress.

Again, try for some kind of activity every day. Even if it's not a hard workout at the gym, just a walk after dinner can do miraculous things with your energy levels. When doing aerobic exercise, it's a good idea to keep track of your heart rate. This is especially important when you are building up to a pace and distance that's comfortable for you.

Exercise on Target

Your maximum heart rate is the fastest your heart can beat. The best activity level is 60 to 75 percent of this maximum rate. The 60 to 75 percent range is called your heart rate target zone. In this zone, your muscles are moving, you're breathing deeply, your blood is delivering ample amounts of oxygen to your body systems, and you're burning fat as your major fuel source. At this level, you should be breathing deeply but comfortably enough that you can hold a conversation or sing to yourself.

To find your heart rate target zone, subtract your age from 220. Your exercise zone will be 60 to 75 percent of that number. So, a 45-year-old would subtract 45 from 220, getting an average maximum heart rate (100 percent) of 175. Sixty to 75 percent of this number would be 105 to 131 beats per minute.

When you begin your exercise program, aim for the lower part of your heart rate target zone (60 percent) during the first few months. As you get into better shape, gradually build up to the higher part of your target zone (75 percent).

To see if you are within your exercise heart rate zone, take your pulse periodically throughout your exercise time. Place the first two fingers of your hand at either side of your neck just under your jaw. You should feel your pulse easily at your carotid artery. Using your watch or the clock, count for six seconds, then multiply by ten. This is your heart rate per minute.

If you don't exercise hard enough to get your heart rate up into your exercise zone, you won't produce the changes in your body and brain that recharge your energy level and mood. However, exercising harder than your target heart rate is self-defeating; it can diminish the effectiveness of your workout. Working to such elevated levels causes you to burn more glucose (sugar) as an energy source, detracting from fat loss and conditioning of your body. It can also leave you feeling exhausted rather than exhilarated.

Cross and Interval Training

Cross training is a technique you can employ that drives up the effectiveness of your aerobic workouts. Quite simply, it is alternating the aerobic activities you do. Instead of using a treadmill four days a week, alternate it with two days of biking. Instead of running every day, run three times a week, swim for two, and cycle for another. Your body perceives the different forms of exercise as more demanding (even though they may seem less demanding), and will trigger greater internal exertion. As a result, you will burn more fat for fuel and become a more efficient energy producer.

Interval training is a technique in which you vary the intensity at which you exercise. If you normally jog at a slow pace, periodically pick up the pace to a run, maybe for a minute, and then return to a slow jog. Alternate this during your entire exercise time. It can give a significant boost to your fitness gains and energy levels.

Conditioning/Strength Exercise

Conditioning or strength exercises are those that tone the muscles through repetitive movements. Either hand-held weights or a weight machine can be used to shape and define the muscles. More important for the Energy Edge, conditioning exercises make demands on the muscles that change their chemistry, making them more energy efficient.

As sedentary people age, from about age twenty or so, they lose 1 percent of their muscle mass each year. By age forty, it's 20 percent. Between the ages of twenty and sixty, inactive people can lose up to 40 percent of their muscle mass. And the flabbier muscles are, the less muscle fuel (energy) they can store. That means less strength and stamina for you. By the age of forty, up to one-half pound of muscle—and the energy stocked inside—is generally replaced with a half-pound of fat.

By reversing this process, weight training can see you into middle age with the strength and vigor of your younger years. As your muscles grow and become more active, the level of energy within the muscles increases, making you even more energetic. In addition, stronger muscles offer more support to your joints, pump up your sports performance, improve your balance, and help prevent injuries. Strength training workouts also maintain bone density and thus may prevent osteoporosis, which afflicts 20 million women in the United States.

Building muscle is also a terrific way to boost an ailing metabolism. In 1993, researchers at King's College, University of London, found that people with more muscle burned more calories constantly, even while they were sleeping. They found that those who weight-trained moderately for about an hour a day burned 8 percent more calories than sedentary people. Athletic types who trained harder and longer burned 14 percent more calories around the clock.

Any kind of repetitive resistance training is effective, whether it's an arm workout with barbells or full soup cans, circuit training on weight machines, or arm and leg extensions with exercise bands. Even push-ups, abdominal crunches, and leg squats are weight-bearing activities—it's your own weight you are bearing!

Just doing a few simple ten- to fifteen-minute strength-training routines at home, two times a week, can turn the tide on muscle loss. A few years ago, I made a $20 investment in a pair of three- to five-pound dumbbells and a rubber exercise band, which is about four inches wide and three feet long and comes in different resistance levels. Each day, I do two to three sets of abdominal crunches and eight to twelve repetitions of each of the following exercises to strengthen my upper body.

* Keeping my arms parallel to the floor, I hold the band or weights (I alternate) in front of my chest (at armpit level) with my hands about six inches apart. I slowly bring my elbows toward my back, like I'm squeezing a pencil with my shoulder blades. I hold for two seconds, then bring them forward again. (If this is too difficult for you, use lighter weights or a band with less resistance; if it's too easy, switch to heavier weights or a band with more resistance.)
* When I'm using my band, I stand on one end and hold the other in one hand. With my palm facing upward, I slowly bring the band up to my shoulder, using only the lower part of my arm. It's important to keep the elbow close to the body and the

upper arm straight. With weights, use the same motions. Repeat with the other arm.

Stretching for Flexibility

Flexibility workouts are critical for maintaining a wide range of motion, allowing you to perform better at daily tasks—from bending over to tie your shoe, to lifting a baby out of a car seat, to carrying a heavy computer bag. As with aerobics, you can break up your stretching routine into shorter sessions before and after your other workouts.

Whether your regimen takes the form of classic sport moves or more mindful stretching, the benefits will be same: better posture providing for better breathing, a lower risk of injury, and even lower blood pressure. Best of all, you will enjoy the satisfying feeling that comes from catching your breath, clearing your mind, and touching your toes.

Don't stretch cold muscles—stretch after a light warm-up or after your workout. Stretch until you feel a gentle tension—not pain—in your muscle. Start by holding each stretch for up to thirty seconds, then work toward holding all the stretches for a full minute. Breathe deeply, concentrating on the muscles you're stretching.

The key with exercise is to not let it *become* a stress. Too much, too hard—two to three hours of hammering the body—zaps energy. Moderation in all things, even exercise, is the age-old word of wisdom.

Walk For Life

There are many unquestionably good exercises, but all are not everyone's cup of tea. For those who cringe at the thought of jogging; can't easily get to a pool for swimming; and don't have the time, place, or desire for aerobic dancing, fitness walking is a tremendous alternative. Walking is structured, simple, easy, quick, and cheap—and is guaranteed to make you feel better and look

Stretches

Here are some flexibility exercises to add to your routine. The ideal is to do two thirty-minute flexibility workouts each week, or ten minutes each day.

Hamstring stretch. Sit with your right leg extended in front of you, your left leg bent with your left sole resting against your right thigh. Place your right hand on the floor slightly behind you as you slowly reach forward with your left hand. Grasp and flex the toes of your right foot, if you can. Repeat four times, then switch legs.

The Big V. Lie on your back with legs straight and stretched out to the sides so that they form a V in the air. Your feet should be flexed. Place your hands on the inside of each thigh just above the knee and slowly press until you feel a gentle tension in your inner thighs. Repeat four times.

Towel stretch. Stand with your feet together, knees soft. With your arms overhead, hold a towel taut (if you feel too much tension, get a longer towel so that your hands are positioned farther apart). Take the towel a few inches behind your head, then slowly lower it. Keep your elbows soft. When you feel the stretch across your chest, take a few deep breaths and hold it. As your flexibility improves, slide your hands closer together.

Triceps stretch. Stand tall, with your feet shoulder width apart. Reach down the middle of your back with your right hand, pointing your elbow toward the ceiling. Keeping your shoulders down, use your left hand to gently pull your right elbow toward the center of your body. Repeat four times. Switch arms.

Cross-legged pull. Lie on your back with your right leg bent, foot planted on the floor. Cross your left ankle over your right thigh. Clasp your hands behind your right thigh and gently coax the leg toward your chest. Feel the stretch in your left hip. Repeat four times, then switch sides.

better in just a couple of weeks. It's also a social contribution: researchers have concluded that you help the national economy just by taking a walk. Two doctors at Brown University have calculated the amount spent nationally each year on heart-disease treatment and the added amount wasted as a result of lost employee productivity. They estimated that $5.6 billion in health care costs would be saved if only one out of ten nonexercising adults started a regular walking program!

Even if you haven't exercised in a long time, remember that walking is natural and easy. You need not "gear up" mentally, so walking is easy to build into your life's routine. Even if you don't walk far, just get out and move.

Turning a Walk into a Workout

Find a block of time in the morning (before breakfast) or after work (ideally, before dinner) to go for a brisk walk around your neighborhood. If you are traveling, or don't feel comfortable walking in your own neighborhood, stop off on the way home at an area where you feel safe. Just remember to pack your walking shoes!

Look for a shoe that offers stability, good arch support, and durability, with a half-inch maximum heel height. The heel should be rolled and tapered. Combine good shoes with good-quality athletic socks that fit smoothly and evenly on your feet. Don't wear running shoes for walking; walking shoes help your feet roll along in a heel-toe motion and have more flexible soles for faster walking.

Before and after each walk, gently stretch to keep muscle soreness and tightness to a minimum. Do gentle, nonbouncing stretches for your shin muscles, calf muscles and tendons, hamstrings and front thighs with a slow, steady pull until you feel the muscles ache slightly. Hold each stretch for fifteen seconds. Do these stretches even on days you don't exercise, to keep your muscles from tightening.

Walk fast enough to work up a light sweat (swing your arms, take long, but comfortable strides), but not so fast that you become breathless. This is your ideal "aerobic" pace. You should always be able to talk to a companion (or hum to yourself) during exercise. If you can't do this, slow your pace. When you feel like extending yourself a bit more, research indicates that you will benefit as much from extending time as from increasing pace.

Walking will satisfy all your body's needs for aerobic exercise if you do it in such a way to raise your heart rate to its training zone. If your heart rate is not elevated at the end of a forty-five minute walk, try walking faster, at least part of the time, or look for some long, gradual hills to climb. You may also try walking with weights.

Plan to get some walking in every day, or at least four to five days a week. In a few weeks, your exercise program will be a habit and you'll feel uncomfortable if you have to miss a day. I've done a lot of different forms of exercise at different times in my life, but I always come back to walking. It's simply the best exercise for me to rely on to keep my body operating at its high-energy best.

Feeding Your Workout

Going to an aerobics class later? How about mowing the yard? Any kind of exercise requires extra energy, so get ready for it. Here's what you need before you start.

EXTRA WATER. Why? Because water regulates your electrolytes, the mineral salts that enable your nerves to send signals and your cells to absorb nutrients. When you're exercising, your electrolytes need all the help they can get—and drinking enough water can make a real difference in your energy level. Drink one glassful an

---

Building Your Walking Program

WEEK 1: Walk briskly for five minutes. Walk slowly for three minutes. Walk briskly for five minutes. Repeat for a total of thirty minutes of walking.

WEEK 2: Same as Week 1, picking up pace a bit (without becoming breathless). Work on improving your speed gradually before lengthening the time of your workout.

WEEK 3: Same as Week 2, but increase brisk walking to eight minutes at a time. Increase time for a total of about thirty-five or forty minutes of walking.

WEEK 4: Same as Week 3. You may find you can pick up the pace and be walking thirteen- to fifteen-minute miles for forty-five to sixty minutes. At this level, vary your walks by climbing hills or stairs—extras that work your buttocks, thighs, and calves, as well as your heart.

hour before your workout and another about fifteen minutes before. During exercise, drink six to eight ounces for every fifteen to twenty minutes of activity.

EXTRA CARBS. A high-carb snack before you exercise will enhance your performance and fat-burning potential. If you exercise up to an hour a day, have a handful of crackers, a slice of whole-grain bread, or a baked potato an hour to an hour and a half before you train, and a piece of fruit within a half hour of exercising.

Don't exercise on a full stomach. Wait at least one hour after a big meal to allow your body to digest the food. When you exercise, blood is diverted away from the digestive tract to other parts of the body, which can cause stomach upsets.

EXTRA REPLENISHMENT. If you exercise for more than an hour, take a break at the sixty-minute point for juice, fruit, or a power bar.

EXTRA PROTEIN. Have protein (from chicken, turkey, meats, milk, cheese, or soy products) balanced with carbohydrates *after* your workout to help repair and maintain your muscle tissue. (Stick to carbs beforehand; they provide the quick form of energy to get and keep you going.)

Sticking With It

Just knowing the benefits of exercise isn't enough; more people *don't* exercise than do. What's the problem? For a lot of us, it's just that exercise is no fun—and it's hard to stick with something every day that's not. To "Just Do It," and keep on doing it, we have to find an exercise that matches our lifestyle, our fitness needs, and our own definition of enjoyment. Follow these guidelines to increase your enjoyment of an exercise routine.

Know Yourself

The exercises you'll find most enjoyable will probably be those you feel you can best handle. If you have difficulty with eye-hand coordination, you may be frustrated by a sport like tennis, but would do well with walking or swimming. If you are not naturally flexible, you may be happier with bicycling than ballet. And you may just want to choose aerobic gardening! Exercise doesn't have to be running a marathon—you just need to get moving, get your heart rate up to your training zone, and keep it there for at least twelve minutes. Playing with your kids or grandkids may work just fine!

Consider Your Current Condition

If you are overweight, beginning with an activity that involves pounding on your feet, such as running or aerobic dance, may stress your joints by placing too much weight on them. Try riding a stationary bike or swimming instead. And remember, if you're over thirty-five, see a health professional for an "all-points" check before beginning an exercise program.

Use the Buddy System

Exercise with a friend will not only give you an opportunity to socialize, but you'll also be more motivated to show up and keep your commitment. Other people's enthusiasm and energy may be just the inspiration you need.

Distract Yourself

If your exercise of choice isn't particularly interesting, combine it with something that is. Use the Stairmaster while listening to books on tape, or sing along to uplifting music while walking on the treadmill.

Have Fun

Take up a sport that allows you to get exercise while working on skills and having fun. Volleyball, racquetball, in-line skating, even badminton, are activities that provide terrific fitness benefits but don't feel like you're exercising. Pick activities that reduce stress, not those that add to it. If risk-taking isn't your idea of fun, leave skydiving to someone else!

Remember the Payoff

Keep your focus on how good you'll feel after you exercise. Keep envisioning exercise as a sword that cuts away at the stress response. Remind yourself of the long-term benefits you're getting: better energy, a better body, and better health. Choosing to exercise daily is giving yourself a precious gift. And your body was created to reward you by strengthening your "armor": building up protective barriers against heart disease, diabetes, bone loss, arthritis, even cancer.

If you are ready to move beyond the reasons of why *not* to exercise and join the ranks of those who successfully develop a regular exercise routine and enjoy its benefits, take note: initiating a well-designed exercise plan will create a wave of positive changes in your life. You'll work with a higher level of energy, think with greater mental clarity and concentration, build confidence, quell negative anxiety, cut away at the stress mechanism—all the while losing body fat; building and toning firm, lean muscle; stabilizing blood chemistry; and increasing your strength. It's an incredible package that shouldn't be hard to sell, even to ourselves!

Nourish your brain

The human brain is amazing. It weighs slightly more than three pounds and has about 100 billion nerve cells. It conducts life with every breath we take and every bit of food we eat. You may not be aware of how much your thinking, your memory (particularly short-term memory), and your intellect depend upon a well-nourished mind.

During the past twenty years, science has learned that our well-being is delicately controlled by a powerful group of chemicals in the brain called *neurotransmitters*. These neurotransmitters can be affected, often quite dramatically, by a wide variety of everyday behaviors.

One of the neurotransmitters responsible for enhancing your overall feeling of well-being, good will, and zest for life is *serotonin*. It increases your ability to concentrate on a particular subject or problem for extended periods of time—and to care about the problem. Serotonin also provides you with deeper and more restful sleep. When your serotonin is high, you are relaxed and loving life. When serotonin is low, energy will also be low, as you are apt to be immobilized with bad moods and depression. It's difficult to concentrate and sleep is fitful.

Dopamine is another vital neurotransmitter, having the opposite effects of serotonin. High levels of dopamine also bring high levels of energy but in an alert, aroused, "get-things-done" manner. Abnormally high levels of dopamine result in high anxiety, to the point of aggressiveness and paranoia.

The body's stress response causes the production and even flow of these chemicals to go awry, causing chemical gymnastics. Plummeting energy and brain fatigue are the result of falling off the chemical high bar. A poorly nourished brain is not able to protect against fatigue and aging, but a mind that is fit and fueled has an energy edge, and a mental edge as well.

Are you getting enough of the right fuel to nourish your brain and keep you alert and energetic? If you have difficulties remembering what you were just in the middle of saying; or what you came into a room for; or remembering names, dates, and places, your brain may be in need of certain nutrients found in everyday foods to help sharpen your mind and bring clarity and alertness to your thinking abilities.

> *A poorly nourished brain is not able to protect against fatigue and aging, but a mind that is fit and fueled has an energy edge, and a mental edge.*

Every time you grab an orange for a snack, or include carrots with your lunch, or choose whole wheat bread for that turkey sandwich, you are providing yourself with brain insurance for a lifetime. A study on the mental function of older Spaniards was recently released in the *American Journal of Clinical Nutrition* (Volume 6, 1997). It showed that those who achieved perfect or satisfactory test scores were those with the healthiest eating habits. Their daily diets included more vegetables and fruits, vitamin C, folate, beta-carotene, and zinc—and much less saturated fat and cholesterol. Wise eating is a power prescription for staying sharp! But just eating, and eating often, is the first part of the equation.

Your brain has only one fuel source: glucose. If deprived of its energy source, the brain functions at a deficit. Tiredness, mood swings, headaches, depression, and poor short-term memory are the early symptoms of insufficient blood glucose levels available to the brain. Remember that your personal sinking spells can be prevented by eating small amounts of food evenly spread through the day, catching the blood glucose levels that will normally crest and fall every three to four hours. Not eating starves the brain, and the resulting drop in glucose pushes you into a brain fog.

You can clear the fog, and even prevent it, by eating the "power" mini-meals of the Energy Edge eat-right prescription. Power snacking is a valuable tool for energized living and thinking, giving you a supply to meet the demand. Plan ahead; a hungry brain will not function at peak performance.

Brain Power Boosts

In addition to fueling the brain with a constant supply of glucose, there are a number of other key ingredients that will keep your mind sharp, clear, and effective.

B's for the Brain

Fuel-carriers are also needed to get the needed supply of glucose to the brain. These vehicles are the B-complex vitamins, serving as catalysts for the body's important function of utilizing glucose as energy and nervous system fuel. When the brain sputters along without adequate amounts of B vitamins, disorders like depression—even dementia—may be the result. Homocysteine levels are kept in check by an adequate daily intake of vitamins B6, B12, and folic acid. These will be discussed in more detail in later chapters, but your basic goal is to aim for the daily values of 2 milligrams (mg) of B6, 400 micrograms (mcgs) of folic acid, and 6 mcgs of B12.

Remember the Choline

One of the more controversial aids to brain power is choline, another member of the B-complex family. It has a unique role: it is one of the few substances able to penetrate the blood-brain barrier passing directly to the brain cells and stimulating the production of *acetylcholine*, a central nervous system neurotransmitter. Acetylcholine is a transmitter used by the cells for the transmission of messages from one nerve to another, and is used by the brain in the formation of memory.

The controversy is based around the fact that there has not been a proven nutritional need for choline—the body produces it on its own. And getting it isn't too difficult; choline is present in many foods, particularly eggs, meats, seafood, nuts, and soy foods, though it has become more scant in the diets of those avoiding cholesterol in foods.

A particularly concentrated source of choline is found in lecithin granules, a food made from soybeans and sunflower seeds. Choline enthusiasts suggest one to two tablespoons a day of lecithin, sprinkled on cereal or in yogurt or whipped into a smoothie. The problem here is the added fat to the diet: one teaspoon of lecithin contains two grams of fat. A better choice may be to eat the soy food itself; many are available in fat-free forms.

Go Fish

Ever heard that fish is "brain food"? That's because it's an excellent source of the amino acid tyrosine. This amino acid increases the production of dopamine and norepinephrine, which help the body to buffer the effects of stress. Known as *catecholamines*, these chemical compounds work to regulate your blood pressure, heart rate, muscle tone, nervous system function, and brain metabolism. They are known to be the "alertness" chemicals of the brain. People who get an increase in tyrosine foods perform better at mental tasks and show a significant edge in alertness and quick response time. They also experience less anxiety and have more clarity of thought.

Fish is the single best source of tyrosine, and delivers it to you in an almost-no-fat form. Cold-water fish like salmon, swordfish, tuna, and mackerel (along with human breast milk!) are also the best source of valuable EPA oils, known to increase the IQ of developing babies. Whether or not adequate EPA oil intake helps the aged brain has not been established.

Supplement with Vitamin E

Because the membranes of brain cells can be injured by free radicals (atoms that trigger damage by altering cellular structure), your brain may benefit from the same anti-oxidants that buffer your body. A study at Columbia University found that high dosages of vitamin E even slowed the progression of dementia connected with Alzheimer's disease. A reasonable dose for a healthy person is 200 to 400 I.U.s a day.

Help Out Your Hormones

The brain's center for memory and reasoning, the hippocampus, contains countless estrogen receptors. Scientists suspect that a shortage of estrogen may be the reason post-menopausal women seem to experience memory lapses and episodes of confusion. If you're female, ask your doctor to assess your estrogen level, and consider synthetic or natural options for replacing it if necessary. If you have concerns about the possible risk of breast cancer from estrogen therapy, or the negative side effects, you may want to speak to your physician about natural hormones and/or the use of soy products for their phytoestrogens. Both can alleviate menopausal symptoms.

A Fit Brain

As mentioned in the discussion on energizing exercise, physical activity also helps you *think* with greater clarity and creativity. It ignites your ability to creatively solve problems, thrive under pressure, and perform at peak levels of effectiveness. Keeping your body fit and fueled is essential for peak mental performance, and keeping the brain itself at optimal fitness is vital as well.

Studies reveal one powerful link to mental clarity, even in old age: intellectual challenge. When we exercise our brains, our nerve cells actually sprout extra branches, or dendrites. Aerobics for the brain are education classes, crossword puzzles, music lessons—anything that stimulates your mind can cause nerve cells to blossom. These are also pleasant diversions that become de-stressors for the body and power boosts for the brain.

Chronic stress taxes the body, but it carries a mental price as well. In animal studies, exposure to stress killed brain cells in the memory and reasoning center, a result which may or may not apply to humans. The evidence is compelling enough to justify an effort to curb your stress level, or at least explore tension-relieving routines.

Here is a quick checklist to make sure you're nourishing your brain and keeping it at optimal performance:

❖ Remain intellectually active.
❖ Have regular physicals to detect vitamin B12 deficiency, thyroid disease, elevated glucose levels, or depression.
❖ Avoid excessive alcohol consumption to save as many brain cells as possible.
❖ Quit smoking; control your blood pressure.
❖ Eat to stabilize blood sugar and maintain a constant fuel supply for the brain.
❖ Eat protein to fuel the brain with tyrosine—a speedy brain power booster.
❖ Exercise to improve blood flow to the brain, reducing the risk of tiny strokes that can cause memory loss.
❖ Don't count on ginkgo biloba, although it has been shown to aid blood flow to the brain, which *may* perk up memory or concentration. (If you try it, only use products that contain 24 percent flavone glycosides and 6 percent terpene lactones, with a daily dose of 120 to 240 mg.)
❖ Get extra vitamin E in foods like nuts and seeds, or by supplementing with 200 I.U.s daily.
❖ If you are a female approaching menopause, be assessed for proper hormone replacement therapy.
❖ Keep a positive mental attitude!

CHAPTER NINE

Manage your moods

A positive mental attitude is a vital spoke in the energy wheel. In contrast, a negative attitude is an energy sapper. When a bad mood overcomes us, we tend to allow it to color our world. A slip-up becomes a life sentence of being no good, a bad-hair day gets translated into an "I've always been so ugly" week. Next thing we know, we're sabotaging our energy with activities and attitudes that are guaranteed to keep us stuck in Gloomsville.

Take Ned, for example. Ned's days were not very different from those of many business owners—demands, stress, and decision-making filled his hours, leaving little room for self-care. Although he had sought my help on several occasions to lose the added pounds he'd put on during periods of intense stress, the weight issue was a tangent from his real problem: the roller-coaster ride his body chemistry took him on all too often—and the impact it had on his moods.

Always feeling "thirty days from being out of business," Ned's personal road to discouragement and exhaustion was a short one.

> *A positive mental attitude is a vital spoke in the energy wheel. A negative attitude is an energy sapper.*

Yet he had attended enough motivational seminars to be acutely aware of how important his attitude and perspective were to keep him focused and successful. He wasn't quite as aware of the energy-draining effect his fluctuating mood was having—and how much of a boost he could get by managing his mood through better food and activity choices.

The exciting news is that it's possible to lift bad moods by becoming aware of such behaviors and thought patterns and consciously working to change them. The next time something happens that puts you into a funk, make a mental list of what's going right. You didn't get that desperately needed raise? Oh well, you do have lots of friends, and your boyfriend and your dog love you. You're very smart. Your life is definitely worth living, even without the extra money!

The key to sealing up the energy leaks caused by bad moods is to learn techniques to short-circuit negative emotions and downward swings. The first step to managing moods is to pay close attention to them. Begin by becoming conscious of precisely how you feel at different times of the day. Journaling will help with this. Make notes about your state of mind after your daily phone call to Mom, your workout at the gym, before lunch, after a package of M&M's. The goal is to identify your mood rhythms.

Mood awareness can help you match activities with your energy levels. If you are sharpest in the morning, that's the time to deal with potentially stressful work—confrontations, difficult meetings and phone calls, deadlines. If you routinely feel drained in the afternoon, reserve these hours for tasks that don't require much emotional energy: opening mail, organizing files, cooking dinner, exercising. This is *not* the time to undertake anything emotionally taxing—making decisions about your future, reconciling relationships. Wait until you are at your best.

Mood awareness will also make living on the Energy Edge more of a priority. Once you see the natural pattern to your highs and lows, and come to understand that you really can take charge by incorporating the energizers into your daily routine, taking care of yourself will no longer be a chore. Instead, the energizers will become your tools for mood magic.

Your Tool Chest For Mood Management

We're already talked about many of the simple things you can do to increase your energy, but you may not be aware of how the same things, and others, affect your moods. Consider the following mood-managers your "lucky thirteen"—use them to maintain the Energy Edge.

1. WORK YOUR BODY. Nothing will overcome a worn-out, dragged-down feeling better than a workout. Just a brisk ten-minute walk can lift your mood for an hour or more. People begin working out for many different reasons—weight control, muscle toning, back pain relief—but stabilizing moods is a number one reason to stay with it. Exercise improves mood by prompting chemical changes in the brain, but aerobic activities also reduce tension and increase energy—the recipe for upbeat moods. Just the ritual associated with the workouts—putting on your shoes, stretching, seeing familiar faces, taking a warm shower afterwards—can pep you up.

2. GO OUTSIDE. Exposure to light stimulates a powerful release of serotonin, the feel-good chemical in your brain. Even in the midst of winter, when you can't see the sun, your body responds to natural light. So bundle up and get outdoors!

3. FOLLOW THE EAT-RIGHT PRESCRIPTION. Eat early, eat often, eat balanced, eat lean, and eat bright! And take a multi-vitamin that contains at least 150 percent of the RDA for B-complex vitamins.

4. DRINK LOTS OF WATER. Remember to keep your body well hydrated. The resulting lift in your energy levels will lift your mood as well.

5. AVOID REFINED SUGARS. Chocolate may be the object of your obsession, but it won't erase a bad mood—and apple pie won't either. Though sweets may give you an initial burst of energy, within an hour you'll feel even more tense, sluggish, and irritable because of the resulting dip in your blood sugar. Battle the blues with a power snack and an energizing walk.

6. FOREGO ALCOHOL AND DRUGS. Many people turn to alcohol and recreational drugs to relieve feelings of stress or to combat fatigue. These substances produce results right away—but once the buzz is gone, so is the good mood. Drinking at night may relax you, but may also disrupt your sleep, which makes your bad mood hang on.

7. TURN OFF THE TUBE. Although a good way to zone out and avoid your feelings, watching television won't stamp out a bad mood. That's because TV makes you even more sluggish. After you hit the off button, you may feel more tired, drained, and guilty for wasting time. And it's hard to lift a guilty spud off the sofa.

8. BANISH BOREDOM. The very act of *doing* shakes away many of the doldrums that make you tired to begin with. Become more active. Put more sizzle into your life! Bring your fatigued body and mind to a social group. Do some good things for yourself. Think of something personally pleasurable—and indulge! It will ignite your energy sparks.

9. CHOOSE REPLENISHING ACTIVITIES. What activities make you feel worse? Which make you feel better? Commit yourself to making room for the replenishing activities in your life.

10. DON'T SUFFER ALONE. Share your negative thoughts with a trusted friend, minister, or counselor. And don't forget the power of prayer. Studies have shown that as little as twenty minutes a day in reflective prayer can produce an ongoing sense of calm and well-being.

11. HANG OUT WITH WINNERS. Spend time with upbeat people doing upbeat activities. Positive attitudes and good moods are contagious!

12. HELP SOMEONE ELSE. Encourage a friend. Pray for others in need. Being in a bad mood can be a good excuse to isolate or wallow in self-pity, but the faster you get outside yourself, the sooner you'll feel better!

13. GET UP AND GET GOING. If you have a job, go to work. If you're in school, go to class. If you're home, make plans that force you out of bed and off the couch. Go to church. Go out for a walk.

Last spring, Ned determined to start managing his mood proactively. He decided to take control of what he could, and let go of the rest. He began eating evenly and well, and exercising every day. He did lose weight, but for the first time, that wasn't his main goal. Instead, it was to gain energy and perspective in his daily life.

In the midst of his personal energy initiative, he got a lucrative offer from someone who wanted to buy his business, and he entered into an exciting, yet stressful, time of negotiation resulting in the profitable sale of his business. The stability from his eating, exercise, and body chemistry gave him the ability to stand mentally tough throughout a very wild ride. "I could not have held it all together without feeling as good and calm as I do," he says. "I've finally grabbed hold of the secret to living well—taking an active role in managing my own body and mind. It's made all the difference!"

CHAPTER TEN

Energize your domain

The 3 PM slump. It's a powerful enemy and many are its victims. Energy drops, moods plummet, tension soars, and the overwhelming feeling is, *How am I going to make it through the day?*

Does it sound familiar? Is there a time in your day when you feel "done in," yet the workday is *far* from done? You may dream of just escaping—getting a change of scenery. And a day at the beach or the mountains would no doubt give you a much-needed boost. But it's key to your mental well-being to look for ways to bring energy into your everyday surroundings.

There is little question that your environment affects your energy level—positively or negatively. Some of what you naturally do when you're feeling "closed in" are the very strategies that will ener-

> *Color is felt, not just seen.*

gize your workplace or any living space. You may seek silence, away from barking dogs or noisy teenagers. You may play soothing or upbeat music. When possible, you might throw open windows and curtains to let in fresh air and sunshine. And beyond these, there are many power-boosting strategies that can make your domain pulsate with energy. You may be astounded by the enormous effect that modifying your environment can have. Try these power boosters.

Take Control Of Your Workspace

The chronic chaos that reigns on your desk could be sapping your energy. So could those drab-colored walls and carpets in your office. Researchers have discovered that warm colors send impulses to your brain that may raise your pulse and blood pressure and give you more energy. Cool whites, blues, and blacks (i.e., paperwork, piles of work, newspapers) may cause your pulse, blood pressure, and energy level to drop.

Gain control of your domain by scooping all those papers into a couple of neat piles and shoving them into a filing cabinet or drawer. Hide them under the rug if you must—just get them out of your eye's view. You may still be miserably disorganized, but the clutter won't be staring you in the face and stealing away your most precious commodity—your energy.

The power of rearranging one's space has been well-demonstrated in studies since the 1960s when it was first reported. Simple action steps, like ones taken by a young woman having trouble studying in her dorm room, can make dramatic differences in performance. She simply got a better desk lamp, moved her desk away from her bed, and drowned out the hall noise with soothing music through earphones.

For years, Weight Watchers and other eating modification groups have used this strategy to help countless people to lose weight by modifying their behavior and "stimulus environment." For example, eating from smaller plates, eating only at the table with a place mat, or maybe rearranging the refrigerator. External changes can have a huge impact on the "inside you."

Clearing the clutter can let the energy flow, so start today! Then look for ways to *brighten* your life.

Add Color To Your Space

Warm up the colors in your surroundings. Energize by adding splashes of yellow, orange, or red. Colors actually give off electromagnetic wave bands of energy that send impulses to the energy control glands in your brain. Just painting a wall or wearing a certain color shirt can energize your day. Fascinating studies have shown that even the blind respond to wavelengths of color in the same way that those who see the colors do—in both energy levels and moods. That's an amazing thought, that color is *felt*, not just seen.

The yellow shades have the most energizing effects on people, followed by the other warm colors of orange and red. Although painting an entire wall an energizing yellow is a bright move, you may not be able to accomplish this. But anything that adds these colors of fire—a flowering plant, a painting or poster, Mexican pottery—will help keep your senses more alert. Just be careful not to overdo—too much color can be just as damaging as too little. Extroverts who are easily overstimulated and distracted often respond best to the calming colors of blue or green.

If you have limited control over your workspace, at least bring your color with you. Dress in energizing brights, or include them in accessories. Or go for bright objects on your desk: a single vase of fresh yellow flowers can brighten up an entire office. Make them fragrant roses, and you'll energize your domain even more though the power of aromatherapy.

Clear The Air

Pleasant scents stimulate a nerve in the body that triggers wakefulness. Conversely, chemical-heavy, stale air that typically fills offices can get you dragging just hours into your workday. So clean up any contribution you may be making to the sniffing stew. Get rid of the stuff piled up in the corner of your office—the gym bag, the leftovers from yesterday's snacks, used coffee cups.

Now, add the scents that trigger alertness. You don't need fancy fragrances or potpourri—they sometimes overwhelm the olfactory sensors, particularly when synthetic. Go the most natural way you can: keep a basket of oranges or lemons on your desk, and slice one when you're feeling fatigued. Just a sniff will do! A mint plant on your desk will provide the same alertness boost when you break off a leaf to breathe in its aroma. Intriguing research has resulted in many Japanese corporations piping the scent of peppermint through the air conditioning system mid-afternoon to perk up energy and boost concentration and productivity.

Another energizing scent is jasmine, found to actually alter brain waves and energy levels. It increases the beta waves in the frontal lobe of the brain, stimulating alertness. Jasmine plants or essential oils will supply the refreshment.

Splitting headache, and still more to do on the report? Well, a green apple a day may keep your migraine away—smelling it, that is! Research done by Alan Hirsch, M.D., of the Smell and Taste Treatment and Research Foundation in Chicago found that for those people who like the smell of green apples, and had the ability to smell, the green apple scent produced a marked reduction in the severity of their headaches. This may also be related to the alteration of brain waves.

Feeling overwhelmed by the stress of the day? The scent of lavender has been found to induce alpha waves in the back of the brain which relaxes and calms. There are even certain scents, such as those from strawberries and popcorn, that can distract you from the stress you are feeling.

The easiest way to provide the specific scent you need is to purchase a small vial of an essential oil, a concentrated mixture extracted from a plant. (Be sure to get pure, natural scents only, available from natural foods stores, bath and body shops, and certain drug stores). An effective way to get the scent where it counts is with a small atomizer (costing less than a dollar) filled with water and just a few drops of the essential oil. Shake before using, then lightly spray on the pulse points of your wrists, or into the air as a freshener. Use sparingly, and don't overwhelm anyone else. They can always fight back with offensive perfumes or colognes!

Some of the more stimulating scents are lemon, peppermint or spearmint, pine, rosemary, eucalyptus, jasmine, and basil. Among the known relaxing scents are lavender, chamomile, orange blossom, rose, marjoram, sage, and patchouli.

Sometimes what we need to breathe is just fresh, clean air! When you can, take fresh air breaks by going outside for a brisk walk. If you're stuck indoors, you may find that surrounding yourself with house plants can rescue you from a perpetual energy drain.

Purify The Air With Plants

Plants give off low levels of hundreds of different chemicals that serve to purify the air. Although the chemicals are designed to protect the plant against insects, they also help and energize *us* by protecting against "sick building syndrome." In addition, plants absorb many toxins like formaldehyde and benzene; the root systems of plants actually feed off pollutants and toxins in the air. After absorbing the contaminants, the plants "breathe back" clean air.

The build-up of air contaminants that occurs in many buildings and homes can cause flu-like symptoms and fatigue, even cancer. Plants are a friendly, "green" way to clear the air. Just seeing the plants may stimulate well-being. One study of surgery patients showed quicker recovery rates when their hospital rooms gave a view of a garden or treed area.

It is suggested that maximum air purification comes when you have a minimum of 1 plant for every 100 square feet of living space. Don't worry about overestimating—the more the better, especially if you have central heat and air. The plants will help control the humidity of your living space, absorbing the humidity when it's thick in the air, releasing it when it's dry. That adds up to you being more comfortable—and energized.

To get the best humidity control from your plants, keep them well-watered but not drowned. Water them like you need to be watered—when needed. This will keep your plants thriving, and is healthier for them than a massive watering once a week. They also need more water in the winter when the humidity is low, just like you do. A good watering can do you both a world of good.

Get Showered In Energy

When you have the time or the place, a brisk shower can truly wash away fatigue! The spray of the water from the shower peps up your body through a powerful energizing reaction that comes through exposure to negative ions (molecules with an extra electron). Although not completely proven, the theory holds that showers, waterfalls, and ocean waves multiply the negative ions in the air, which in turn affects brain chemistry, releasing energy and positive feelings.

You can get a quick, cheap stand-in for a shower with a small atomizer. Fill it with mineral water, hold it six inches from your face or pulse points, and spray. It's amazingly refreshing, like a rain or waterfall mist. It humidifies the air, hydrates your skin, cools you, feels good, and wakes you up.

See The Light

We were created to live in the light! Our brain's neurotransmitters respond well to sunlight. That's why we feel oppressed and trapped in urban centers or enclosed spaces. The more oxygen we get, the more alert we feel. And the more sunlight we get, the more feel-good chemicals the brain produces.

Sunlight, even on cloudy days, helps to set your biological clock, lifts your mood and immune system, and even produces vitamin D to keep you strong and well. Sunlight is made up of a full spectrum of wavelengths or colors that, as we discussed earlier, each produce an effect on your body. The full-spectrum wavelengths produced by the sun create feelings of emotional well-being and physical energy. A few minutes by a sunny window will brighten your day—and a walk outdoors can give you a tremendous boost!

Though not a replacement for natural sunlight, only one type of artificial light helps you maintain proper energy levels: warm incandescent light. It also puts you in a good mood, while cool incandescents have been shown to depress you and deplete your energy reserves. An increase and improvement in office lighting has been found to result in decreased absenteeism and errors—and increased productivity.

Bring a lamp with a warm-tinted light bulb to work, even if you have overhead lighting. You'll cut down on computer-screen glare and improve your concentration levels. If you are at all able to take control of the room's lighting, ban fluorescent lights. They flicker at high enough speeds (about sixty times per second) to cause headaches and fatigue. Fluorescent lighting has also been shown to increase the production of stress hormones. If you can't rid your space of fluorescents all together, attempt to have the widely used cool-white bulbs replaced with warm-white fluorescents. They are readily available for only pennies more.

If you are desperately in need of light, or are suffering from SAD (seasonal affective disorder), you may need full-spectrum bulbs that more closely simulate natural sunlight. SAD can cause serious depression and needs to be treated appropriately. Although full bright light exposure is necessary to lift up from SAD, full-spectrum lights are now readily available for both home and commercial use. Some of these lights operate electronically rather than magnetically and flicker at 60,000 times per second, actually making them much softer on the eyes. They can be found at home improvement centers or lighting stores.

Another great energy investment are dimmer switches. These energy boosters let you control the amount of light you need throughout the day, resulting in less glare. They also give you a sense of being in charge of your domain. That's particularly important if you really aren't! There's nothing worse for energy and productivity levels like glaringly bright fluorescent lights—and noise.

Turn Down The Volume

Noise is an invisible fatigue factor, but an ever constant one in today's world. You can't always see this ear-thumping energy sapper, but you can hear it. Whether it comes from loud music, heavy machinery, traffic, airplanes, lawn equipment, or the television, it's noise pollution and it causes excessive blood pumping and an accelerated heartbeat. Both leave you fatigued.

Normal conversation falls between 45 and 65 decibels. Anything above 85 decibels—like prolonged exposure to a lawnmower—can cause hearing damage and chronic fatigue. A single exposure to noise over 125 decibels (next to a jet at takeoff) can leave you exhausted, and in extreme cases can affect your hearing permanently. Chronic noise exposure damages the delicate hair cells of the inner ear, which cannot be repaired or replaced.

If you can't turn off a noise, like the neighbor's barking dog or teenage drummer, you may want to block it out with ear plugs (the foam kind you squeeze before inserting and then let expand in your ears). You can buy these at the drugstore or sporting goods store for less than a dollar, but the energy savings is worth millions. I use these during airplane travel, and they provide an incredible plug for the energy drain that comes from the noise assault.

You can also drown out energy-sapping noise with the more pleasant tones of white noise (such as sounds of waves, wind, or waterfalls) or of music. But even with these more positive sounds, take care not to blast your ears at more than 110 decibels, or wear earphones too long.

Turn On The Tunes

We all know how difficult it is to not get moving and grooving when fun music is playing, but you may not be aware of the energizing impact that music has on your performance. A study conducted at the University of Illinois found that employees who were allowed to listen to music of their own choosing on headphones had significant improvements in job performance and satisfaction. In addition, they rated themselves as less tired and were noted to spend less time in idle chatter with coworkers.

If you're in a slump, music can lift you up. If you're stressed, music calms you down. Music can open the door to your emotions, stimulate you, restore you, and awaken your creativity. The best brain power response will come with listening to music with a gentle rhythm such as that of the piano or flute—and without lyrics or loud drums. It should be music that keeps your mind focused rather than distracting you. Lyrics force your brain to sort out the words, which can interfere with your attempts to focus or perform. Rhythmic music impacts brain waves in a similar way as color, particularly by inducing alpha waves which have been linked to enhanced concentration.

> *Music can open the door to your emotions, stimulate you, restore you, and awaken your creativity.*

This impact on the alpha waves of the brain is only one of the examples of music's power to relax. Studies show that listening to rhythmic music can reduce blood pressure, heart and breathing rates, and even impact stress hormone levels. Relaxing music doesn't necessarily make you sleepy, it just opens the doorway of the mind for feelings of peace and serenity. This is a necessary part of reducing stress and releasing energy. Again, just ten minutes of Mozart has been shown to rein in the racing mind—relaxing you and enhancing performance.

Shake Things Up!

Using the power boosters will energize your domain by bringing in zesty color, radiating light, grooving music—but they will bring in something else as well: *change.* We humans are very prone to ruts in life—in the way we eat, the way we live, the way we interact with others. These ruts may provide safety, but they also bring boredom and weariness. So shake things up! Giving yourself a different point of view will remind you that you are in control of your choices and can change things. It can do a world of good for your energy levels because it breaks you out of a sense of entrapment.

You probably have a suitcase full of habits and ruts that you aren't even aware of. By becoming conscious of these routines and then breaking or altering them, you can stir up your old thought patterns and emerge from your slump. Consider moving the furniture; mix up your schedule of doing things in the morning; do your work in a different location; eat a different breakfast; listen to some new music; cross train in exercise; take a new route to the office or school; change the lighting; paint a room; try some fruits and vegetables that are unfamiliar. Believe that you are the wisest person in the world!

Whatever you do, changing your daily domain and choices will propel you out of an energy sapping rut. It can also clear the air and bring fresh perspective into areas of your life that are screaming for a breather from the daily grind. Energizing your domain may provide the wherewithal to make time, and take time, for recharging time-outs.

CHAPTER ELEVEN

Take time-outs

Mary is tired, empty, and feeling like she just won't make it through the day, let alone the rest of the week. Driving car pool, her eyes are glazed over and her body is aching. *Where have my energy and concentration gone?* she wonders. *And why am I feeling so irritated at these innocent children?*

If this sounds like you, you're in good company—a good number of others are walking in the same zombie-like shoes. Life is just plain busy, with too much to do and too little time to do it. The demands come faster than we can keep up with, but we try. Many of us push ourselves into prolonged periods of exertion without adequate periods of rest and relaxation. Some of us push ourselves through long days with barely time for a bathroom break, and definitely no time for lunch. Some go months, even years, without a vacation, or even a weekend with no demands. No wonder we get run down and easily robbed of the joy and peace we so desire.

Yet we were created with a need to rest, to recreate, to reflect, and to be regenerated. In addition to honoring sleep, making rest a part of your lifestyle is choosing to "let go and let God" in our waking as well as our sleeping hours. We enter rest when we let go of all the stuff we don't want, won't use, and don't need. We feel uplifted and drawn to the new because we aren't struggling to carry the old. But without rest—time-outs from our hectic schedules—every aspect of bright, abundant living is dimmed.

Chill Out!

Countless studies have documented the benefits of chilling out. Anything that relieves stress also boosts physical, spiritual, and emotional energy. Fatigue disappears; backaches vanish; colds and flu are kept at bay; blood pressure drops; and chronic conditions such as migraines, irritable bowel syndrome, insomnia, even acne, improve.

But it used to be a little easier to get a break. Ten years ago, most stores were not open on Sundays. Now, Sunday is a day for shopping. There is no longer a notion of the Sabbath, a day of rest. You can go to the all-night supermarket and get your entire week's food at 3 AM. And holidays—even those like Labor Day and New Year's—are a merchant's delight: a time for some of the biggest clearance sales of the year.

To really enjoy life spiritually, emotionally, relationally, and physically, we must have a way, and take the time, to recharge our physical batteries and renew our spirits. Otherwise, we get depleted, sick, and tired.

You may protest, "But you don't know my life! You don't understand the demands. I couldn't possibly squeeze out another moment!" And you're right, I don't know your particular situation. But I do know what happens when we are overcome with responsibilities, and end up burned out, sometimes sick, and sometimes bitter. It *is* possible to find time-out in the midst of our busy lives. And we don't have to run away to do it. Here's how.

Trim Your Calendar

Brutally cross out unnecessary scheduled events in your calendar. Time pressure is a huge zest zapper. Research tells us that although we feel more rushed and harried than we did twenty or thirty years ago, we actually have more free time than we used to. We just feel pressured to fit in more as a result of our super-speedy culture. So go ahead, cancel some social events and not-so-vital work commitments and do *exactly* what you want. It will energize you beyond words.

Make A Date With Yourself

At least once a week, carve out one hour (or longer!) for your own—an hour in which you'll have nothing to do. Plan ahead on when the hour will be, but don't plan what you'll do—otherwise it will become one more thing on your "to do" list. Allow yourself to lay aside the weight of responsibility for that period of time.

Start Your Day With A Time-out

Many of us have learned the power of starting the morning in a quiet time of reflection and spiritual connection. This is a daily part of my life because I know that there is nothing more important that I should be doing, and there is no other way

> *We were created with a need to rest, to recreate, to reflect, and to be regenerated.*

to start my day operating from strength. It is a time in the midst of my busyness to divert and reflect on what my source of strength really is, who I really am, and that nothing—*nothing*—is worth being robbed of the joy of living life. Starting my day with a time-out for reflection is like the warm-up for the exercise of my day—a time to spiritually stretch and get my soul circulating.

Take Power Breaks

Research shows that as busy as people are, they would work better, faster, and more productively if they took time for a break. Brief but effective breaks in the middle of a hectic day will help maintain a focused, but energized state. A short downtime can dramatically improve your long-term wellness and your short-term performance.

True, withdrawing from your endeavors for a few moments temporarily halts your output, but research shows that doing so can erase tension, enhance optimistic attitudes, focus the mind, jump-start creativity—and give a significant energy boost. Why work hours on end at a slightly unfocused 75 percent performance, when a fifteen-minute power break can help you work at an extremely efficient 100 percent for the next few hours?

And that's exactly what happens. Research shows that after every few hours of focused activity, your brain and body take a downturn in performance capability. Blood sugars begin to drop, energy levels fade, alertness dims. You need to get up, get a snack, get water, get moving, and get your mind off the work at hand. If you ignore this need, or try to shake it off, you'll only be rewarded with a lower level of vitality and focus. But planning strategic break times can make all the difference in your performance and energy levels.

Do strategize and use the break time to power snack, relax, and reflect. You may need to write breaks into your schedule as a priority appointment—as important as any other meeting. It *is* that important. Even the most difficult schedules of my clients—that of a surgeon doing open-heart surgeries, a judge hearing back-to-back cases—can be manipulated to allow for break time. If you realize how important it is, you can make it happen. Ask yourself these questions:

* What kind of work exhausts you the most?
* What kind of work invigorates you?
* How long a period can you work at your best?
* What kind of breaks leave you refreshed?
* What kind of breaks leave you unfocused, distracted, even disoriented?
* How do you procrastinate taking breaks?
* What is your attitude about breaks?
* How do you work best?

Understanding your patterns of work and rest is important in maximizing your energy. Remember this: *More breaks, more breakthroughs!*

End Your Day With A Time-out

I have recently begun to end my day with a time-out. This is very difficult for me; I have to tell myself that *there is nothing more I should be doing.* I enjoy some of my favorite things that don't seem very productive in the scheme of life, yet I know are vital to recharge my energy: reading travel magazines, listening to favorite music, journaling, whatever.

Again, it doesn't come naturally for me to do this; I'm a "doer" by nature. The first one up in our household, I go nonstop till the sun goes down and beyond. Even my "breaks" have always been purposeful: planning, researching, meeting with a small group. I have laughed for many years about being a "human doing" rather than a "human being," but only in recent years have I realized it's not something to laugh about. Ending my day with a time just to "be" reaffirms in my own mind that I am only human—and that's more than enough!

Making Time

Does all this sound more like the ideal than reality? It needn't be. There couldn't be a more meaningful time to carve out these personal moments of renewal, because living in contemporary society has made the need desperate for all of us. With determination and a little creativity, anyone can make the time for time-out.

Divert Daily

I use my exercise time as my daily diversion. I awaken and eat breakfast (body fuel) while reading (soul fuel). Then, I walk. While walking, I'm also reflecting—not just going through a mental checklist and to-do list, but taking a step beyond to look at the "why" of my life: what's the passion, what's the purpose, why am

I doing all these things, and why am I spinning all these plates? Sometimes I need to focus more on what I need to say no to, more than on what to say yes to. After this time of listening and reflecting, journaling is my way to get my thoughts and feelings into an arena where I can take action.

Sometimes we need to divert just to do something *different*. When things get too structured, we get bored and lose energy. Curiosity increases our performance capability. When devoid of stimulation, people become disorganized, lose intellectual ability to concentrate, and decline in coordination. So read a new book, paint your masterpiece, seek out new situations, work opportunities, and challenges. We are stimulus-hungry beings, and denying our nature can lead to inertia and listlessness.

Withdraw Weekly

I try to spend one day a week in time-out rest. Whether it's Sunday or another day, I need a weekly withdrawal to do replenishing activities. A day of rest for me means a day of activities that personally revitalize me. It may mean reading novels; taking leisurely walks; napping; enjoying friends; window shopping; or just sitting, daydreaming, and journaling.

For some people, this kind of activity would *provoke* anxiety. To relax and be replenished, they need to be skydiving, or driving a race car! And that's fine. Not everyone is replenished by the same activities—"relaxing" means different things to different people. Just switching to another activity, even if it's physically strenuous, can often revive you.

Read your symptoms to choose the activity to relax with. If you're tense, you may need quiet activities like reading and walking for relief. If you're mentally or physically fried, you may need physically demanding activities to work out the tension

Something happens to me when I choose to relax and be replenished. I return to what I was created to be: a human *being*. With time invested into recharge I can review how I'm normally spending my time and reevaluate according to the purposes that have been placed in my heart. Otherwise, I stay too busy for issues of the soul.

Abandon Annually

At least once a year, completely change your scenery. Even if it's only for a weekend, physically separating yourself from your daily obligations can do a world of good for your energy level. Leaving your familiar environment is a surefire way to recharge and refresh your batteries and open yourself to new activities. Viewing life in a new context is itself invigorating. When you return, you will have a new perspective.

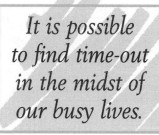

It is possible to find time-out in the midst of our busy lives.

Even in the midst of a very busy "vacation," take some time for soul care. I try every year to plan a personal retreat, a time to journal and reflect on where I've been and where I'm going. Is it what I want, propelling me toward my dreams?

Let your time away build motivation for making your day-to-day world more beautiful, more relaxing—and definitely more energizing.

CHAPTER TWELVE

Boost your immune system

You don't have to be a hypochondriac to worry about getting a pesky cold or flu. You have lots of enemies out there: 200 cold bugs and a variety of flu viruses that are circulating around and looking for a victim. These invisible raiders are responsible for the estimated 1 billion colds and 35 to 50 million cases of flu that afflict Americans every year. And it's not just the winter months that bring on the sniffles; as summer temperatures and humidity soar, so do the common cold bugs, the *rhino* viruses. Our relief from the heat—air conditioning systems—constantly recirculates these bugs and other irritants into crowded, closed spaces. And, during pollen season, many allergy-sensitive folks develop swollen, puffy sinus membranes that are ripe for infection.

Although science has yet to discover a cure for the common cold, there are ways to outsmart these bugs! Researchers have begun to unlock some of the secrets of the body's protective shield, the immune system. It *is* possible to boost the immune system to get well, and to stay strong and healthy. Just because flus and viruses come knocking at your door, you don't have to let them take up residence. A stronger immunity not only better protects you from infections and sicknesses, but also helps to keep you feeling good, looking great, thinking clearly, and brimming with energy.

Your Personal Border Patrol

The best way to picture the immune system is as a disciplined and effective personal "Border Patrol," with soldiers and scouts on permanent duty throughout your body. These warriors include several different types of white blood cells, each with its own special mission. Together they work to identify a threatened enemy invasion, call an alert, and divide into army battalions to attack and destroy the enemy: bacteria, viruses, parasites, and fungi. It all happens so quickly, you often don't even know you were threatened.

It's all part of the plan to keep you living life abundantly. Energy is not the only thing scripted into every cell in your body—healing is as well. Your body has been designed with protective mechanisms against enemy attack—but they all require energy. Malnourished, starving people are not good candidates to get well or stay well. An inadequate diet will not provide enough calories or nutrients to enable your body to heal itself.

In order to keep your border patrol officers alert and strong, I suggest following this immune boosting prescription:

1. EAT POWER FOODS.
2. TAKE A HIKE.
3. LIFT UP THE STRESS SHIELD.
4. DRINK FOR YOUR HEALTH.
5. GET SWEET SLEEP.
6. BE A GIVING FRIEND.

Eat Power Foods

Eating for the Energy Edge, as described in Chapter 5, strengthens your barricades to sickness and feeds your army of disease-fighting cells. For example, whole-grain carbohydrates not only fuel your energy, but they supply much-needed B6, selenium, and magnesium—all nutrients that are critical for activating the infection-fighting troops within. Power proteins strengthen your force shield against attack. They also provide vitamin D, iron, and zinc, which are vital for maintaining a healthy immune army. Remember to look for lower fat sources of protein and use little added fat; studies are showing that as fat goes down, immune power goes up.

You need optimal amounts of the essential vitamins and minerals to keep your immune system humming along. The best way to get them is to eat a variety of brightly colored fruits and vegetables such as carrots, sweet potatoes, tomatoes, broccoli, spinach, romaine lettuce, strawberries, etc. Generally, the more vivid the color, the higher in nutrients it will be. Bright fruits and veggies are loaded with beta-carotene and vitamin A, folic acid and other B vitamins, along with vitamin C. These nutrients help to prevent viruses from multiplying and stimulate your fighter-forces.

In one study, when volunteers consumed five half-cup servings of kale, sweet potatoes, and other vegetables every day at lunch time for three weeks, the strength of their immune systems rose 3.3 percent—enough to enhance their ability to fend off colds and flus.

Nutraceuticals for the New Millennium
If you have been eating foods just to lose weight, or gain weight, or just because it's dinnertime, you are missing an important and exciting truth: food is filled with pharmacological agents that energize and power you. Food is *medicine* for your body. If you desire to get well, stay well, and live a life filled with energy, you must expose your body to food because of what's *in* food: natural healing agents, mood enhancers, and energy boosters. There are certain foods that pack a powerful punch when it comes to wellness. In addition to their wealth of vitamins and minerals, these foods contain *nutraceuticals*, the food pharmacy for the new millennium.

This may be a new thought for you. Most of us are much more aware of the food/*disease* connection: if a person has diabetes,

refined sugar is a bad thing; if he's allergic to shellfish, eating lobster is a bad thing; if she has high cholesterol, saturated fat is a
very bad thing. Yet most people are just becoming aware of the
food/*wellness* connection. And it's the most exciting part of health
research today—a focus on the essential building blocks in food
that make us well and keep us well. This new perspective takes us
beyond Mom's chiding to "eat your vegetables" because they're
good for us. Instead, it's an understanding of what is in broccoli,
for instance, that makes it exciting to eat—indoles and sul-
foraphanes that protect against cancer and aging, folic acid that
protects against heart disease, and vitamin C that boosts the
immune system.

These truths are why I'm a "food pusher." While eating for
energy, we are eating the foods that make us well. This perspective builds appreciation and awe for something like lycopene in
tomatoes—a substance that strongly protects against prostate and
cervical cancer; or for the b-glucan in whole oats that does medical magic by reducing cholesterol levels, increasing protection
from cancer, regulating blood sugars, and serving as a gastrointestinal stabilizer.

These are just a few of the foods in my "Nutritional Top Ten"
that can make all the difference for a life filled with vitality and a
body protected against disease. Review this list, and then review
your food choices over the past week. How are you measuring
up? It may be time to go to the grocery store!

Start eating more of the best and less of the rest. The real world
can be a deadly place, so protect yourself with power foods. And
outsmart the invisible invaders that get you sick by keeping your
natural medicine chest stocked with the right ingredients.

Outsmart the Bugs
VITAMIN E. Supplementing a healthful diet with vitamin E may
offer many benefits—a primary one being the boosting of your
immune system and keeping you safer from infectious diseases. In

The Nutritional Top Ten

1. OATS: The b-glucan in whole oats reduces the risk of coronary heart disease. The soluble fiber is instrumental in lowering cholesterol and stabilizing blood sugars.

2. SOYBEANS: The bioactive ingredients in soy products suppress formation of blood vessels that feed cancer cells. Soy helps stabilize hormone levels in women, as well as decrease the risk of heart disease; osteoporosis; and ovarian, breast, and prostate cancers.

3. TOMATOES: Lycopene, a potent antioxidant, is a carotenoid that fights the uncontrolled growth of cells into tumors. It fights cancer of the colon, bladder, pancreas, and prostate. Men who eat ten servings of tomatoes per week have been shown to decrease their prostate cancer risk by 66 percent.

4. COLD WATER SEAFOOD: Healthy EPA/omega-3 oils are shown to decrease risk of coronary artery disease, stabilize blood sugars, increase brain power, and reduce the inflammatory response. Seafood reduces LDL cholesterol and triglycerides, while raising levels of HDL cholesterol.

5. FLAXSEED: A unique source of lignans, powerful antioxidants that are believed to stop cells from turning cancerous. Flaxseed also contains alpha-linolenic acid, the plant version of the omega-3s found in fish oils; it makes a great healthy option for people who won't eat fish.

6. GARLIC: Rich in allicin, which boosts immune function and reduces cancer risk. Garlic also has strong anti-viral effects and has been shown to lower blood pressure and cholesterol levels.

7. HOT PEPPERS: A source of capsaicin, a vital immune-booster with powerful anti-viral effects. Capsaicin is linked to decreased risk of stomach cancer due to its ability to neutralize nitrosamines, a cancer-causing compound formed in the body when cured or charred meats are consumed. Capsaicin also kills bacteria believed to cause stomach ulcers.

8. SWEET POTATOES: A rival of carrots as a potent source of beta-carotene and other carotenoids, which help prevent cataracts and protect the body from free radicals and cancer—particularly cancer of the larynx, esophagus, and lungs.

9. GRAPES: Grape skins contain a high concentration of resveratrol, which appears to block the formation of coronary artery plaque, as well as tumor formation and growth. Red grape juice or red wine is considered a better source of resveratrol than white, which are made without the grape skins.

10. CRUCIFEROUS VEGETABLES: Broccoli, cabbage, cauliflower, and Brussels sprouts contain indoles, sulforaphane, and isothiocyanates, which protect cells from damage by carcinogens, block tumor formation, and help the liver to inactivate hormone-like compounds that may promote cancer.

testing the effects of vitamin E on the immune systems of healthy older people, researchers at Tufts University in Boston have shown boosted immune defenses with 200 I.U.s of the vitamin. There was actually more protection seen from supplementing with this amount than with 800 I.U.s—suggesting that 200 I.U.s may be the optimum immune-boosting dose. When it comes to supplementation, more isn't always better.

ECHINACEA. German studies have found this flowering herb to be an immune-system stimulant that can minimize the symptoms of a cold, or head it off entirely. Echinacea is best taken in a tincture (a dropperful in water, four times a day), or freeze-dried in capsules (two capsules, four times a day) at the first sign of a sniffle. Be sure to get *Echinacea purpurea* or *E. augustifolia*, standardized for echinacoside (the active ingredient). Take it for no more than two weeks, as it loses its effectiveness over time.

VITAMIN C. Although there is great controversy over this vitamin's power to prevent colds, there is general agreement that taking moderately high dosages of vitamin C (about 1 to 2 grams per day) at the first sign of illness may reduce the duration and severity of your symptoms. But beware: ingesting too much, too quickly, can cause gastrointestinal upsets. If you are working up to 2,000 mg, start with 500 mg twice a day for three days, then boost up to 1,000 mg twice a day for three days before taking the full 2,000 mg.

ZINC. Zinc has been shown to inhibit cold-virus replication in test tubes, and study subjects who took zinc-gluconate lozenges within twenty-four hours of a cold onset got better in roughly half the time. The recommended intake is one lozenge every two hours when you're awake, for no more than seven days. Longer use or higher dosages have been found to actually suppress the immune function. Be aware that you may experience minor side effects from zinc, such as a bad aftertaste and nausea. And only take lozenges with glycine, the only formula shown to work. Avoid those tablets containing citric acid, tartaric acid, mannitol, or sorbitol; all are additives that neutralize the zinc.

GARLIC. This major-league anti-viral is also a mild decongestant and expectorant. Eat one raw clove a day to boost immunes, two raw cloves a day to stay in the cold-free zone. If you take garlic capsules (not the first choice), go for coated capsules of dried garlic powder that release 8 mg of alliin or 5000 mcg of allicin (two of the active immune-boosting ingredients) in the small intestine. If you get the first symptom that a sniffle is about to strike, go out for a heavy garlic meal—and add chili peppers as well. The heat factor in fiery foods works medicinal wonders by boosting immunities, sometimes right over the bug!

Try this version of Grandma's Chicken Soup—it's guaranteed to get you feeling chipper!

Take A Hike

In addition to cutting the effects of stress on the body, moderate regular exercise has been shown to boost the immune system over the long term. One study found that those who walked forty-five minutes a day, five days a week, had as much as a 57 percent increase in one kind of immune-cell activity, and were half as likely to be sick with colds or flus as those who were not exercising. Frequent, moderate-intensity exercise appears to increase the activity of white blood cells and natural killer cells, both of which help the body seek out and destroy viruses. Those who exercise regularly simply get fewer colds than their couch-loving counterparts.

Grandma's New Chicken Soup

28 ounces chicken broth
1 bulb garlic (about 15 cloves)
2 jalapeno peppers, seeded and sliced
5 sprigs of parsley, minced
6 sprigs of cilantro, minced
1 tsp. lemon pepper
1 tsp. minced sweet basil leaves
1 tsp. curry powder
1 tsp. Tony's creole seasoning

Stir all ingredients together in a medium stock pot. Bring to a boil, then reduce to a simmer for 15 minutes. Sip 6 ounces every 2 hours.

The key with exercise is to not let it *become* a stress. Too much, too hard has been shown to impair immunity. It takes a lot of exercise to make this happen—two hours or more of hammering the body—much more than what most of us would do. Moderation in all things, even exercise, is the age-old word of wisdom.

Lift Up The Stress Shield

A number of studies have indicated that people who are under chronic stress are more likely to get sick than people whose lives are consistently less pressured. There is even some preliminary evidence that shows that just one bad day may be enough to make a strike at our internal defenses.

Hormones released during stress-producing situations suppress the activity of immune-system cells, making us more susceptible to attack. It doesn't appear to be the circumstances alone that are damaging, but our stress response. Unprocessed emotions, particularly negative ones like bitterness and resentment, are especially threatening. For help in identifying and healing feelings, read about the power of reflection and journaling in Chapter 28.

Overcoming stress is seeing that although we don't always get to choose our life's circumstances, we do have a choice in how we respond to them—as victims or victors. King Solomon advised in the Old Testament that laughter is the best medicine (Proverbs 17:22). Science concurs, with research showing that laughter helps us fight infection by releasing hormones that can cut the immune dampening effects of stress. So next time the enemy attempts a strike, laugh in his face—and do whatever you can to keep stress from getting you down. It may be taking a hot bath, talking to a friend, praying, journaling, breathing deeply, getting a massage, or exercising. The key is to get it before it gets you!

Drink To Your Health

Low humidity and overheated buildings dry out moist nasal passages that would normally trap and eliminate viruses. The anti-

---

Don't Let Your Emotions Make You Sick

Intriguing research is affirming that chronic, insidious feelings of hopelessness or unforgiveness can affect the immune system. For instance, doctors at the University of Ohio have shown that significant stress (like loss of a loved one) can actually lower several of the major immune factors in your bloodstream. Other studies suggest that this type of stress can increase the risk of infection from a cold or virus, or even more tragic diseases.

Medical researchers in California, Florida, and North Carolina have found that stress-induced irritability and unresolved anger may increase production of hormones that are responsible for reducing the body's ability to fight disease and can lead to high blood pressure and heart attacks. Anxiety and fear often affect the digestive system, contributing to the development of ulcers, colitis, and irritable bowel syndrome.

---

dote? Stay well hydrated by drinking at least eight to ten full glasses of water a day. Also, mist your nostrils with a salt-water nasal spray several times a day while you're indoors. Keep the heat down and a humidifier going in your bedroom at night. (Be sure to clean the machine regularly so it doesn't harbor bacteria and mold, which can trigger allergies.)

Get Sweet Sleep

Just one late night is enough to lower your resistance to the viruses that cause colds and flu. Many studies have shown that people who are sleep-deprived experience as much as a 50 percent drop in the natural killer cells that fight viral invaders. The good news: the body bounces back quickly. After the subjects got a good night's rest the following evening, their reduced cell counts returned to normal levels.

Be A Giving Friend

Studies show that people with a solid network of friends and opportunities for giving of themselves are nearly four times less inclined to pick up colds and flus they are exposed to. It's theorized that the feelings of self-worth, responsibility, purpose, and meaning in life make people more motivated to take care of themselves. There is also evidence that shows that just the expression of love and feelings of being in love give an amazing boost to immunities.

When The Bugs Outsmart You

Sometimes, no matter how hard we try to protect ourselves by boosting our immune system, a pesky virus will take up residence. When that day comes, try these natural remedies.

Bug Zappers

BUG	OVER-THE-COUNTER	NATURAL HOME REMEDY
Stuffy nose	A decongestant spray containing oxymetazoline; use only for three consecutive days.	Inhale steam to thin secretions. To soothe nasal passages, add sage or eucalyptus leaves to a bowl of hot water; inhale with a towel draped over your head.
Runny nose, sneezing	Antihistamines, even though they cause drowsiness.	Saline solution spray.
Sore throat	Lozenges with benzocaine or dyclonine for temporary relief.	A salt-water gargle (1 tsp. salt per 8 oz. warm water three times a day to soothe passages.) Sucking on zinc lozenges at the first sign of a cold may cut its duration.
Headaches, body aches	Aspirin, ibuprofen can relieve pain.	Hot bath or whirlpool helps alleviate muscle aches. For headache, use treatment for stuffy nose, and apply cool or warm compresses to painful areas.

BUG	OVER-THE-COUNTER	NATURAL HOME REMEDY
Fever	Acetominophen, aspirin.	Drink lots of water and juice to prevent dehydration.
Dry hacking cough	A syrup that contains a suppressant.	A spoonful of honey and lemon.
Chest congestion	An expectorant with guaifenesin to loosen phlegm.	Water, warm broth, spicy food (such as Grandma's New Chicken Soup).

Now What?

Once high levels of energy are being released through the energizers, it is vital to look for the lifestyle blocks to energy-filled living. Where are your energy leaks? You'll need to analyze your current lifestyle so you can root out the *neutralizers* and *vandalizers* that are wreaking havoc with your energy system.

In the next section, you'll face the energy enemies head on and begin to outsmart them. It's time for you to claim all the energy you're entitled to as a human being who is wonderfully made!

PART THREE

Energy neutralizers

CHAPTER THIRTEEN

Are you sleep deprived?

Patti was about as perky as you can get. Her friends and coworkers would often marvel at her perpetually sweet nature, upbeat attitude, and ability to brighten any room. So they were disconcerted when her usually calm and sunny self was replaced over a period of a few weeks by forgetfulness, crankiness, and a short fuse.

Patti recognized her personality changes right along with everyone else, and felt guilty about her frequent outbursts. She blamed the new stressors in her life—her elderly mother had come to live with her, and caring for her had added demands to her already hectic schedule. And being busier definitely played a role in Patti's energy drain—but it was not the primary cause. Her days were not only busier, but her nights were shorter. She was getting to bed later, and she often had to care for her mother's needs in the middle of the night. Patti's schizoid personality changes were actually the result of her natural energy being neutralized by sleep deprivation.

Chances are you're in the same boat. Experts report a near epidemic these days of people who short themselves on sleep. In the past year, one-third of American adults had trouble falling asleep or staying asleep. A National Sleep Foundation survey found nearly two out of three people do not get the recommended eight hours of sleep each night. A third of those get less than six hours of sleep.

Small sleep losses can build up day by day and be cumulative. Soon, this chronic lack of sleep drains natural energy reserves, causing slow thinking, impaired memory, erratic behavior, mistakes on the job, and irritability. Many people seek professional help, believing they have some serious mental or physical disease, but their problem may be just a lack of sleep.

Rest For The Weary

Rest is something we read about, talk about, and long for, but often don't get enough of. How many of us fall into bed at night, literally "dead to the world" (or is it dead *from* the world?), seeking a few hours of relief from the days of our lives? We're physically exhausted, emotionally weary, and spiritually empty. Too many days of doing whatever it takes have taken their toll. Too many hours of getting through have gotten us. Bedtime comes, but refreshing sleep may not.

For some, it's as difficult to turn off the day as it is to turn off the TV. There is simply too much to do and not enough time to do it, and robbing from sleep seems an easy way to make up the difference.

Just staying faithful to a bedtime does not seem to be a new millennium virtue. Ask ten people how disciplined they are with a sleep schedule and you're likely to hear variations on the same theme: "I go to bed when I finish doing what I have to do." Bombarded by increasing demands from work, travel, play, family, and social obligations, most people steal time from sleep. They may even put on a smug attitude: many are downright *proud* of under-sleeping. Sleep loss is a power thing for some; getting by on four hours is a matter of pride for those who want to sport a superhuman aura. Society places great value on sleeping as little as possible and on staying awake beyond normal limits.

Believe it or not, however, research continues to prove that the average adult needs seven to eight hours of deep, restful sleep each night to stay healthy and alert. There are exceptions: one in ten people needs ten hours of sleep each night, one in 100 can be refreshed with five. We think we can lose sleep and be a little tired, but otherwise we'll be fine. The truth is we won't—we ultimately have to pay the piper. We may be living life in the modern age, but we still have the same bodies, living by the same principles, that we were created with.

New studies show that cutting back on sleep to below the seven and one-half hours most of us need can be as dangerous to health as a poor diet and no exercise. Eve Van Cauter, a University of Chicago sleep researcher, has discovered that cheating on sleep for even just a few nights increases brain levels of cortisol, a potentially dangerous stress hormone. Cortisol, released by the adrenal gland in response to stress, prepares the body to take action for survival. Production of the hormone is programmed to subside once the stressful event is over. But as we've discussed, when stress is chronic and takes on a life of its own, people can have long-term exposure to abnormally high levels of cortisol. This can damage brain cells, causing shrinkage in the hippocampus, the critical region of the brain that regulates learning and memory. Van Cauter's research showed cheating on sleep for only one night increased evening cortisol to levels that could impair memory if it occurred regularly as a result of chronic sleep deprivation.

There appears to be a biological feedback loop between the body's use of energy, its need to resupply it, and the brain's mechanism for maintaining the proper energy balance. This need of the brain for energy helps to explain why lack of sleep dulls the brain, saps energy, increases irritability and depression, and makes people more accident prone. People who are sleep deprived are operating their brain on a metabolically depleted level—sleep is needed for the brain metabolism to be working in an optimal way.

The Sleep Foundation study results concur, with one out of three participants reporting that sleepiness interfered with their daily activities, and one of four reporting falling asleep at the wheel in the past year. An estimated 100,000 car crashes are blamed on sleep-deprived drivers each year. We may need an organization to educate against these sleepy folks getting behind the wheel: "Friends don't let friends drive sleepy!"

Other studies have shown that robbing ourselves of sleep, or being robbed of *restful* sleep, steals half of our mental powers to carry us through the next day. We run on just a few cylinders. The symptoms can stay hidden though, because we're experts on coping. After a while, sleepiness can even start to feel *normal*, and we forget what waking up refreshed feels like. The danger signs are subtle and easy to deny: we turn grouchy, we become forgetful, our mind fogs when forced to make quick decisions, we lose our sense of humor, and our creativity seems to lock up. Tests show that spontaneity, flexibility, and originality in the thought process can be seriously undermined by as little as one sleepless night.

Perhaps you're well aware that sleep deprivation is draining your energy reserves, but you're in a bind: *you just can't sleep.* Going to bed may be a welcome respite, even an escape from the demands of life; but once you get snuggled in, you can't *rest.*

When A Good Night's Rest Eludes You

For some of us, the late hours designated for sleep become a copy of our days: we fight through them. Tossing, turning, trying to count sheep, but counting our debts, tasks, and tears instead. Two-thirds of those in the Sleep Foundation's survey said they had sleep-related problems such as insomnia, snoring, or restless legs.

Insomnia

Occasional sleep problems are common, and most can be overcome with lifestyle upgrades. But if insomnia has become your life's pastime, it's high time to seek out medical help. If you've tried some of the sleep remedies described in Chapter 6 for a month, but your sleeping problem persists and begins to interfere with your ability to function, pay a visit to your physician.

To help break your sleeplessness pattern, your doctor may suggest a two- or three-week course of sleep medication until your other self-help strategies kick in. Prescription drugs, such as Valium, Lithium, and Ativan, are widely used but can lead to dependence and other side effects. A newer generation drug, zolpiden (Ambien), enables more natural sleep and isn't as likely to lead to addiction.

An herb tea being used as a sleep aid has shown some promise. In a Swiss study, subjects were given *valerian* (a wild herb) before bed. Those taking the valerian fell asleep much faster and awakened more refreshed and recharged than those receiving the placebo. The recommended sleep remedy is 300-500 mg of a standardized valerian extract or a cup of

What About Melatonin?

Made by the pineal gland, this hormone regulates our sleep/wake cycles and has been glorified as a remedy for jet lag and insomnia. Because production dwindles as we age, supporters say that taking synthetic supplements helps turn back the clock. Unfortunately, there's no evidence of this effect in humans, and even the animal study on jet lag has been discredited. However, there is evidence that supplementation with melatonin can decrease fertility by affecting estrogen production in women and may constrict arteries in the brains of rats. It's bad news; avoid it for long-term use.

valerian tea before bed made from 1 teaspoon (1 to 2 grams) of the dried root. No worry about addiction—it smells awful! You won't be drawn to it. And it's not been shown to be addictive anyway—although there may be minor side effects. Most common is the occasional stomach upset—but headaches, restlessness, and morning grogginess have also been reported. Valerian should not be taken when pregnant, given to a child, or if using other prescriptions or over-the-counter tranquilizers or sedatives.

The key is to not allow any medication—or even "natural" remedies—to become a Band-Aid for a bigger problem. Beyond lifestyle hindrances, insomnia can be triggered by a number of medical conditions, from an overactive thyroid to clinical depression to narcolepsy. When the illness is properly treated, the insomnia is relieved.

Sleep Apnea

A common cause of sleep deprivation results from a medical condition called *sleep apnea*. More often seen in men than women,
the condition seems to stem from a combination of aging, being
overweight, and blood sugar fluctuations. It is characterized by
poor breathing, frequent waking, heavy snoring, and periods of no
breathing at all. Sleep apnea results in agitated, interrupted sleep;
the person keeps trying to breathe, and tosses and turns until he
can get air into his lungs. The result is waking up markedly unre-
freshed and being extremely tired and sleepy during the day. There
are increased risks of traffic accidents, and even an increased incidence of cardiovascular disease, among sleep apnea sufferers.

It is important to get a proper diagnosis for the condition, and
then get proper treatment. The problems can be cured with a
breathing device worn during the night, or minor surgery. Speak
to your health care provider if you suspect you may be doing
more than a loud snoring job—or if you think your loved one may
be struggling to breathe while sleeping.

Restless Legs

After lying in bed for an hour, an odd sensation began to creep
through Bill's calves. He shifted around and tried to ignore it, but the
urge to move kept coming back. It felt like ants crawling on his bones.

Bill is suffering from a condition known as restless legs syndrome, or *anxietas tibiarum*, which can occur while sitting or lying
down. It can make people like Bill miserable—and can rob them
of precious sleep. The pulling feeling in the legs acts like an alarm
clock and prevents getting adequate rest.

Pregnant women are most apt to develop a problem with restless legs; one out of ten complain of the problem. People with
nerve damage in their legs, often caused by diabetes or disc problems (Bill's happened in the military) are also prone to restless
legs, as are people with kidney disease.

Although an exact cause is not known, there are medications

available to treat the condition, and home remedies can alleviate the sensation for some. If you are suffering, and your sleep is as well, try any or all of these tactics:

Get up and move. First, try stretching your leg from your hip, and pointing your toe back toward your leg five times, holding to a count of four each time. If that doesn't stop the ants, get up and move around. Avoid evening exercise—it seems to promote restless legs.

Take calcium. Five hundred milligrams of calcium citrate or carbonate at bedtime, along with proper amounts of dietary calcium throughout the day, has been a cure for many. Iron and folic acid are also found to help. Be sure you're getting the right amounts of all, being careful not to megadose.

Try tonic water. The quinine contained in tonic water, horrible tasting as it may be to you, has a medicinal calming effect.

Narcolepsy

A college friend of mine suffered from narcolepsy, a nervous system condition that affects a surprising one out of every two thousand Americans and brings on overwhelming feelings of fatigue. Narcoleptics regularly fall asleep when they don't want to: at the dinner table, at the grocery store, even while driving. Some of Ted's more famous nap attacks occurred at the circus, on railroad tracks, on his dresser—and of course, in class. He had cataplexy, a muscle weakness that would come upon him suddenly and would almost paralyze him for several seconds. The nap attacks during the day often resulted in disturbed sleep at night and kept a vicious cycle in place.

Ted's narcolepsy was finally diagnosed and treated. This is a very serious condition affecting one's quality of life, and can be life threatening due to accidents. If you suspect you may be suffering, get checked. For more information, call the National Sleep Foundation at 202-347-3471 or Sleep/Wake Disorders Canada at 416-483-9654.

Depression

Feeling depressed can also be a cause of insomnia. Similar to many interwoven health problems, sleep deprivation and depression are hard to isolate as a singular culprit because they compound one another. If both sleep and energy are being robbed, it's vital to identify if you are carrying around emotional baggage. Nothing will weigh you down more, so lifting your emotional and mental outlook is a major spoke in the energy wheel.

CHAPTER FOURTEEN

Depressed or ill?

Mood colors everything we do: what we eat, what we wear, whether we'll make love with our spouse tonight, or end up in a disagreement. We all know what it is to be in a great mood—we feel strong and energetic and have a great self-image. We love, we're lovely, our potential is unlimited, and life is bathed in light.

Bad moods are also easy to identify. We're off, drained of energy, overwhelmed, and irritable. Bad moods hit us all—only 2 percent of us report feeling cheerful every day. Most of us swing in and out of bad moods fairly regularly, and fairly predictably. Polls show that the average person spends about three days out of ten trying to lift up and over a bad mood.

As we discussed in Chapter 9, your moods probably have more rhyme and rhythm than you realize. They are most often based on natural biological patterns and chemical changes from lifestyle and food choices you make throughout the day. You may blame your funk on the day's frustrations, but chances are it's more related to your daily low points, when energy drops. Becoming an observer of your moods will help you to track them and influence them for the better.

Sometimes, however, a bad mood is more than the blues—it's depression, and it's tough to shake. When you're depressed, you feel out of control, hate yourself, hate life, hate the people in your life, and feel hopeless and overwhelmed. Everything is dark and grim.

Because a positive mental attitude is so crucial to living on the Energy Edge, and a bright, hopeful perspective is necessary to make the lifestyle upgrades that can lead to vitality, I address the possibility of depression with every one of my clients who is fighting fatigue.

Slaying The Monster

What exactly is depression? And how can you fight it? Depression is both a physical and mental condition marked by sadness, hopelessness, and fatigue. It's a monster of a disorder that causes the entire body to slow down, pulling you down and back from life.

You may wonder, "Which comes first—the depression, or the fatigue?" Is depression a side effect of extreme fatigue, or is fatigue a symptom of depression? Is the fatigue stemming from the insomnia that often accompanies depression, or is the depression being triggered by the sleep deprivation?

Depression can have many triggers—both internal and external. Internal triggers include brain chemical imbalances, hormonal changes, nutritional deficiencies, or illness. Depression may be caused by certain high blood pressure medications, birth control pills, and the hormonal changes that come with menstruation, menopause, childbirth, or breast feeding cessation.

Depression can also be externally triggered by any loss and its resulting grief. The death of a loved one, financial problems, or life changes such as a move, job loss, children leaving home, or divorce can send you into a downward spiral.

Even the most healthy grieving response includes a period of depression, but sometimes losses are compounded or intensified in such a way that you can't resolve them—and you get stuck in the depression. You can also get stuck if you don't give yourself permission to grieve—believing that you are somehow showing weakness or ungratefulness if you give in too much to your sadness. But natural grief in response to loss cannot be denied; the more you refuse to acknowledge your authentic feelings, the more depressed you get. The converse is also true: the more you allow yourself to grieve, the more rapidly you recover from the loss.

When a person gets sucked into a downward spiral, the blues can rapidly progress into clinical depression. The body stuck in depression loses the capability to produce the brain chemicals (neurotransmitters) that fight dark perspectives. Clinical depression is accompanied by several telltale symptoms, including profound sadness, a loss of interest in things once enjoyed, feelings of worthlessness and hopelessness, anxiety, changes in appetite (usually resulting in significant weight loss or gain), sleep disturbances, digestive problems, problems concentrating, thinking, remembering, or making decisions, and recurring thoughts of death or suicide.

A positive mental attitude is so crucial to living on the Energy Edge.

This is why, if fatigue is rooted in depression, a professional evaluation is necessary. Antidepressant medication, often necessary to correct and replenish brain chemistry gone awry, can often turn around serious depression—saving lives, families, marriages, and careers. However, antidepressant therapy is rarely enough to stabilize the body's chemistries for life—it's just a jump start. The long-term answer for depression-related fatigue comes through getting help to deal effectively with life issues and hurts, along with embracing a lifestyle of self-care.

Dying For Energy

The physical body often shoulders the weight of things that take a toll on our energy, emotional well-being, and spiritual vitality. The result is a body incapable of proper functioning for peak performance.

Picture energy as steam produced in the center of your soul. Steam is a powerful energy source. It can move machines, heat buildings, and cook food, but only when guided into the proper channels. If it is capped, there is not only an energy deficit; steam's pressure can rise to an explosive level—producing a big bang!

We've already discussed many of the ways our amazing bodies adapt to stress and the endless demands we place on them. But no body can withstand a terminal lack of TLC. Eventually, it gets sick. That sickness may be only as serious as a common cold—or it might be the "big bang" of heart disease, cancer, fibromyalgia, or what has been called the "yuppie flu": Chronic Fatigue Syndrome.

Fatigue To The Nth Degree

It felt like a bad case of jet lag that first morning, but Sally hadn't left town. On Thanksgiving Day in 1994 she woke up dizzy and disoriented, determined she had the flu and *had* to go back to bed. Forget the feast; a day in bed was in order.

But Sally didn't get well after her day of rest. By Christmas, the television producer could no longer remember her guest's names, explain how her show should be put together, or find her way back to her desk. It was spring before she admitted she could work no longer.

It took Sally two years—and dozens of doctor visits—before she found someone who could diagnose her problem: she had Chronic Fatigue Immune Dysfunction Syndrome (or CFS for short). She's working again, but nothing is the same for her. "I've had to downsize my life," she says. "I don't try to do more than I'm capable of doing—which isn't much. My body simply short-circuits."

Our frenzied world is filled with people who are really tired, but people with CFS are *bone-achingly tired*, debilitated, immobilized. Their fatigue has taken on a life of its own—and taken away life as they once knew it. This potentially devastating illness remains cloaked in misunderstanding and medical uncertainty. By the time I see a patient with CFS, she is usually coming to me as a last resort. She is often unable to work, and sometimes is too weak to hold a phone or even walk into the kitchen. She's been feeling terrible for a long time, as if she needs an awful lot of sleep. But when she does sleep, it's a scrambled, fitful rest.

Although no one knows how many people have CFS, the American Association of Chronic Fatigue Syndrome reports that the syndrome affects an estimated half-million Americans. It strikes men and women, Caucasians and people of color, religious people and those without faith. However, the Centers for Disease Control and Prevention reports that most people diagnosed with CFS are women—mostly Caucasian and mostly between the ages of twenty-five and forty-five.

The cause of CFS is not known. It often strikes suddenly after physical or emotional trauma such as surgery, divorce, bereavement, or a flu-like illness. Although not considered contagious, most researchers theorize that the trigger is a viral infection, chronic stress, or some on-going trauma to the immune system.

Besides crushing fatigue and weakness lasting six months or more, CFS patients

> *My experience with Chronic Fatigue Syndrome and fybromyalgia patients convinces me that there is a way to resolve these debilitating illnesses.*

battle a complex mix of symptoms that may include sore throat, tender lymph nodes, muscle and joint pain, headaches, low-grade fever, and tumultuous sleep patterns. They are more likely to have allergies, and many suffer a distressing impairment in neurocognitive function, from short-term memory loss to word-retrieval problems.

Because of its potential to affect any of the body's primary systems, CFS often mimics diseases like multiple sclerosis, mononucleosis, and lupus. And a recent report issued by the Royal Colleges of Physicians, Psychiatrists and General Practitioners in Great Britain estimates that after the illness' onset some 50 to 70 percent of CFS patients experience depression, anxiety, or other psychological disorders. These symptoms may be rooted in the illness, or the result of the syndrome's effect on the patient's life, such as not being able to work and having no energy for socializing. Almost all patients are forced out of the fast lane and must avoid any physical or mental stress that could set them back even further.

It is estimated that only 2 percent of CFS patients fully recover, although most get better over time. Recovery is slow and uncertain. Because the cure for CFS is even more of a mystery than the cause, doctors can only treat the symptoms. They might prescribe an antidepressant to reset a patient's sleep rhythms, or anti-inflammatory drugs for joint pain. Some physicians, especially those not familiar with all the manifestations of CFS, discount its validity or brush it off with a "just take it easy" prescription.

The lack of consistent, clear treatment can make a CFS diagnosis a very lonely affair—and can result in some desperate measures to find relief. Some patients seek out alternative therapies including large dosages of herbal or vitamin-mineral supplements or tonics. Natural remedies can bring a measure of healing answer for some; for others, they are just a dead end, or worse.

Most CFS sufferers ultimately discover that a total life change is the only path back to wellness. A comprehensive plan of self-care focused on boosting the body's immune response and stabilizing body chemistries is critical. It's important to accept that the body has been attacked, to understand the M.O. of the attacker, and to grieve the personal loss of health. But recovery must also focus on changing the way the illness and treatment are perceived and the way the patient perceives himself or herself. People with CFS must learn to celebrate their gains. Rather than viewing themselves as victims who can't walk even a block, they must work on seeing themselves as overcomers who are able to walk a quarter of a block this week, and maybe half a block next week.

Fibromyalgia: First Cousin Of CFS

Fibromyalgia (FM), a form of arthritis, is an illness characterized by fatigue; intense, widespread muscle pain and/or stiffness; and soft tissue pain and tenderness of certain points of the body—particularly the neck, the lower back, along the spine, or over the chest. Although FM can occur without fatigue, when intense fatigue is a prominent symptom, this illness is strikingly similar to Chronic Fatigue Syndrome. And like CFS, it involves sore throats and sleep disruption, which adds to the debilitating tiredness and mood changes.

Unlike CFS, however, fibromyalgia pain and fatigue is lessened with exercise and stretching. Exercise intensifies CFS. Other than this variance, many of the same treatments help both CFS and FM sufferers. Eating strategically for the Energy Edge is key; eating the right foods at the right times helps edge out the fatigue accompanying the chronic pain of FM as well as stabilizes sleep patterns.

My experience with CFS and fybromyalgia patients convinces me that there *is* a way to resolve the physical and psychological issues that underlie these debilitating illnesses. It's a long, slow climb back onto the Energy Edge, but the prescription is the same for those who are sick as it is for those of us who remain relatively well: seal up the energy leaks and diligently utilize the energizers. Neither illness nor depression need be a permanent lifestyle.

CHAPTER FIFTEEN

Caught in a hormone hurricane?

A s we've discussed, hormone fluctuations can wreak havoc with a woman's energy levels—not just during menopause, but on a monthly basis. And not just a day or two before her menstrual cycle—many women experience lethargy, mood changes, and fatigue from ovulation through the end of their period. They barely get a breath of energy before the symptoms begin again. If a woman is to seal up her energy leaks and keep her natural reserves from draining away, she must understand and deal with the hormones that play major roles in her energy and well-being.

Two of the hormones most familiar to women are *estrogen* and *progesterone*. Estrogen not only serves in the regulation of the menstrual cycle, but it also acts as a mild antidepressant and greatly enhances a woman's sense of well-being. When estrogen is not produced at proper levels, memory, mood, and drive all suffer—which explains the many changes associated with menopause when estrogen production dramatically falls off. Before menopause, estrogen levels peak in the first two weeks of the menstrual cycle and decrease during the last two weeks after ovulation.

Progesterone is also involved in regulating a woman's menstrual cycle, and works to prepare the lining of the uterus for pregnancy. Progesterone begins to increase at ovulation, at the time the estrogen levels decrease, and stays high over the last two weeks of the cycle. Progesterone is the hormone culprit for PMS-related symptoms: irritability, fatigue, depression, decreased sexual desire, and achiness. Energy and sexual drives are thought to be diminished due to progesterone's suppression of dopamine, the brain neurotransmitter that keeps us alert, motivated, and poised for action.

The hypothalamus, the body's control center, plays monitor to the levels of hormones produced by the ovaries. And this control center is affected by external as well as internal factors. It is the hypothalamus that is battered by the stress chemicals, causing the metabolism, blood sugars, and fluid balance to go awry in times of intense stress. Little wonder that the symptoms of a hormone hurricane are metabolic slow-downs; blood sugar fluctuations resulting in irritability, fatigue, and food cravings; and fluid retention and bloating.

Proper nutrition, exercise, and sleep can be tremendous stabilizers, but can fuel the hurricane if they are at a deficit. Women who skip meals or go long hours without balanced eating are setting themselves up for fatigue and moodiness.

Here are some stabilizers you can count on to calm the hormone havoc within.

Calming The Storm
Eat Smart
Go easy on sweets and alcohol. Although most often the object of cravings, these substances trigger a response like throwing gas on the fire of PMS symptoms. Refined sugars have been shown to aggravate just about every symptom of PMS.

Instead, focus on eating whole carbohydrates throughout your day to even out the blood sugar response. If you eat whole grains, you will also get the blessing of vitamin B6 and magnesium—two nutrients particularly helpful in stabilizing and soothing brain chemical production.

Beyond whole grains, good food sources of vitamin B6 include fish, chicken, turkey, potatoes, and bananas. And a daily supplement of 150 mg can help alleviate PMS symptoms for many women. If you supplement with B6, limit yourself to less than 300 mg per day—higher levels of supplementation has been linked to neuromuscular damage and paralysis.

A magnesium supplement may be helpful as well, although a well-balanced diet including green, leafy vegetables, soy products, and lots of whole grains is apt to fill your magnesium need. The recommendation by most PMS researchers is 350 mg of magnesium per day to lessen the intensity of symptoms. Magnesium gluconate and magnesium aspartate are the most absorbable forms. Read more about these nutrients in Chapter 17.

Add Calcium
Recent research shows that menstruating women who supplemented with 1200 mg of calcium had significantly less intense symptoms of PMS, and some had no symptoms at all.

Limit Caffeine
It aggravates fibrocystic breast pain, and complicates the energy and mood seesaw of PMS.

Go for Soy
Soy foods have been shown to alleviate many of the symptoms of hormone fluctuations—even the hot flashes of menopause. Substitute soy-based foods (tofu, soy cheese, soybeans) or soy protein powders for meat proteins at least once per day. To be effective, soy products must contain 35 to 45 mg of soy protein isolates. Read the labels.

Exercise Every Day
Although this may be the last thing you are motivated to do, regular exercise can change your entire hormone and brain chem-

istry makeup. The stress-busting endorphins exercise releases can calm your personal storm.

Hormone Replacement Therapy

Approaching menopause is another hormone struggle altogether; the hormonal fluctuations that tended to intensify once or twice a month now can take on a life of their own. To calm the hormonal hurricane induced by menopause, you have the option of replacing dwindling hormones with synthetic forms of progesterone and estrogen. There are certainly risks and side effects with these hormones, factors that need to be discussed with your health care provider. As previously mentioned, natural hormones are now available and can be intricately mixed for your individual need. Soy foods also play a part in alleviating symptoms. Just don't ignore the hormone replacement issue; there is more at risk than moods or hot flashes alone. Hormone deficiency increases the risk of osteoporosis, heart disease, and Alzheimer's—risks that are not worth taking. Find the right choice and balance for you.

Thyroid Disorders

You may not have identified it as so, but your thyroid gland is also a part of your hormonal system. It's a mysterious gland, most often getting the blame for fatigue, weight gain, and slowed metabolism.

The thyroid gland does impact energy levels in big ways—it controls the metabolism of body energy, regulating the speed of your metabolic rate and the number of calories you need to keep your body operating. It does so by releasing hormones to regulate your body systems. One of the more important thyroid hormones secreted into your bloodstream is thyroxine, which serves to regulate your heartbeat, metabolic rate, body temperature, and even GI motility.

If the thyroid gland becomes overactive, it releases too much hormone; if it is underactive, it releases too little. The reason for an adult's loss of thyroid function are unclear. One possibility appears to be a viral infection which triggers the body into an immune response directed against itself. A common target for this autoimmune response is the thyroid gland.

The hyperactive thyroid gland works too hard, accelerating the heartbeat and producing an anxious, uncomfortable excess of energy. A sluggish thyroid function, on the other hand, causes low energy, dry skin, hair loss, lowered immunities, poor appetite, intolerance to cold, weight gain, and constipation. Some women may experience an irregularity in heart rate and headaches as well. One out of five women over sixty have hypothyroidism, often unbeknownst to them. What they do know is that they are experiencing overwhelming fatigue, chilliness, and a host of other maladies that may be called aging.

If a woman is to seal up her energy leaks and keep her natural reserves from draining, she must understand the hormones that play major roles in her energy and well-being.

Because exhaustion and depression are often the most pronounced signs of thyroid problems, it's important to get a thorough physical when fatigue lasts for an abnormal period of time, or when it doesn't respond to positive lifestyle changes. Treating an underactive thyroid is not difficult, once diagnosed; it just requires a daily dose of a synthetic thyroid hormone.

Along with the medication, your body can be energized by treating the symptoms naturally. Keep your slow metabolism revved up to a higher gear by following the Energy Edge eat-right prescription. Eating balanced mini-meals every two and a half to three hours and getting quality proteins throughout the day also helps to stop hair loss and skin maladies. Also keep a sluggish GI tract on the move with adequate fiber and a high water intake.

A hormone imbalance can be a powerful neutralizing force on our energy and vitality. Hormone levels gone awry affect every part of the body—and soul. Because of the intricate interplay between hormones and the neurotransmitters of the brain, being caught in a hormone hurricane can bring destructive winds into our energy picture—often referred to as our national pastime.

CHAPTER SIXTEEN

Are you worrying yourself sick?

Jana Brown's teenage daughter was due home at 4 PM; it's now 5:10. Jana has gone through every reason possible why her daughter might be delayed (heavy traffic, stalled train, prolonged after-school conversation). Jana's given herself a twenty-minute deadline before she starts making phone calls. She's filled in every second in between with panicky, paranoid thoughts of disaster (car crash, kidnapping, assault). By the time Katie nonchalantly strolls in, starving and wondering why dinner isn't ready, Jana is tied in a miserable knot of stress, fear, and worry. It isn't a happy night at the Brown household.

If you've ever spent hours mentally replaying a conversation, or ruined a weekend because you couldn't quite stop thinking about work, then you have an idea of how energy draining worry can be. Worry is not a passive pursuit—it requires energy and even burns calories.

Most people worry at one time or another, and some forms of worry may actually be productive, helping us to think through worst-case scenarios and prevent dangerous and defeating activities. Some degree of stress and worry can keep us on our toes and boost performance. Being concerned causes us to think hard about solutions. But concern isn't worry. Worry keeps us hyperfocused on the problem, not on the solution.

Energy is neutralized when worry becomes obsessive and chronic. To keep healthy concern from morphing into draining worry, we must take appropriate action—always the positive response to stress. When there is no action to be taken, that's a clue that continuing to worry is nothing more than spinning our wheels. It only exhausts our strength without bringing us any closer to solving the problems that cause it.

To stop your worry wheels from spinning out of control and into obsession, try these quick fixes for your fixations.

Calm Yourself

Sit quietly in a comfortable position, eyes closed. Choose an empowering thought, phrase, or word that is rooted in your faith. These are some of my favorites: *I can do all things through Him who gives me strength. I am more than a conqueror through Him. Be still, and know that I am God.*

Now, breathe naturally, and as you exhale, repeat your chosen affirmation silently to yourself. When other thoughts come into your mind, push them out by returning to your affirmation. Continue for ten to twenty minutes, as your schedule allows. You may feel better after just one session.

Listen To Yourself

Whenever you feel depressed or exhausted, you need to stop, take a few slow, deep breaths, and consider what you're thinking or telling yourself. You may find that your internal voice is yakking away about how bad things are going, and how you'll never get this done, and you'll never do that right. You may be feeding yourself irrational drivel that is making you feel worse—or even sick.

By simply acknowledging that your mind is filled with too much busybody thought, you can start slowing it down and cleaning it out. If you're not a regular journaler, read Chapter 28 for help and motivation to get started with this very worthwhile pursuit. Writing your thoughts and feelings brings them out of your head into the more sane light of day.

Set Aside Designated Worry Time

To ward off that free-floating sense of doom, schedule a half-hour in the morning or after work—on the ride home, in the tub—to sort out your anxieties. (Bedtime is *not* the time!) For particularly nagging problems, it can be helpful to write in your journal or talk with a trusted friend. If you start worrying during the day, resolve to hold off until your scheduled "obsession session." Whatever you do, don't let worries play over and over again in your mind, like a broken record. Instead, vent them—get them out of your worry whirlwind where you can look at them more rationally.

Give Yourself a Reality Check

If you're dreading an upcoming event, consider the absolute worst-case scenario (*Even if I do this exactly right, I still won't do it up to the standard of perfection and I'm going to be fired and I'll never be able to get a job again and I'll lose my house and family and will become a bum!*). Sometimes when you ask the question, "What's the absolute worst thing that can happen?", you realize that it probably won't. You can remind yourself that, even if disaster were to strike, you could and would survive.

> *If you've ever spent hours mentally replaying a conversation, or ruined a weekend because you couldn't stop thinking about work, then you know how energy draining worry can be.*

Once you've played out your scary stories, try to assemble in your thoughts real assessments of what is likely to happen (*My boss may tell me I need to make a few minor changes before sending this report out....*) Tell yourself, "I can handle it." It will diminish the negative chatter, enabling you to relax and release your natural energy once again.

Correct Negative Thought Patterns

When you feel overcome by stressful thoughts, recognize that you need to calm down by saying something gentle to yourself like, "Oh, there I go again." Just the admission tells you that the stress is from within your own thinking, not just the outside world. When you can, sit down and write down the thoughts that are bothering you. Then identify the mistakes in your thought patterns (often called "stinkin' thinkin"!) These are the most common:

PERFECTIONISTIC THINKING: *Everything must be perfect; everything I do must be right and correct every time.*

AWFULIZING OR CATASTROPHIZING: *Assuming the worst, that a certain event or happening will be horrible.*

OVERGENERALIZING: *The holidays were bad last year, and they'll be bad every year.*

After you identify mistakes in thinking, replace your draining, negative thought with a realistic, positive one. If you're worrying about a business party you have to go to, replace the focus on the people you don't enjoy with excitement about seeing people you enjoy. Write down, "I'll be happy to see Joyce and Ed, and I'll spend a lot of time talking to them."

Zap Negative Thinking with Positive Action

Instead of staring at your credit card bill in despair, make an appointment with a financial counselor. Instead of dwelling on how much you hate your job, work on your resume. Instead of agonizing that you may have offended a friend, call her and talk to her about it. Call it "obsession rehab": you replace a virtual addiction to certain fears with productive, restorative activity.

Try Classic Thought-Stopping Techniques

To banish an unwanted thought the moment it occurs, speak to it: Say STOP! Or, wear a rubber band on your wrist and snap it to snap yourself out of obsession. You may want to try mindful breathing: Inhale slowly through your nose, expanding your diaphragm; hold a moment, then focus on exhaling through your mouth as fully as you can. Taking deep breaths from the abdomen will calm you, helping to ease you out of the panic mode.

Don't Try to Control Everything

If you have a tendency to obsess, chances are good that you're also a perfectionist. Realize that going over something again and again will not magically produce the "right" answer or perfect solution.

More important, accept that you don't always have the power—or the responsibility—to make everything flawless or everyone happy. Some things that weigh you down are way beyond your control or potential to change; others just aren't worth the worry. Be more selective about the things you allow to rent space in your head. Remember, *you* pay the rent on your well-being.

> *Energy is neutralized when worry becomes obsessive and chronic.*

Get Moving

Because of its power to burn off anxiety-causing adrenaline and release endorphins, exercise is a sure bet to change your emotional and mental state, right along with the physical you. Even a quick walk around the office will help you walk away from your worries.

Get Involved

When you're self-absorbed, you're much more prone to worry. However, when you strike a balance of investment in yourself, along with being involved with others, your life is enriched. When you are giving of your time to a cause you care about, trouble in one part of your life doesn't overtake or overcome you as easily. You realize that there's more to your life than whatever is bothering you.

Get Help

This is critical when you're miserable. If exhaustion persists and physical maladies have been ruled out, seek out a trusted friend, pastor, or a counselor to confide in. Your energy levels, and your fullness of life, are much too precious to be neutralized by stinking thinking.

The energy neutralizers are pervasive—and easy to accept as "this is your life" material. It is quite normal to feel trapped and helpless to change. But the power to make changes and begin to lift out of the muck and mire of fatigue *is* available! It begins with desire— a passion to feel better. Your energy levels, and your fullness of life, are much too precious to be neutralized any longer.

In addition, there may well be a storehouse of available strength and energy within you that is being vandalized every day by your lifestyle choices and habits. The energy vandalizers may be lording false power over you in the name of "friendly" energy. But their promise is empty and undeliverable. Read on to identify, and arrest, these fraudulent criminals that have been stealing from you for much too long.

PART FOUR

Energy vandalizers

CHAPTER SEVENTEEN

Do you have a junk diet?

uzie's days start early, look grim, and don't get a whole lot better. She reports hitting a wall every afternoon. "My brain just goes to grits around 3.00!" she confesses in her very Southern drawl. At this time of day, things just aren't efficiently working for her any longer. She gets irritable, snappy, and can't think clearly. "Sometimes I'll be right in the middle of an important phone conversation, and forget who I'm talking to," she says. That's when she heads for a Snickers bar and double cappuccino.

She gets through the afternoon, but describes her homecoming this way: "When I get home at night, I go straight for the fridge when I walk in the door. I eat an entire meal's worth of calories while preparing dinner—and then finish off dinner as well!" She finishes her meal feeling full, yet not satisfied—and just wanting *something* sweet!

"If I don't fall asleep on the couch at 8:30, I finally snuggle up to a bowl of frozen yogurt and then go to bed and fall into a coma—dead to the world!" But then Suzie is awakened at 2:30 to 3 AM, feeling anxious. Is it a call to the bathroom, her snoring husband, or that bad dream? Whatever, she doesn't get back into a restful sleep the rest of the night. Instead, she fights with sleep; she catnaps.

It's no surprise that Suzie's answer to my question, "Do you wake up in the morning saying 'Good Morning, Lord!' or 'Good Lord, Morning!'" is a snarl. She stumbles out of bed in the morning, feeling anything but refreshed. She can't think of exercise, and she won't face breakfast.

Suzie starts to feel a little low midmorning and goes looking for a cookie or Danish, but usually comes back with a diet soda. Lunch may be a full meal if entertaining clients, but is more often some cheese crackers or another diet soda. And then her mid-afternoon slump comes, and every cell in her body starts screaming for food and a nap.

Interestingly, Suzie didn't seek out my counseling for herself. She came for nutritional guidance in feeding her three-year-old picky eater. She worried that she was creating a fast food junkie before her eyes because of being too tired to battle with him over dinner. If fries made him happy and kept him quiet, then a nightly run through the drive-through was called for.

True, Suzie did need help in setting boundaries for her toddler, but her greater need was help in filling her personal energy void. She needed a plan for *living* life rather than going through the motions. With energy, she could better deal with family meals and her son's behavior. But to do so, she needed to identify the vandals that were stealing her energy.

Suzie's days are so typical that I can almost script them. Also typical is how unaware she is of being a victim of her own food choices. In order to get off the fatigue merry-go-round, Suzie needed to recognize that her typical diet was zapping the zest from her days.

Starving For Nutrition

Living life in the fast lane (and often, the fast food lane!) means that food choices are often about convenience instead of nutrition. It adds up to more than a junk food diet; it's more of a *junk diet*: lots of calories, lots of fat, lots of sodium, lots of sugar—all promising energy on the run. But it's energy that runs out.

A diet low in nutrition but high in fat is a recipe for fatigue, yet only 23 percent of Americans eat the recommended five or more servings of fruits and vegetables a day. And in 1995, the average American ate twelve pounds of candy—up from ten pounds in 1983.

The classic junk diet is notoriously low in the nutrients that provide for consistent, long lasting energy. The problem is not so much what we are eating that's bad—the grease, the white flour, the refined sugars—it's what we're *not* getting that leaves us in the fatigue lurch. The vitamin and mineral value of our meal-time treats is at an all-time low. We are more apt to eat chips than fries, eat ketchup than tomatoes, and drink orange soda instead of orange juice. And because of these choices, most of us are deficient in the vitamins and minerals that would keep us healthy and energetic.

Deficient From A To Z

A vitamin deficiency takes you down over time. It takes months, and it's a slow decline into fatigue and weakness. As your body becomes depleted of certain vitamins, various biochemical changes take place that result in a general lack of well-being. This occurs long before any symptoms of a specific vitamin deficiency can be seen. For example, a thiamine deficiency can ultimately exhibit itself as nerve damage, but appetite loss, weakness, and lethargy will proceed it.

Vitamins are organic minerals that the body does not produce on its own but cannot do without. As chemical catalysts for the body, they make things happen. Though vitamins do not themselves give energy, they help the body convert carbohydrates to energy and then help the body use it.

Minerals, unlike vitamins, are inorganic compounds. Some minerals are building blocks for the body structures such as bones and teeth. Others work with the fluids in the body, giving them certain characteristics. Some thirty minerals are important in nutrition, though most are needed in small, yet vital amounts.

Like an insufficient intake of vitamins, mineral deficiencies are also energy sapping, particularly when there is a lack of the high-energy nutrients: iron, magnesium, and zinc. Let's take a look at what these deficiencies mean to our energy levels, and how to get our stores back to an optimum.

Ironing Out Anemia

There's no doubt that iron-deficiency anemia is the best-known and most often diagnosed nutrition-related cause of fatigue. When you're anemic, you tire easily and are more susceptible to infections. You may experience shortness of breath, along with a lowered attention span and memory capability.

One out of every five women will have low iron levels at some time during her life. But that doesn't mean that fatigue is a sure bet that you are low on iron. As we've discussed, there are many causes of fatigue. You should never supplement with iron unless you have been advised to do so by your physician or nutritionist after reviewing recent blood work for your hematocrit and hemoglobin, or for your ferritin levels, a storage form of iron. Too much iron can be as detrimental as too little, just causing different problems. This is why iron should never be taken just because "you think you need it." Heavy dosages of iron can interfere with your zinc absorption, bringing on even more fatigue and zinc deficiency symptoms. In addition, too much iron can trigger immune system problems and may increase your risk for heart disease. Those who have had cancer or who are at risk for it should also avoid taking excess iron; some disturbing research has linked cancer to an iron excess.

Nonetheless, when in short supply, iron can wreak havoc with your energy levels. That's because the body needs iron to make red blood cells. These red blood cells contain hemoglobin, the protein in blood that carries oxygen from the lungs to your tissues. Remember, oxygen is used by your cells for energy metabolism, just as it's needed to get a fire burning. With too little iron, you'll have too little hemoglobin, and less oxygen. Without adequate amounts of oxygen circulating, you'll feel as if you are in slow motion. And the fatigue may be accompanied by shortness of breath, an irregular heart rate, inability to concentrate, and chronically cold hands and feet. Many people suffer from iron-poor, tired blood, and as a result, operate at an energy deficit all the time.

Premenopausal women are more prone to have iron-deficiency anemia because of menstrual blood loss, particularly those with a heavy flow. Pregnancy and breast feeding can also drain iron stores. And of course, inadequate intake or absorption of iron also plays a major role.

Unless you have been shown to need an iron supplement, and if you aren't pregnant, you will get all the iron you require from a wisely chosen diet. A premenopausal woman needs 18 mg per day; a man or postmenopausal woman needs 10 mg.

If an iron supplement *is* recommended for you, the most efficiently absorbed forms of iron are ferrous gluconate and ferrous fumerate. These are best utilized when taken with your power snacks, between meals. Avoid enteric coated or delayed-release iron formulas, as they can interfere with your iron absorption. So can calcium or zinc supplements and antacids. If you experience GI distress when supplementing, you may want to split the daily dose and take it in two installments. Generally, an iron supplement will be necessary for six months to build up iron stores.

Even if you are taking an iron supplement, you should include food sources highest in iron, most notably: dried apricots, raisins, prunes, prune juice, dried beans, dark, green leafy vegetables, whole grains and cereals, well-cooked oysters and clams, tuna, shrimp and sardines, lean red meats, and poultry. (Lean meat supplies the most absorbable form of iron.) In addition, follow these tips to help iron's absorption and use by your body:

EAT SMALL, FREQUENT MEALS THROUGHOUT THE DAY. This allows your body to absorb iron more effectively. The more iron you put in at one time, the less the body absorbs.

HAVE A PROTEIN AT EVERY MEAL AND SNACK, as protein enhances your iron absorption.

EAT FOODS HIGH IN VITAMIN C AT YOUR MEALS AND SNACKS to increase iron absorption. These include fruits such as citrus, strawberries, and pineapple, and vegetables from the cabbage family (broccoli, cabbage, cauliflower). If supplements are prescribed for you, take the supplement with orange juice or another high vitamin C food or juice.

AVOID DRINKING TEA, COLA, AND COFFEE with your meals and snacks, as these contain tannic acid which hinders your absorption of iron. Never use these beverages to take your supplements. Drink wonderful, pure water instead.

Pernicious Anemia

This second type of energy-depleting anemia is caused by shortages of vitamin B12 or folic acid. Both are needed to allow oxygen-carrying red blood cells to mature and function properly.

If you have intestinal absorption problems or are vegan (you eat only plant foods which contain no B12), then you may be at risk for vitamin B12 deficiency. Meat, eggs, and dairy foods easily supply the B12 the average person needs each day. Inadequate intake or absorption will cause B12 levels in the blood to slowly drop, and energy levels follow. B12 injections may be needed to bring the levels back to a healthy zone.

Folic acid is a celebrity nutrient these days, especially for women of childbearing age. Proper levels of folic acid can help protect against the birth defect spina bifida. Women who are considering becoming pregnant are encouraged to supplement with 400 mcg of folic acid every day. Women who take oral contraceptives should supplement with 800 mcg daily.

Dietary studies reveal that only 61 percent of Americans get even half of the 200 mcg RDA of folic acid. Symptoms of folic acid deficiency come on slowly and, for that reason, are easily not identified with this type of anemia. The first symptoms are fatigue and depression.

There is no need to fall into a deficiency; it's easy to get adequate amounts of folic acid from your daily diet. All dark, leafy greens are rich in folic acid as are dairy products, eggs, meat, oranges, papayas, strawberries, and beans. Go for vegetables raw or lightly cooked, as this vitamin is easily destroyed during cooking.

Energize with Magnesium
Magnesium is also essential for many chemical reactions in your body, including energy production. Every cell in your body requires magnesium to get its generator cranking out the energy you need. It has been theorized that a magnesium deficiency is a primary cause behind fatigue.

Power B Foods	
VITAMIN B6 (NEEDED: 2 MG DAILY)	
Brewer's Yeast	.16 mg
Potato	.91 mg
Banana	.73 mg
Whole Grain Cereal (1/2 cup)	.50 mg
Lean Beef or chicken (3 oz.)	.48 mg
Salmon (3 oz.)	.80 mg
VITAMIN B12 (NEEDED: 6 MCG DAILY)	
Clams (3 oz.)	84.0 mcg
Atlantic Mackerel (3 oz.)	16.0 mcg
Beef (3 oz.)	3.0 mcg
Tuna or Salmon (3 oz.)	2.0 mcg
Milk (8 oz.)	1.5 mcg
FOLIC ACID (NEEDED: 400 MCG DAILY)	
Brewer's Yeast (1 tbsp)	313 mcg
Chickpeas, cooked (1/2 cup)	140 mcg
Lentils, cooked (1/2 cup)	179 mcg
Spinach, cooked (1/2 cup)	130 mcg
Orange Juice (1 cup)	110 mcg
Strawberries (1/2 cup)	80 mcg

A British researcher found that 80 percent of the fatigue patients he studied experienced a vast reduction in symptoms with magnesium supplementation.

The required level of magnesium for optimal energy production is 400 mg per day. Most women get only 200 mg, and most men only 300 mg. Here's how to get more.

GO FOR THE GRAIN. And make it whole. Refined grains have lost about 80 percent of their magnesium, and none is replaced in the enrichment process. For this reason, brown rice has four times the magnesium of white, and whole wheat bread has six times as much as white, refined bread. To get a power boost of magnesium, add bran to your diet. Bran is the magnesium-packed outer layer of grain that is removed in refining. Add it to hot cooked cereal, homemade breads, or sprinkle it on salads. Wheat germ is also rich in magnesium.

GET NUTTY. Just about any nut is loaded with magnesium, but also generally loaded with fat, so take care with portions. The fat is generally not saturated, but is a fat nonetheless. Pack extra magnesium into your diet by using, the Trail Mix (containing nuts) power snack (page 50), or lightly spreading nut butter rather than butter onto bread. Seeds are also filled with magnesium, particularly sunflower and pumpkin seeds. These are also great additions to a Trail Mix. Other good sources of magnesium are fish (particularly halibut and haddock), beans, tofu, leafy greens, and avocados.

Be cautious, however, with your magnesium intake. Magnesium is one of the nutrients that can, if taken to an overdose, backfire and cause extreme fatigue. It's almost impossible to get toxic levels from your food, but many people unknowingly get an overdose from certain magnesium-filled antacids and from supplements (it's in a variety of multiple-type supplements, and is often combined with calcium). Check with your pharmacist or physician if you OD on antacids—there are better options to deal with an angry gut.

Zinc Sense

Four million Americans—most of them women of childbearing age—are deficient in zinc, getting only 75 percent of the RDA. This is unfortunate because, even though needed in small amounts, zinc is an essential trace mineral, crucial to literally hundreds of biological processes. It's necessary to keep the immune system in top condition, and provides for tissue growth and repair. Zinc improves muscle strength and endurance, along with enhancing healing. Zinc is necessary for the formation of insulin, which functions to get energy into your cells to be burned. And, it protects against fatigue—chronic or otherwise.

Zinc from meat, fish, and poultry is more available to the body than from other sources, particularly grains. Grains contain a substance called phytates which may hinder zinc absorption. For this reason, vegetarians are at higher risk for zinc deficiency and should be sure to supplement properly—and wisely.

Like magnesium, too much zinc can actually depress your immune system and cause fatigue. And men taking 50 mg per day have been found to have a

> ## Mineral Tonics: Do They Help?
>
> So-called tonics of "colloidal" minerals (tiny particles of minerals suspended in liquid), which are touted to increase energy, are brisk sellers in multi-level marketing organizations and health stores alike. But there's no evidence that these drinks do any good, and because they contain potentially toxic heavy metals, they may do a great deal of harm. Many contain arsenic and dolamite, which can build up to toxic levels in the body.

dangerous lowering of their protective HDL cholesterol. For this reason, it is not wise to take more than 30 mg daily.

The beautiful thing about good, balanced nutrition is this: everything fits together in such a perfect way that just eating a wide variety of different foods in their whole form will more than likely give you an adequate intake of essential nutrients. Eating well is the time-tested answer to the vitamin-mineral question, so don't let a junk diet vandalize your energy stores any longer.

CHAPTER EIGHTEEN

Are you seduced by sugar?

Patrick had been receiving counseling from me for seven months when the holidays rolled around. Although rejoicing in his new healthy life (and a weight loss of fifty pounds), he was now gripped with fear that holiday sweets would sabotage all the progress he'd made. "Honestly, Pam," he confided, "I feel like an addict—and my drug of choice has always been sweets. It may start as just a piece of Thanksgiving pie, but it's a dozen cookies before I go to bed. And, once I've started, it doesn't stop 'till New Year's. I just *have* to do it different this year!"

Patrick's experience is a familiar one. Surely sweets do taste great, but for many the pull is much stronger than a taste bud tickle. It takes on an unnatural drive. Here's how it works: When memories, moods, or just avail-

Contrary to much popular literature, sugar is not "white death"; its darkest crime is its vandalizing effect on our energy.

ability trigger a heavy sugar intake, it brings a pleasurable rise in body chemistries that will be followed by a quick fall a few hours later. That dip triggers "eating for a lift" to relieve the fatigue, brain fog, and mood drop. Usually the chosen food is again high in sugar, and the seesaw effect continues. Then the guilt tapes begin to play: *You've already blown it, go ahead and finish the cookies before you get "back" to healthy eating.*

In our stressed states, we are easily pulled toward those oh-so-available sweet treats that promise an energy boost and stir our memory buckets of happy, carefree times. So what's so wrong with that? Well, maybe not what you think. Contrary to much popular literature, sugar is not "white death"; its darkest crime is its vandalizing effect on our energy. And it has partners in crime: sugar-laden treats are usually loaded with saturated fats and calories as well. And generally, these treats prevent us from choosing healthy foods that work to stabilize our body chemistry.

Kicking The Sugar Habit

If sugar is affecting your well-being, make it your goal to cut back on your daily use of sugar or sweets and eat fruit to satisfy your natural craving for sugar. Sugar is not worth robbing yourself of your precious energy and stamina. For help in kicking the sugar habit, use these tips.

Know Your Enemy

Sugar is called by many names—honey, brown sugar, corn syrup, fructose, and so on—but it's all sugar! Much of our problem with sugar lies in the fact that it is hidden in nearly every packaged product on the grocer's shelf. American consumption has risen to 146 pounds per person per year, mainly from prepared foods.

Beware if sugar or a name for sugar—like any word ending in –*ose*—is in the top three ingredients in a packaged product. You are getting more than you are bargaining for!

Know Yourself

How much is enough for you—and how much triggers the desire for more? Does nibbling a little bit of sweets lead to a lot? Patrick found that even occasionally eating high-sugar foods was impossible for him—he *was* hurt by "just a little bit." It wasn't about the calories or sugar's health risk, it was the effect it had on his body. The seesaw effect resulted in a "more he has, more he wants" syndrome. It may be necessary for you to "just say no" to sugar-laden foods for long enough (twelve to fourteen days) to allow your blood sugar levels to stabilize, and to allow your energy and appetite for healthy foods to return.

Know When You're Vulnerable

Identify—and avoid—resolve-breakers like fatigue, hunger, anger, or loneliness. These are often the music playing in the background of temptation! If your life response has been to eat when you're tired, to "get through," it is more difficult to choose to break for a nap than to reach for cookies. If you have spent a lifetime pushing down anger with food, it is more difficult to choose to journal your anger or discuss its cause when you are furious. Eating with a frenzy is more natural, and food is so accessible.

Resist the "I've Already Blown It" Syndrome

Even when you succumb to temptation and consume foods you know interfere with your health, be assured that a lapse in healthy eating doesn't ruin all the health you have attained over weeks of wellness. A lapse in your healthy lifestyle is just that—a lapse. Don't let it become a relapse, another relapse, and finally a collapse. Look at each meal and snack as an event—don't wrap it all into one bad day or one unhealthy weekend. Instead, get right back on track with the next meal or snack. Your body will stabilize quickly, you'll feel great, and you'll be thanking yourself the next day!

Know That It Will Get Easier

Although we are born with a natural preference toward foods with a sweet taste, these taste bud preferences have been overdeveloped and fueled by a lifetime of high sugar intake and erratic eating patterns. As you cut back, over time, your cravings diminish and your taste buds regain their ability to pick up the sweetness in a carrot or piece of fruit.

"Power snack" throughout the day

Just in case it hasn't sunk in yet: eating every two to three hours throughout the day keeps your energy okay and a ravenous appetite away! Go for energy-boosting combos like fresh fruit or a box of raisins with low fat cheese or yogurt, a half sandwich, or a Trail Mix of dry roasted peanuts and sunflower seeds mixed with dried fruit. Keep power snacks available wherever you are—they will serve as a lift to your body and prevent the drowsiness and sweet cravings that often follow meals.

Avoid Artificial Sweeteners

As you become aware (and possibly alarmed!) about your intake of sugar, you may be tempted to use sugar substitutes. Don't. There are no absolutes in the safety of chemicals—saccharin, aspartame, or any new one to come along. The long-term effects of their use will not be known for years.

For example, in the short time since aspartame has appeared on the market (as Nutrasweet™), cautions concerning its use have accelerated. Questions have been posed about its allergic reaction in some, its impact on the brain chemistry due to its crossing the blood barrier of the brain, its danger with possible breakdown in hot foods, and its effect on children and the unborn.

The battle will continue, for even though aspartame is made from natural sources, it is still made in a laboratory and is not found in nature. The possibility for problems to occur as a result of its frequent use are endless. As bad as sugar may be, and whatever the health hazards associated with its overuse, at least it's not a chemical. It has been used for centuries. The best wisdom to use about artificial sweeteners is, "When in doubt, leave it out."

Also understand that as long as you continue to use sugar-laden foods or sugar substitutes, you will keep your taste buds trained for sugar. The goal is to cut back on its use so you no longer need everything to taste sweet. Allow your taste buds to change so that the desire for sweetness can be met in a safe way—from fruits and other naturally sweet foods that are natural outlets for our inborn sweet preference.

Rely on the Natural Sweet Treat

Fruit is the natural fulfillment of our sweet desires. Go for the fruit, not the fruit juice; the fiber slows the release of the fruit's carbohydrate, which prevents blood sugar spikes and insulin surges.

Consume Enough Fiber

Fiber is the part of plants not digested by the body. There are two types of fiber: the *water-soluble fibers* found in oats, barley, brown rice, apples, dried beans, and nuts, and the *water-insoluble fibers* found in wheat bran, whole grains, and fresh vegetables. Dietary fiber offers many health benefits, including controlling constipation and hemorrhoids and lowering serum cholesterol and triglyceride levels. Water-soluble fiber also serves as a "time-release capsule," releasing sugars from digested carbohydrates slowly and evenly into the bloodstream. This helps keep your energy levels up and even.

Save the Best for Last

If you must have sweets, add a dessert on to the end of the meal rather than having the treat as your meal, or as your snack. This allows the balanced meal to temper the insulin surge, keeping blood sugars more stable.

If chocolate is your sugar seductress, you may be hooked on more than the sugar alone. In addition to the chemical impact of chocolate on the neurotransmitters of the brain (research shows that it releases substances similar to those released when we're in love!), chocolate packs a one-two punch with a double hit of sugar and caffeine. If that double mocha latte calls your name every afternoon, then your energy is probably being robbed by more than sugar.

Read on for insight into some possible "old friends" that may be cheating you out of your personal vitality.

CHAPTER NINETEEN

Are you being robbed by miscellaneous menaces?

aving a friend be revealed as a thief is shocking, disappointing, and discouraging. You trusted him! He was always there for you, guaranteed to provide for you. How could he have been stealing from you all along?

Good question—and important to ask when it comes to "friends" like caffeine, alcohol, and nicotine. Like hanging out with a bad crowd, you end up getting more than the good time you bargained for: you get robbed of vital energy.

And, similar to breaking free from the power of a gang, breaking free from the these felons can be very difficult. But it's not impossible. Understanding their true character is a good start.

Are You A Java Junkie?

Caffeine is among the world's most widely used and addictive drugs—yet it remains a relatively acceptable way to artificially stimulate the brain. Caffeine works by blocking one of the brain's natural sedatives, a neurotransmitter called *adenosine*. Caffeine stimulates the central nervous system, accelerates your pulse rate and heartbeat, and can give quite a boost to your mood. A single cup of coffee can seem to work energy miracles when needed. Your eyelids open, fatigue dissipates, you're more alert. All in all, it's powerful stuff!

Like other drugs, however, there is a downside to caffeine. Too much causes a surge of adrenaline, but when the spurt is over, energy levels plummet. As discussed earlier, even small amounts of caffeine may cause side effects, including restlessness and disturbed sleep, heart palpitations, stomach irritation, diarrhea, and fibrocystic breast disease. It can promote irritability, anxiety, and mood disturbances, as well as aggravate premenstrual syndrome and mood swings in women.

The Power of a Jolt

PRODUCT	MILLIGRAMS OF CAFFEINE
5 oz. automatic drip coffee	110-150 mg
gourmet brews	280-550 mg
5 oz. instant coffee	40-110 mg
5 oz. decaffeinated coffee	2-5 mg
5 oz. hot tea	50-90 mg
12 oz. iced tea	35 mg
decaffeinated iced tea	less than 1 mg
1 oz. unsweetened baking chocolate	58 mg
5 oz. hot chocolate	10 mg
1 oz. milk chocolate	5 mg
12 oz. Mountain Dew	55 mg
12 oz. Coca-Cola, Tab	45 mg
12 oz. Mr. Pibb, Mellow Yellow, Surge, Sunkist Orange	42 mg
12 oz. Pepsi, Dr. Pepper, RC Cola, Diet Rite	35 mg
12 oz. 7-Up, Sprite, Root Beer, Fresca, Ginger Ale, Diet Sunkist Orange	0 mg
No Doz, Vivarin, Caffedrine, Dristan	30 mg
Anacin, Midol	64 mg
Excedrin	130 mg
Dexatrim, Dietac	200 mg

The stimulant effect is thought to kick in with consumption of 150 to 250 mg of caffeine—the amount in one mug of brewed coffee or three glasses of iced tea. And because caffeine is also found in soda (regular and diet), chocolate, and even some pain relievers and decongestant cold pills, it adds up quickly.

The levels soar when you get java from a gourmet coffee bar. New analysis shows that these specialty brews often contain two to three times the caffeine found in a cup made from your typical supermarket brands. Gourmet coffees are stronger because more grounds are used to give the brew its rich flavor, and the beans are often specially roasted, making the coffee even more potent. In fact, one large cup of gourmet coffee packs a walloping 280 mg of caffeine, and some specialty brews contain 550 mg. It's at these higher levels of intake, about 600 mg, that you can get *too* energized—and start to feel the java jitters: frazzled nerves, the shakes, insomnia, and ultimately, fatigue.

Do you need to cut out caffeine altogether? Not necessarily. Despite its drawbacks, it's definitely an energy jolt. I do encourage you, however, to cut back slowly to a 250 mg ceiling. And if, after cutting back to this amount, you still experience any of the above-mentioned side effects, I encourage you to withdraw completely. If you're not ready to give up your caffeine boost altogether, you may want to try green tea, now known to have powerful antioxidant benefits.

If you decide to cut back on your caffeine consumption, the word *withdrawal* will take on new meaning for you. Again, caffeine is a powerfully addictive drug, and withdrawal symptoms are real and sure. Many people experience zombie-like fatigue, irritability, lethargy, and headaches from going "cold turkey," and the symptoms may last for up to five days.

So cut back *gradually*, a quarter of a cup at a time, over the course of a week to ten days. Or substitute a decaffeinated product for the real thing in the same reducing amounts. Withdrawal will be less painful if you follow the Energy Edge eat-right prescription; small, balanced meals throughout the day will stabilize your body chemistry and reduce your reliance on caffeine for energy.

On a personal note, I believe that if you're going to cut back on your coffee drinking to one cup, make it spectacular—choose fresh ground, dripped on the spot, strong flavor, first rate! It's kind of the same feeling I have about desserts: if you are going to have a sweet, with all the health negatives accompanying it, make it great. Don't waste sugar and fat intake on a dry, packaged Danish or cookie—make it Tiramisu!

Caught In The French Paradox?

You may have watched it on *Sixty Minutes* or read about it in the newspaper. It's called "The French Paradox," and it's all about wine, particularly red wine, being good for you. The argument is that a moderate amount of alcohol, in any form, actually extends life, and may help to offset the negative health effects of a high-fat diet. A glass of Merlot every night is a great idea, we hear.

But is it true?

It is true that a moderate intake of alcohol has been found to have positive health benefits, and the research is strong and promising enough to result in many physicians actually *recommending* a glass of wine to their patients. But how does that advice play into the Energy Edge? Does that happy hour drink give you the happy energy boost you need?

The reality is, no. Although a drink or two a day *may* be a health boost in some ways, it is actually a depressant to your energy levels. Alcohol in any amount slows down your reflexes, your metabolism, and your brain. It may relax you momentarily, but it ultimately depletes your energy and takes the edge off your peak performance.

Over time, alcohol consumption can result in a chronic energy drain; its impact on your blood sugars interferes with your sleep and prevents you from absorbing many of the energy nutrients. Alcohol inhibits production of a key pituitary hormone, causing more water to leave the body. The result is that your brain cells become dehydrated—which spells hangover. The extra calories liquor adds to your diet can contribute to weight gain, another energy drag. And more than moderate intake can damage your internal organs (such as your liver, intestines, and heart) and increase your risk of cancer, particularly of the liver and breast.

The medical benefits of wine or other spirits are *not* compelling enough to encourage people who don't drink to begin. And considering alcohol's depleting effect on energy, it's important to moderate your drinking, or stop altogether. Moderation is considered a 4 to 6 oz. glass of wine, a light beer, or 1 1/2 ounces of liquor a day. The minute you drink more, your health hazards soar and your energy levels fall dramatically. Like with desserts and coffee, I believe if you are going to enjoy a glass of wine, and its possible health benefits, make it a great one—and make it part of the mealtime experience.

Are Your Medications Zapping You?

You may know that certain antihistamines, cold medications, and cough syrups can make you drowsy. But you may not realize that the list of potential energy sappers features many other familiar drugs that can cause drowsiness in some people. These include certain blood pressure medications and even some diuretics.

Some medications, like sleeping pills, are meant to make you feel tired, but often have a longer life than you are seeking. Others, like appetite suppressants and decongestants, initially have a stimulant effect, but the rebound effect brings on fatigue. And common over-the-counter antihistimines are almost a prescription for being sedated.

It you feel tired or run down, ask your doctor or pharmacist whether the medications you're taking might be the cause, and what alternatives may be available. You may be able to switch to a nonsedating prescription, or change the time of day you take your dose. Or, there may be more natural alternatives to relief than the drug you're taking—alternatives that won't wipe out your energy along with other unwanted symptoms.

Are You Puffing Yourself Sleepy?

Aside from killing you, smoking is an energy depleter. Nicotine is a central nervous system stimulant but, as always, what goes up must come down—and fast. And, as ugly as this sounds, smoking also gives you bad breath, discolored teeth, sallow, wrinkled skin, and shortness of breath—all of which make you feel and look decades older.

The great news is this: Quitting smoking is likely to make you feel loads better almost immediately. After quitting for twenty minutes, your blood pressure decreases, your pulse rate drops, and the temperature of your hands and feet increases. Within eight hours, the carbon monoxide levels in your blood drop, your blood oxygen levels rise, and your breathing returns to normal. Within two days, your nerve endings start regenerating, walking and breathing become easier, and food smells and tastes better. After two weeks to two months, circulation improves, exertion becomes easier, lung function increases, and coughing and sinus congestion decrease. Within three months, fatigue decreases. Within one year, your heart disease risk is half that of a smoker!

Trying to quit smoking, but dying for a cigarette? You actually may be dying for the deep breathing you used to do when you smoked. Think about it. With each drag on a cigarette, you would breathe in, and then slowly breathe out. Granted, the oxygen was polluted with unhealthy things, but you were getting the benefits of the relaxing breathing.

Try your old breathing again—without the cigarette smoke. Sit still, with your hands flat on your lap. Breathe in, fully; then breathe out. Do it ten times, every time you feel that tension and craving building up. Remember when you were a kid and got angry, and some adult would say "Count to ten!"? A slow, breathing count to ten can dissipate a stressful situation—the same set of circumstances that would have you reaching for a smoke.

You will also find that the Energy Edge Meal Plan will give stability to your body chemistry and a boost to your metabolism to help stave off many of the nicotene withdrawl symptoms—including keeping the dreaded weight gain at bay.

If learning more about the effects your "friends" have on your health and energy leads you to realize that caffeine, alcohol, or cigarettes are major-league vandalizers in your life, you may say, "It's time to stop." If so, remember: practicing the energizers in Part 2 is a great first step. When your body and mind are stronger and more stable, it's easier to find the power to whip the thieves that are robbing you blind.

CHAPTER TWENTY

Are your relationships dragging you down?

"**P**lease understand, I just don't want to go! I don't have the energy to do this tonight." I was trying to get out of plans that were made for me by my loving husband. Friends had called and had sort of "corralled" Larry into agreeing that we'd go out to dinner with them that evening. He thought it would be a treat for me because we hadn't gotten together with these friends in quite a while.

I didn't receive the news well—and that was my fault. My fault because I hadn't communicated to Larry that it wasn't just our busy schedules that had kept us away from frequent contact with these folks—it was that time with them was exhausting to me. As fun as our friends were on one level, there was only a certain depth to our relationship. Over time, I had learned that there were certain places our conversation could not go, and parts of our lives that couldn't be shared. We have very different beliefs about children and family, and how my husband and I manage our careers. I know, from past experience, that I can't talk about this or that, nor tell them about some of the exciting things going on in our lives. Before I even open my mouth, I have to go through a mental checklist of what is acceptable to say. The energy required to keep a façade in place had to be prepared for. And I was not prepared for a surprise dinner that night!

Debbie has a much more intense energy drain than mine—from times with her husband's family. She comes from a different religious background, and her marriage to the first-born son was actively fought by her husband's mother and sister right up to the wedding-day "I do's."

"Actually, I know they are still fighting it, and me, but now it's a silent, cold war," Debbie laments. So holiday times, especially religious ones, are horrible for her. "I feel as though I have to watch every word I say, every action I take, every look on my face. I go into every conversation, every dinner, every special occasion with a bullet-proof vest around my feelings, expecting an assault missile to be launched at me at any moment." Debbie's husband Marc adds, "It takes enormous energy for Debbie to go through the mental rehearsals beforehand, and even more to keep her armor in place. She is left exhausted afterward, and I am left furious at my family and the whole situation."

I am working as Marc and Debbie's wellness coach, helping Debbie to deal with symptoms of fibromyalgia. It's no surprise that she has a tremendous flare-up around holidays.

Connecting with other human beings is vital to our lives; we have been wired for relationships. But the power of connecting can be drastically short-circuited by crossing wires with the wrong people. Just as good relationships can fan the flame of energy, difficult relationships can douse it. Let's take a look at both types.

Take Stock Of Your Relationships

For years it's been known that romantic love stimulates a chemical reaction in our bodies. When we first fall in love, for example, our brain produces dopamine and norepinephrine, the chemical cousins of amphetamines that cause the sweaty palms, fluttering hearts, and overall euphoria associated with new love. More mature love can prompt the release of endorphins, which bring that calm, peaceful feeling.

New research indicates that it's actually our *attitude* toward love that energizes and empowers our immune system. Those who value love and friendship have been shown to have higher levels of microbe-fighting NK cells, better rations of T-helper/T-suppressor cells, and more of the other important body chemicals that keep us energized and strong. Just the memory of having loved or felt loved can boost these power chemicals.

We are social beings who need regular contact with others to produce and perform optimally. Contact with friends, especially those in whom we can confide, has been shown to promote mental health and well-being. A Duke University study of nearly 1,400 people with heart disease revealed that those with even one good friend were three times less likely to die of a heart attack. And many studies have shown

Just as good relationships can fan the flame of energy, difficult relationships can douse it.

that people who have an array of social contacts seem to be more energetic and even get fewer colds than their less social counterparts. The simple truth is that friendship is good medicine!

But the deeper truth is that it's *replenishing* relationships that energize us and improve our health. Some friends and family members recharge and refresh us in wonderful ways. But we all have others that leave us drained and down. Do you have some relationships that are downright exhausting, even toxic?

A Relationship Inventory

In order to identify the energizing and de-energizing people in your life—and to contain the drain that some of your relationships may be having on your reserves—I strongly advise you to do a relationship inventory. Here's how:

1. Write down the names of all the key people, friends, and relatives in your life. This will, of course, include spouses or significant others, children and parents, and other close family members. It will also include neighbors, colleagues, and church or civic relationships that play a role in your life.

2. Across the top of another piece of paper, write these four headings: "Replenishing," "Neutral," "Draining," and "Toxic."

3. Look at the names on your relationship list and think about how each one makes you feel. If time with that person makes you feel energized and enhanced, put him or her under the "Replenishing" heading. These people are the ones who appreciate who you are and are there for you when you need them.

Under "Neutral," list the people you relate to who don't impact you particularly negatively or positively. Your connection with them isn't highly significant.

Under the "Draining" heading, list the people who deplete you. They may be very needy and take a great deal from you, but aren't able to offer much in return. They may be very self-centered or unreliable, or may not be available enough or have the emotional resources for a reciprocal, replenishing relationship.

If time with certain people on your list leaves you feeling very bad, depressed, or condemned, put their names under the "Toxic" heading. These people can poison your self-esteem through criticism, attacks, exploitation, or competitiveness.

Take Charge Of Your Relational Health

After you have completed your assessment of your relationships, look back over each name and think about why you are in that person's life. In some cases, you're in the relationship through no choice of your own—you were born into their family, they were born or married into yours. Others are in your life because of circumstances—work, your neighborhood, organizations you're involved in. Others are there because you are meant to meet their needs in a specific way—or they are meant to meet yours.

This is what I came to realize about our very draining friends.

They wanted to get together with us because of what we could bring to them. We were really doing them a disservice by not being fully ourselves, and communicating the reality of the challenges and struggles in our lives. It felt harder to be real than to keep up our façade because we knew it was important to communicate in a way that was respectful of their beliefs, but honest about our own. Sometimes it just seemed easier to avoid the "touchy" subjects.

Realistically evaluating this particular relationship enabled us to prepare for draining times, and strengthened our resolve to bring our authentic selves into our get-togethers. The truth is, the only thing we had to lose, if they really didn't want to be with the authentic Pam and Larry, was unwanted invitations!

Replenishing relationships challenge us to be our best—they provide a new lens through which to look at ourselves and our lives.

If it's family gatherings that drag you down the most, fill up the schedule with lots of activities. This helped Debbie and Marc. They started planning movie outings, bike rides, and duck-feeding expeditions with the kids. They also found that it was easier to get together with the family in a restaurant—the "neutral" and public space was a safer harbor. They would take along energy-boosting friends or loved ones to serve as a buffer. Debbie found that if she prepared herself to be an "observer" of the happening, she could detach herself and not take the guaranteed attacks so personally. The problem was not hers; although she could not control the behavior or words of some of her in-laws, she could make choices about how to respond. She would not be a victim!

Through counseling, Marc also learned skills of communication that enabled him to gently say, "That comment was very hurtful to me, because it hurt Debbie. Did you really mean for it to be as hurtful as it sounded?" Or, "When you rolled your eyes at Debbie just then, did you mean to hurt her the way you did?" Calling his family members on their behavior began to impact the frequency of their hurtful actions. It actually made them want to get together with Debbie and Marc less and less! And that was fine, for this young couple came to realize the power of energizing relationships, and committed themselves to investing time in them as much as possible.

Replenishing relationships challenge us to be our best—they provide a new lens through which to look at ourselves and our lives. Once you've identified the people who replenish you, resolve to spend quality time with them. The energy and healing they bring into your life is precious and vital.

PART FIVE

Energy practicals

CHAPTER TWENTY-ONE

The energy edge in sports

As a wellness coach working with athletes (professional and potential!), I am often consulted for "eat to win" strategies. As you've probably picked up, the advice I give is actually focused on *living* to win—a whole lifestyle approach for getting the body operative from a point of physical strength, allowing natural gifts and learned skills to flow freely for peak performance.

My goal is to get the athlete's body strong and stable. The body will work at its best energy level, ready to go for the gold, when the metabolism is functioning optimally, the blood sugar is stable, and the tissues are sufficiently hydrated and undergirded with energizing nutrients. To win consistently—in sports and in life—the body has to stay properly fit and fueled.

These are the principles upon which I build my eat-to-win action plan.

Fill The Energy Edge Eat-Right Prescription

I can't say it enough: eating early, often, balanced, lean, and bright naturally fills the bill for the human body—athlete or not. So...

❖ Eat breakfast: It's the most important meal of the day!
❖ Eat every two and a half to three hours to keep energy high and concentration focused.

❖ Eat power meals and power snacks, balanced with energy-filled carbohydrates, power-building lean proteins, and brightly colored fruits and vegetables.

❖ Choose foods that are low in fat. Fat increases stomach acids and stomach upsets as well as slows down the metabolism—and the athlete.

Drink To Win

Avoid carbonated, high sugar drinks, and drink plenty of cool water instead. Water is more quickly absorbed, providing adequate hydration to the muscles.

In addition to drinking your minimum of eight 8-ounce glasses of water every day, super-hydrate with an additional 16 ounces before a competition or practice, and replenish with 6 to 8 ounces more for every twenty minutes of activity. If the event lasts more than one hour, add in a carbohydrate fuel source—either through a sports drink or diluted juice.

Eat To Build

We've already talked a lot about essential nutrients that produce and support energy. Iron, magnesium, and calcium are especially important for peak athletic performance.

Because iron carries oxygen through the body, keeping iron stores high is critical for meeting an athlete's energy demand. Magnesium plays a vital role in muscle recovery and immune boosting. And calcium helps prevent muscle cramps as well as decreases the risk of osteoporosis in the future. Teenage female athletes are especially at risk for a calcium deficiency and decreased bone density.

Top Ten Proteins for Building Health and Muscle

1. Egg whites
2. Tuna
3. Lentils and rice
4. Nonfat yogurt or skim milk
5. Steamed clams
6. Lean beef
7. Roasted or grilled chicken breast
8. Salmon
9. Roasted turkey
10. Tofu and grains

Eat To Gain

If you want to gain weight, do it the right way. The goal is not to fatten up, but to build up lean muscle. This is best accomplished with eating *every two hours* and eating a balance of carbohydrates and lean proteins. Proper fueling should be combined with a strength and conditioning program in addition to aerobic training.

Eat To Prepare

It's important to go into a competition well-fueled and hydrated, but many athletes make the mistake of not eating enough before competition, and simply run out of energy. Some athletes were trained with the notion that if they played hungry, they played "mean" or more aggressively. This is a hard mindset to shake.

> ## Power Shake
>
> 1 cup skim milk
> 2 tbsp. nonfat dry milk
> 1 coddled egg white, or 1/4 cup eggbeaters
> 1 tbsp. honey
> 1/2 cup frozen fruit
> l tsp. vanilla
> 1 tbsp. wheat germ
>
> *Put all ingredients in a blender, and blend till smooth and frothy.*

The first day that Shaquille O'Neal ate breakfast on a game day, he had his career-high score, at least at the time. It made him a believer in the power of breakfast! The right pre-game meal can make all the difference in an athlete's level of competition and energy.

Energy is stored in your muscles and liver in the form of *glycogen*. The amount you have available in storage determines the length and quality of your athletic performance. Low glycogen stores can force you to slow your pace, or stop competing altogether, as you fatigue. Running out of glycogen is described by endurance athletes as "hitting the wall"; it feels like your legs are weighted down with lead, that you simply can't go on another second. Your body automatically slows in response to low glycogen and switches to burning fatty acids for energy, which dumps waste products into your bloodstream. This usually occurs when exercise lasts longer than sixty to ninety minutes.

If pre-game or pre-race jitters make it difficult for you to even *think* of eating, try this power shake, two hours before the event. The marathoners I've worked with have had great success using this shake before the run's incredible endurance test on their body.

For endurance events, it's also important to pack extra energy into glycogen storage sites. This is best accomplished through carbohydrate loading: simply eating extra carbohydrates the day before an event, while giving your muscles a rest.

Through the years, there have been many schemes of carbo-loading including starving the body of all carbohydrates for several days and then bingeing on starch. Radical weight loss or weight gain, weakness, and heart rhythm problems have been observed as a result of this classic type of carbo-loading. There's a better—and safer—way.

Studies have shown that the best way to increase glycogen stores is through a modified carbohydrate loading the day before an event. Exercise should be light or skipped altogether, and carbohydrate intake should be doubled. Glycogen stores of the well-trained athlete can be fortified as a result, increasing the normal energy stored by up to 600 calories. It's been compared to giving the body another ten slices of bread to feast on!

It's important to stay away from unfamiliar food the night before competition, and to not experiment with a new sports bar or gel during the event itself. Try new food choices only while training so that you can see if the food sits well with you and enhances your performance. You don't need to add a new ingredient into a stomach that is already experiencing pre-competition anxiety.

On game or race day, also load up on carbohydrates three hours before competition by eating 1) a large serving of pasta, rice, or potatoes; 2) a serving of fish, seafood or veal, prepared without fat; and 3) a vegetable or fruit. Skip salad if it tends to leave you bloated or gaseous.

Eat While You Compete

As you are exercising, you are using up the stored carbohydrates in your muscles. The cells turn to the bloodstream for more energy, and the liver would normally readily supply it. But the liver's glycogen stores are being depleted as well. When the stores are at a deficiency and blood sugars drop, you "bonk" and get lightheaded and weak.

You can prevent the drop by drinking a sports drink or fueling with a carbohydrate food (like a banana) when performing for more than an hour at a time. Don't wait for the bonk to hit—start fueling right away if you know you are in for a long haul.

Choose your competition fuel carefully. If it's a sports drink, go for one with the right concentration of sugars, preferably in a form your body can absorb most evenly such as glucose polymers. The drinks made with glucose polymers don't

A High Carbohydrate Day

UPON ARISING
8 ounces unsweetened juice

BREAKFAST
2 slices whole wheat toast with
1 tbsp. all fruit spread
1 1/2 cups whole grain cereal
with 1 cup milk
2 pieces of fruit

MID MORNING POWER SNACK
10 whole-grain crackers or
1 whole-grain bagel with 1 oz.
lowfat cheese
1 piece of fruit

LUNCH
2 sandwiches (4 slices of bread
with 2 oz. lean meat or fish in
each sandwich)
2 pieces (or 1 cup) fruit
Baby carrots or 12 oz. V-8 juice

MID AFTERNOON POWER SNACK
8 oz. plain yogurt mixed with
1 tbsp. all fruit jam
2 homemade bran muffins

DINNER
2 cups brown rice or whole
wheat pasta
2 oz. lean meat or 4 oz. tofu or
1 cup cooked beans
1 cup cooked vegetable
1 pieces of fruit

BEDTIME SNACK
1 1/2 cups cereal with 1 piece of
fruit and 1 cup skim milk

taste as syrupy-sweet as the simple sugar drinks. A good sports drink should have about a 7 to 8 percent carbohydrate concentration; more can slow fluid absorption and cause bloating, nausea, or diarrhea. Remember that there's nothing magic about sports drinks—they simply rehydrate you with water and replace some of the carbohydrates, or sugars, you burn through physical exertion.

I've always preferred that my athlete clients stick to water for fluid replacement, and food for carbohydrate and electrolyte replenishment. These are some of the carbo foods I recommend for fueling while exercising:

bananas	peach slices
dried apricots	baked potato chunks
dates	raisins
fig bars	sport gels or goos
grapes	power bars, Clif bars
pieces of melon	tortellini tossed in a bit of vinaigrette

The tortellini may seem a bit odd, but I've had great success with marathoners carrying it in a waist bag and popping in a few pieces every quarter hour or so. Many of my racing clients have difficulties eating some of the sports bars (they get stuck in their throat like gravel), and the gels are too sweet to them. The pasta is slippery and easy to swallow, and the vinaigrette produces more saliva (always a racing need!).

Some stomachs seem to handle eating during competition better than others. It often times requires a "trial and error" period during training to determine what will suit your system best. Refueling needs during exercise are all about the length of time you're required to perform. You may not require anything but water, but if your exercise time exceeds an hour, your muscles will work at an optimal level if continuing to be fed with carbohydrates.

High-Octane Fueling for the Energy Edge

EXERCISE TIME	WATER	SPORTS DRINK	SOLID FOODS
Less than 1 hour	6 oz. at 20 min.	none needed	none needed
1-2 hours	6 oz. every 15 min.	4-8 oz. after 90 min. in place of water	a piece of fruit
2-4 hours	alternate 6 oz. every 10 minutes with sports drink	6 oz. every 20 min.	100-150 calories
4-6 hours	same as 2-4	same; be sure to drink every 30 min.; drink should contain sodium	100-150 calories include sodium foods like crackers, tortellini, breads

Eat To Replenish

After the competition, replenish your energy stores. Within twenty minutes, have a juice or fresh fruit and lots of water; within an hour of completion, have a meal balanced in complex carbohydrate and proteins. Studies have shown a 50 percent increase in the rate of recovery of depleted muscle glycogen if replenishing begins within an hour—so even if your appetite is less than voracious, push it. And continue to push it: eat balanced mini-meals every two hours the rest of the day following an endurance competition.

If you've been depleted of glycogen from a competition like a marathon, replenishing is tough, but vital. To adequately bring the glycogen stores back to healthy levels you need two carbohydrate calories for every pound of body weight, every two hours over the next twelve. For a 180-pound man that translates to 360 carbo-hydrate calories every two hours. That's six ounces of juice, four slices of bread, and two pieces of fruit. Any wonder why it's so hard to recover?

Live Smart

If you want to perform at your athletic peak, use your common sense. Avoid caffeine, alcohol, and chemicals in food. Pace yourself with activities. Don't burn the candle at both ends. Get uninterrupted sleep, and shoot for seven to eight hours a night. A body under constant demand needs to be treated well and given rest.

Also be careful not to exercise and train *too* much. You don't want to set yourself up for burnout or injury. Here are some warning signs that may clue you in to whether or not you're overdoing a good thing:

* trouble getting to sleep at night or interrupted sleep
* resting heart rate is up in the morning
* frequent irritability
* poor appetite
* sore legs for more than two days in a row
* frequent eye twitches
* a cold that won't go away
* cessation of menstrual cycle

Whatever you choose to eat and drink for the Energy Edge, just remember this: your body, gifted as it may be, requires the proper fuel to perform at its competitive best. Place your bets on good food and water for supplying your energy stores.

CHAPTER TWENTY-TWO

Packaged pep

J enny Martin has a drinking habit: every morning without fail, she whips up a frothy concoction—a cup of orange juice, two scoops of a protein powder, and some ice cubes—in her blender. She says the protein powder gives her the energy she needs to make it through her stressful mornings as a pharmaceuticals sales educator—and she feels absolutely dependent on her morning power shakes. "If I made a regular breakfast, I'd have to cook and clean up, and that takes time. I'm not a good morning person, and I'd really prefer no breakfast at all, but my body just won't do that well—so ready-made food is my solution."

People used to be too busy to cook meals; now they're too busy to eat them. As a result, they're turning to the slew of nutrient-packed shakes that have flooded the market. There are weight-loss shakes with a tad less fat, energy shakes with a touch more carbohydrate, and body-building shakes with a bit more protein. They come in a can, or in a powder form that requires a spin through the blender with water, milk, or juice. And there are now chains of stores that have made a terrific business out of making shakes for their customers. The new-age shake is called a smoothie (to distinguish from the Dairy Queen variety).

The question is: are nutritional shakes and smoothies the panacea they are touted to be? Well... they are certainly a better choice than downing a coke and fries and calling it lunch; but they are a much worse choice than a grilled chicken salad. Better than no lunch at all—but not better than the real McCoy. A can a day *won't* keep the doctor away.

The problem with nutrition-on-the-go is the lack of the complex collection of nutrients in real food that manufactured liquids and bars can't duplicate. They lack adequate fiber and valuable phytochemicals such as isoflavones, carotenoids, and other plant-derived compounds that get you well and keep you well.

Even fruit- and dairy-based smoothies don't comprise a whole healthy diet—although they can be great as a snack or part of a meal. Liquid nutrition can provide a boost, but what about the pleasure of eating? When people turn to liquid lunches, they deprive themselves of the pleasure of real food, with all its varied textures and smells—and oft-times fall headfirst into an order of fries instead.

If you still want a meal-in-a-blender, leave the cans at the grocery store and make your own—using real food and getting the benefits of the good stuff that's not man-made.

Smoothie Tips

The basic smoothie recipe is a no-brainer: wash and cut fruit; add juice and a protein (yogurt, milk, or soy milk), and blend with ice. Here are a few tips to make your smoothie healthy and delicious.

❖ Keep calories low by sticking to unsweetened (no sugar added) fresh or frozen fruit.

❖ Frozen fruit will make a thicker drink. Spread diced fruit on a cookie sheet and freeze for two to four hours; transfer the pieces to a resealable bag when hard. Most supermarkets also carry frozen unsweetened strawberries, peaches, blueberries, raspberries, and melon.

❖ For the creamiest, smoothest smoothie, let the ice sit at room temperature for ten to fifteen minutes before blending. The smaller the ice cubes the better—fill trays half full or set the automatic ice maker to the smallest setting.

❖ Experiment! Flavor with pure vanilla extract, freshly grated ginger, chopped fresh mint, or a small dab of peanut butter. Try using silken tofu instead of yogurt, or buttermilk instead of low-fat milk.

Power In A Bar

"Energy" bars such as Power Bar, Tiger Sport, Stoker, and Clif Bar are the most visible part of the $300 million energy foods industry. Promising "fuel for optimum performance" and "stamina," the bars are carried in lunch bags, briefcases, and glove compartments for snacks and pick-me-ups. Individually wrapped, they cost $1 to $3 each.

Just a few mouthfuls and soon your blood pumps to your muscles the sugar provided by a typical bar's 50 grams of carbohydrate—the same amount as in two slices of whole wheat bread, one cup of strawberries, and one cup of skim milk. Or, go for a protein bar and you'll get as much protein as found in a chicken breast or serving of beef—more than 25 grams.

Unfortunately, however, you're not getting any of the nutrients naturally found in real foods like whole-wheat bread, chicken, strawberries, or milk. And that's the long-term problem when these energy bars become chronic substitutes for meals. The average person, even the moderately active one, doesn't need their energy to come from an engineered bar; they simply need to eat, and to eat often and well. Yet, the "energy" term is very seductive; people feel they're getting more than they are. What you actually get from one of these bars is calories, but the term "calorie bar" wouldn't gross the same sales!

If push comes to shove, and the choice is an energy bar over a candy bar, or no lunch at all, these bars are certainly the better choice and can become good fill-in nutrition. The ones to choose are those that have about 220 to 250 calories, less than 2 grams of fat per 100 calories, over 10 grams of protein, and about 45 to 50 grams of carbohydrate—a snack for a would-be weight-gainer, a meal for a would-be weight loser or maintainer. Just be sure to get real food at the next stop.

If you need pre-exercise fuel, go for fruit if your snack is within a half hour of exercise, crackers or bread if you're fueling an hour before. Have these again after the workout, but add some protein to repair and build lean muscle.

A "Natural" High?

There are other, even more dangerous energy-boosting supplements out there that promise to get you through the day even if you don't eat well. They may fly under the "natural remedy" flag—yet some are deadly and should be avoided at all cost.

Ephedrine

This bad-news drug is often found in Chinese herbals like Ma Huang, or hawked as a natural energy high and weight loss aid as Ephedra. It's also found in herbal Fen-Phen, a diet system's alternative to the diet drug pulled off the market by the FDA. Stronger than caffeine, this stimulant works as a bronchodilator (which is why it is often included in medicines for asthma and allergies) and acts on the central nervous system, thereby increasing heart rate and blood pressure. At certain dosages, ephedrine can bring harmful, even fatal, effects such as tremors, heart attacks, seizure, stroke, hepatitis, and sudden death. *Since 1993, the FDA has received more than 800 reports of adverse health effects, and direct links to as many as thirty-four deaths.* Stay clear of this bad boy, especially if you have a heart condition, high blood pressure, or a neurological disorder, and certainly if you are pregnant.

Guarana

The extract of the guarana plant, grown in Brazil, contains caffeine—many people's favorite pick-me-up. It's chemically the same as an afternoon espresso. Yes, it's natural, but so are coffee beans. Caffeine is a stimulant that acts on your central nervous system and can speed up your heart rate. If coffee tends to make you jumpy, so will guarana.

Creatine Monohydrate

This substance is made from amino acids and is intended to increase energy and build muscle. Touted as a safer version of steroids, it's heavily used by bodybuilders and sports figures. It has been shown to enhance energy production in the muscles and muscle mass, and to be helpful in short, high-intensity activities like sprinting. However, it hasn't been shown to be more effective than eating protein (amino acid's food source). With whole proteins, you get a lot more: essential minerals. No "natural" substance is an adequate substitute for conditioning and good food.

Kola Nut
Grown throughout Latin America, this is another source of caffeine. Although no more natural than coffee beans, it's being hawked as another "natural" stimulant. If you're a java junkie—needing a caffeine fix—this will seem like an energy miracle. But, again, it's just a jolt instead of a real contributor to your body's energy stores.

DHEA
This hormone is produced in the body, but in smaller amounts after age twenty. Enthusiasts claim that taking 50 mg of the hormone daily—an amount equal to levels found in young adults—increases energy and improves immune function. But at this time, no studies investigating these claims have been done on humans; most of the research has been done on mice. Because DHEA hikes levels of sex hormones, it may cause acne and oily skin, unwanted hair in women, irritability, moodiness, and aggressive or hostile behavior. It can also elevate cholesterol levels, increase heart disease risk, disrupt the body's hormone cycles, and may actually increase the risk of breast, ovarian, and prostate cancer. Bottom line: Don't take it—particularly without blood tests by to reveal your present DHEA levels.

There is some evidence that DHEA can be raised naturally by vigorous exercise, keeping a low body fat percentage, meditation and prayer, and other forms of stress reduction. DHEA levels apparently drop from excess alcohol intake, oral contraceptives, chronic illness, or stress.

Pregnenolone

This precursor to DHEA is emerging as a new star in anti-aging—with claims being made that it enhances memory and reduces fatigue. The truth is that little human research has been conducted on this possibility. Since the body converts it to DHEA, it may similarly heighten the risk of certain cancers. Get your health and energy from food instead.

Weed These Out!

Ephedra *Or* Ma Huang *OR* Epitonin—DANGEROUSLY LIFE THREATENING!

COMFREY—used for wound healing. It's carcinogenic and can obstruct blood flow in the liver.

YOHIMBE—used as an aphrodisiac and energy booster. It increases blood pressure and causes rapid heartbeat; can cause paralysis, stomach problems, nausea, vomiting, and dehydration—even death.

GERMANDER—used for weight loss. It can cause liver damage.

POKEWEED—used as an overall body tonic. It is carcinogenic.

MELATONIN—used for anti-aging and as sleep aid. It throws off hormone balance.

SASSAFRAS—used as an energy tonic. It is carcinogenic.

COLTSFOOT—used as a cough suppressant. It is carcinogenic.

DHEA—used to boost energy and slow aging. It throws off hormone balance and may increase the risk of breast, ovarian, or prostate cancers.

Ginseng

This fork-shaped root of the Chinese herb has been used for thousands of years—promising a shot of energy, alertness, and calm. We know a lot about its history, botany, chemistry, and even its effects in small animals (some research has shown a degree of performance enhancement in mice, apparently because of ginseng's effect of stabilizing blood sugar levels and raising levels of serotonin). But there is much less sound information on its effects in people. True, there have been a few clinical trials reporting generally favorable results in terms of health improvement, physical and mental capacities, and various metabolic measurements—with minimal, or no, side effects. The catch is that few of these studies would be thought acceptable by today's medical standards. Reliable research is scarce, and long-term side effects are unknown.

The biggest problem with ginseng is product consistency, sourcing, and quality issues. Many products are mislabeled and have zero effectiveness; others have been laced with pollutants and toxins that can cause liver damage. One of my clients, an NBA player, missed a playoff game due to a "flu"—which turned out to be a ginseng reaction on his liver. It sent him to the hospital for the night; he's never taken ginseng again.

The most promising ginseng research has been done using a carefully measured, standardized extract, G-115, which contained 4 percent ginsenosides. It's not that easy to get such a carefully standardized product in the real world—just because the word "ginseng" appears on the label doesn't mean you're getting the real thing. A host of imitators, hoping to cash in on the reputation of the original, can be found—including Siberian, Brazilian, and Indian ginseng. These belong to an entirely different plant family and don't have any of the same effects. To be authentic, it must be a species of *panax*, such as Asian (*Panax ginseng*) and North American (*Panax quinquefolius*).

These two varieties of ginseng are purported to have different effects in the body. North American ginseng (*Panax quinquefolius*) is prescribed in Chinese medicine for an afternoon pick-me-up. However, if you feel tired in the afternoon, something is wrong with your body chemistry because of choices you've made earlier in the day. You probably just haven't eaten enough at lunch, particularly enough protein. Red (*Korean and Chinese*) ginseng (*Panax ginseng*) is used for a lift, particularly for people who are easily chilled. It also is touted as an aid to heighten sexual desire. However, this has not been established through human research. What has been seen with this species of ginseng is irritability and a raising of blood pressure, sometimes to dangerous levels.

Varro Tyler, author of *The Honest Herbal*, offers this advice: if you purchase a ginseng product, only buy one with a standardized dosage of 4 percent to 7 percent ginsenoside. The acceptable dosage of such a product is two 100 mg capsules daily.

Ginseng should be combined with a healthy lifestyle that includes exercise, good nutrition, and sufficient sleep. It's not going to cure a lifetime of poor habits, but *may* add to the benefits naturally experienced from positive lifestyle upgrades. Any energy boost or stress reducing effect will last only as long as the pills are taken—which is why long-term lifestyle improvements are always the preferred choice.

At best, these herbs and supplements can be a worthless drain on your finances—and energy. At worst, they may make you sick—or take your life. The scariest aspect is that no one really knows—the research on real people in real-life situations is scarce and unreliable. Yet, we swallow the sales lines, and the supplements they hawk, believing that we will feel better—quick.

That's what twenty-year-old Peter Schlendorf believed when he swallowed Ultimate Xphoria, an over-the-counter dietary supplement that is promised to boost energy and sexual sensation. This spring breaker died five and a half hours later from a fatal cardiac arrhythmia caused by the high-octane punch of the active ingredients, Ma Huang (ephedrine) and caffeine in this "legal high." The death of this healthy young man and many others led the FDA to issue a warning about the use of ephedrine containing stimulants. But they are still on the market, and millions are still taking them. And they take them carelessly, dangerously doing "chemical blending" (fifteen million people took prescription drugs last year right along with a natural remedy), leaving the body to deal with the cumulative effects. The "natural is safe" mantra gives the confidence. More than one hundred million Americans are using dietary supplements.

Know this, just because something is natural *doesn't* mean it's safe. Arsenic, after all is natural.

CHAPTER TWENTY-THREE

Peak performance traveling

You're flying on a forty-year-old plane and a forty-day-old airline. You've got to be calm by the time you get to Phoenix... yet you can't be in a power negotiating mode if you're worn out from wondering if Nearly-Free Airlines cut costs by skipping on the wing rivets.

Traveling is stressful and depleting in the best of times—even if you're on your way to a week in the sunny Caribbean. It's not unusual to arrive at your destination dehydrated, drained, and disoriented—or otherwise unfit to be productive and have fun. Yet, it is possible, even for the road warrior, to stay energized, strong, and healthy while traveling. Use these tips to help you trek in tip-top shape, especially when traveling by air.

Travel Savvy

Resist Rushing

One big trigger of flying anxiety is rushing. Try to arrive at least an hour ahead of your departure time for a domestic flight and two hours early for an international flight. If you're racing to get to your flight, the time anxiety can morph into other kinds of flying fear.

Rub in Relaxation

Put your fingers on your collarbone at the point where a suspenders strap would fall. Move your fingers about two inches down the front, then push in with your thumb on that spot. If it hurts, your chest muscles are tight, which can make it difficult to breathe. Gently massage the spot until the pain disappears. When you remove the pressure, you should feel a sense of relaxation spreading through your shoulder area. This self-massage will help you breathe easier and lower your stress level.

Eat Before Boarding

Eat before you're airborne. If your body is hungry, your blood-sugar level drops. When that happens, your body sends out a stress signal. Your adrenaline rises. So does your anxiety.

To short-circuit this sequence, eat adequate pre-flight complex carbohydrates—some whole wheat bread, cereal, or a banana. (This is especially important if you are planning to sleep on the plane.) On a travel day, don't go more than three hours without having at least a snack, preferably a meal. If you tend toward anxiety, stay away from coffee—it will only ratchet up your tension level.

Drink Up

Water, that is! Flying is extremely dehydrating; the pressurized cabin air is ten times more dry than the Sahara Desert, causing you to lose fluid through your skin. This leads to puffy hands and ankles, fatigue, and a generalized bloated feeling. So drink *lots* of water. Even the standard eight glasses of water a day won't cut the anti-jet lag mustard, so add an extra 8 to 12 ounces every hour you're in the air. And limit your consumption of alcohol and coffee; both are potent dehydrators. Even decaf can leave you parched, so stick to bottled water or seltzers, herbal teas, or juice.

Power Up

Want to be bright-eyed and bushy-tailed when you arrive? Moderate your intake of carbohydrates as you get close to landing: they induce sleep and calm. Eat more high-protein, yet low-fat, fare (poached eggs, low-fat dairy products, grilled meats) to boost alertness.

Generally, it's wise to order a special meal for air travel (give your airline twenty-four hours' notice). Diabetic meals are highest in protein, fiber, and freshness, at no extra cost.

Perk Up

If you have a layover between flights, use the time to exercise. And request an aisle seat on the plane so you can get up and stretch. Try to move about the cabin every hour or so.

Power Nap

If you need to catch some shut-eye, take a nap. But limit it to forty-five minutes, the amount of time NASA has shown to improve alertness and enhance performance. Longer naps will make you more tired when you wake up.

Beating Jet Lag

Jet lag is more than just a sense of being tired; rather, it is an actual discrepancy in the body's intrinsic biological sleep cycle or "circadian rhythm." Your body's sleep cycle is controlled by the daily alternating sunlight and darkness patterns you experience. Jet lag occurs when your body's inside clock and outside clock are saying two different things.

When you travel to a new time zone, your circadian rhythm remains on its original biological schedule for several days. This results in your body telling you it's time to sleep when it's actually the middle of the afternoon, or it makes you want to stay awake when it is late at night. Traveling west to east seems to be easier on the mind and body than traveling east to west.

Jet lag can cause fatigue, insomnia, headaches, indigestion, and disorientation—not exactly energy boosters! Here are some anti-jet lag tips to help reduce the strain of traveling across time zones:

❖ If possible, select a flight that allows you to arrive in the early evening, then stay up until 10 PM local time. This is one time you'll want to avoid napping. Instead, try to stay up during the day and go to bed in the evening. If you feel you must take a nap, keep it under two hours and take it several hours before you plan to go to sleep for the night.

❖ The best thing you can do to adjust to a new time zone is expose yourself to natural light as soon as possible. Light acts as a powerful cue, telling your internal clock where you are and what schedule to keep. When you fly east, attempt to exercise at least thirty minutes in morning sun. When you fly west, attempt to exercise at least thirty minutes in the late afternoon sun.

❖ Change your bedtime three nights before you depart. If you're traveling west, go to bed one hour earlier for each time zone difference you will experience. If you're traveling east, do the opposite: start going to bed one hour later for each time zone. If possible, do this both to and from your destination.

❖ Limit your intake of stimulants such as caffeine and alcohol, particularly three hours before you plan to go to bed.

❖ Be careful with sleep medications—they don't resolve the biological imbalance caused by jet lag. What they may do is help to manage the short-term insomnia brought on by travel, so physician-approved short-term use may be acceptable.

❖ Again, drink plenty of water and juices to prevent dehydration.

On The Road Again

Are you car traveler? If so, freeway exercise might be just the ticket for keeping you toned. Sitting tense for hours on end is not great for any part of your body, especially your back. Try to stop for short stretch breaks, at least once an hour.

In addition, doing safe car exercises helps to keep you looking as good as what you drive (hopefully sleek, well-maintained, and at top operating speed!) Two hot selling audio tapes take auto-exercisers through stretching and relaxation movements involving the shoulders and neck, and then continue on to isometric exercises: tightening the muscles of the hands, arms, legs, and fanny. Get a copy of "Freeway Flex" by Sandra Lott Fisher (212-744-5900), or Karkicks by Natalie Manor (800-666-2230).

When You Get There

Jamaica. I needed it so badly—time away, time for refreshing. I needed to come back to my daily life revitalized and renewed. It was to be a different trip than ever before—a retreat of sorts, away from everything except my loving husband, our best friends, and

> *It is possible, even for the road warrior, to stay energized, strong, and healthy while traveling.*

God's creation. And truly, it was a quiet time in which I received gentle words of encouragement and strong words of direction.

But my renewed energy was stolen, because the last two days brought me every traveler's nightmare: food poisoning. My experience wasn't Jamaica's fault (it remains a favorite spot); my own carelessness tripped me up. After my personal bout with toxic travel, no discussion on healthy travel would be complete without a few basic food safety tips.

The Centers for Disease Control issues this food warning about foreign travel, particularly to third-world countries: *If you can't peel it, cook it, or boil it*—forget it! That means yes to bananas (if you're doing the peeling), no to the cut fruit on the plate. It means yes to the cooked vegetables, no to that big salad I had in Jamaica (it looked so good!). It means to drink water or juices *only* from a capped, sealed bottle. Trust me, it's worth the extra care!

In addition to eating safely, eat for energy. There's no reason to get run down when you're on the move—or while you're resting at the beach.

STICK TO YOUR NORMAL ROUTINE. As much as possible, try to get the same number of hours of sleep as you usually get, and try to eat on some kind of even schedule.

PACK SNACKS. They will help keep eating "on the move" more feasible, and will keep your lagging metabolism burning high. With your own snacks, you can keep eating the right foods at the right time, regardless of where you find yourself during the day. Pack foods that don't need refrigeration, such as dried fruits, a trail mix of peanuts, sunflower seeds, and raisins, and boxed milk. These snacks will be allowed into a foreign country, although the U.S. may not let them back in!

STAY IN SHAPE. At the very least, plan on taking a brisk walk every morning or afternoon. Also, attempt to find a hotel with a swimming pool or exercise facility. By having such options conveniently located, you'll be more likely to use them.

CHAPTER TWENTY-FOUR

Eating well while eating out

Dining out is no longer just for special occasions. New research shows that America spends 40 percent of its food dollars dining away from home. For the health-conscious, dining out presents a culinary challenge: to enjoy fine food without compromising energy.

The energy threats of dining out lie mostly in the "hidden fats" of restaurant food preparation. A typical restaurant meal packs the equivalent of twelve to fourteen pats of butter! To sidestep some of the energy land mines of eating away from home, follow these tips.

The Discriminating Diner

Plan Ahead

When you're in charge, choose a restaurant that you know and trust for quality food and a willingness to prepare foods in a healthful way upon request. More and more restaurants recognize that this trend toward healthy eating is not a passing fad; many progressive and responsible restaurants have begun to offer healthy menu selections. Supporting this initiative will ensure it continues.

Order Smart

Restaurant menus give you plenty of clues about what the selections contain. Avoid items with these words attached:

Danger Words

au gratin (in cheese sauce)	**hollandaise** (with cream sauce)	**crispy** (fried)
au fromage (with cheese)	**bisque** (cream soup)	**pan-fried** (fried with extra fat)
au lait (with milk)	**basted** (with extra fat)	**sauteed** (fried with extra fat)
à la mode (with ice cream)	**buttered** (with extra fat)	
escalloped (with cream sauce)	**casserole** (extra fat)	
	creamed (extra fat)	

If you see these words in the description of an appealing entrée, be bold enough to ask for the entrée prepared in a healthful way; that is, if the description says "buttered," ask for it without added butter; if the description says "pan-fried," ask for it grilled or poached instead. Never be timid about ordering foods prepared in a way that suits your energy needs. You are paying (and paying well!) for the meal and service, and *deserve* to have foods prepared the way you desire. You also deserve to know the content of what you are going to eat. Remember: it's your money, your health, and your waistline! Speak up. Don't be intimidated.

Order meats, fish, or poultry broiled or grilled without butter, and ask for sauces *on the side*. Good choices: petite filet, marinated breast of chicken, broiled fish or seafood, steamed shellfish. Entrées that are poached in wine or lemon juice are healthful, as are those simmered in tomato sauces. When fresh vegetables are available, order them steamed without sauces or butter. A baked potato or side of pasta with red sauce is often a better choice than rice pilaf, which is usually prepared with oil. Order salads with dressing *on the side*. Lightly drizzle on one tablespoon for taste, adding extra vinegar and lemon juice for moistness.

Control Portions

As an adult, there are no rewards for cleaning your plate. Restaurant portions can be huge, yet we often eat every morsel. Remember, you do have choices: smaller appetizer portions are often just right, and make a fine meal with a salad à la carte.

Try ordering one meal (and an extra plate) to share with your dinner companion. Never load up at all-you-can-eat brunches or food bars. Your overeating ("I want to get my money's worth") is not going to cheat the restaurant out of anything, but it can cheat you out of precious energy—and many healthy years!

Eat-Smart Ideas

Let's look at the good and bad qualities of various cuisines and restaurants. Use this guide to help you make better choices when eating away from home.

Mexican

Ask that a salad be served immediately (with dressing on the side) in place of the chips. It will help prevent the "munch a bunch" syndrome. And don't eat the fried tortilla shell your salad may be served in; those shells are grease sponges with upwards of twenty-two grams of fat per shell.

Always order à la carte rather than a combo plate, which is often laden with high-fat side dishes such as refried beans (refried beans are made with pure lard). You can also request that the sour cream and cheese toppings be omitted from your dish. These carry ten grams of fat per ounce.

And beware of the margaritas—they are loaded with both salt and sugar, to say nothing of alcohol!

EAT-SMART IDEAS: black bean soup; chili or gazpacho; chicken burrito, tostada, or enchilada; soft chicken tacos; chicken fajitas (without added fat).

Asian

Chinese, Korean, Thai, or Vietnamese food is an excellent choice for dining out, as stir-frying is the main method of cooking. This terrific technique cooks the vegetables quickly, retaining the nutrients, and, if requested, uses very little oil.

Order dishes that have been *lightly* stir-fried (not deep-fried like egg rolls) and are without heavy gravies or sweet and sour sauces. Half a dinner portion is appropriate, with *steamed* brown or white rice; fried rice is just that —fried!

Many restaurants will prepare food without MSG if you ask, and be careful to watch the soy sauce you add. Both are loaded with sodium.

Sushi is awesome for the enthusiast, but be sure you are eating it at a high-quality restaurant that is serving the freshest fish from the best sources. If in doubt, have grilled teriyaki instead.

EAT-SMART IDEAS: bamboo-steamed vegetables with chicken, seafood, or fish; Moo Goo Gai Pan; shrimp or tofu with vegetables (with no MSG and little oil); wonton, hot and sour, or miso soup; udon noodles with meat and vegetables; Yakitori (meats broiled on skewers).

Italian

Controlling the size of the portion is especially important here; the typical plate of spaghetti is five times too much! Although pasta with red sauce is a relatively low-fat choice, order it in a side dish or appetizer portion topped with steamed or grilled seafood, chicken, or fish. Ask for your salad with dressing on the side, and never hesitate to request a red sauce rather than a butter or white sauce.

EAT-SMART IDEAS: grilled chicken with a pasta side dish or bread; fresh fish with pasta side dish or bread; clam linguine with red sauce (be careful about the amount of pasta!); grilled shrimp on fettucine with red sauce; Cioppino (seafood soup); minestrone soup and salad (dressing on side), with à la carte mozzarella cheese or meatballs for protein; side dish of spaghetti with two à la carte meatballs.

Seafood

When possible, order fresh fish/seafood—steamed, boiled, grilled, or broiled *without butter*. A small amount of cocktail sauce is a better choice for dipping than butter (two dips in butter = fifty calories). Remember that small seafood items such as shrimp, oysters, etc., are deadly in terms of fat and calories when fried; the surface area is so high that more breading adheres and absorbs more fat.

EAT-SMART IDEAS: fresh fish of the day—grilled when possible, without butter, sauce on the side; steamed oysters, shrimp, or clams; lobster/crabmeat/crab claws; seafood kabobs; mesquite grilled shrimp; blackened fish or seafood from the grill, prepared without butter.

Steak Houses

Portion control is also crucial here. A 16-ounce steak or prime rib will give you far more protein and fat than you need. Order the smallest cut available, and plan on taking some home!

EAT-SMART IDEAS: petite cut filet; shish-ka-bob or brochette; slices of London broil (no sauces); Hawaiian chicken or marinated grilled chicken breast; char-broiled shrimp (grilled without butter).

Health/Natural Food Restaurants

Do not feel "safe" here by any means! Although you will have an opportunity to get whole grains and nicer fresh vegetable salads, you still need to avoid the fats and sodium. Many foods are prepared in the same way at "health food" restaurants as at the drive-through; they just have healthier sounding names! Beware of sauces and high-fat cheeses smothering the foods, as well as high-fat dressings on salads and sandwiches. If you have a cheese dish, be sure to use no other added fats in the meal; the cheese will contain enough for the day!

EAT-SMART IDEAS: vegetable soup and 1/2 sandwich (avoid tuna/chicken salad due to mayo); "chef"-type salad (no ham) and whole grain roll; stir-fry dishes, asking for "light" on oil; marinated breast of chicken; fresh fish of the day, grilled when possible; vegetable omelet with whole-grain roll; pita stuffed with vegetables and cheese; fruit plate with plain yogurt/cottage cheese and whole-grain roll.

Fast Food Restaurants

If you have to eat in a hurry and can't request special preparation for a sit-down meal, at least become more aware of the hidden fats in the foods you consider while you're on the run.

❖ Special sauces: it's the mayonnaise, special sauces, sour cream, etc., that triple the fat, sodium, and calories in fast foods. Always order your take-out without them!

❖ Stuffed potatoes may seem a healthy addition to the fast food menu, but not if they're smothered in cheese sauce (equivalent to nine pats of butter per potato!). Ask for grated cheese, and no butter, instead.

❖ Chicken is a lower-fat alternative than beef, but not when it's batter-fried! One serving of chicken nuggets has the equivalent of five pats of butter—more than twice what you would get in a regular hamburger. And the fat it's soaked in is purely saturated—usually just melted beef fat. A chicken sandwich is no health package either—it usually has enough fat to equal eleven pats of butter, unless the chicken is grilled.

❖ Croissant sandwiches aren't a whole lot more than a meal on a grease bun! Most take-out croissants have the equivalent of more than four pats of butter, and the toppings add insult to injury.

❖ Salad bars can add fiber and nutrients to a meal, but it's only salad vegetables that do so. The mayonnaise-based salads, the croutons and the bacon bits, should be left on the bar, and dressing used sparingly. Use extra lemon juice or vinegar instead.

❖ Frozen yogurt, although lower in fat and cholesterol than ice cream, contains more sugar—so it is *not* a perfectly healthy substitute. This also applies to frozen tofu desserts. Substitute one of the new sorbet-like frozen desserts that are primarily fruit. They will contain some sugar, but usually not in such high amounts.

While there are many de-energizing foods in the fast lane, there are some choices that can make eating "fast" healthy and safe. Use this guide to help you eat smarter at the take-out counter.

❖ **BURGER KING.** Although no burger is truly lean, the smaller the portion, the less fat you get. A Hamburger Deluxe without mayo is filling and tasty, and delivers twenty-eight fewer grams of fat than the Big King. Also try the B.K. Broiler Chicken Sandwich (without dressing or mayo) or Chunky Chicken Salad with reduced-calorie Italian dressing and crackers.

❖ **MCDONALD'S.** Choose the McGrilled Chicken Classic (try it with barbecue sauce); Chunky Chicken Salad (with your own whole grain, low-salt crackers for carbohydrate) and lite vinaigrette dressing; or a small Hamburger (no mayo).

❖ **WENDY'S.** Order a baked potato (plain, without cheese sauce; get it with chili instead). Or try the salad bar, filling up on raw vegetables rather than potato salad, macaroni salad, etc.; use garbanzo beans or chili for protein. Other smart choices include the Single Hamburger (without mayo), Caesar Side Salad (without dressing) with grilled chicken; or the Grilled Chicken Sandwich.

❖ **HARDEE'S.** Choose the Chicken 'n' Pasta Salad; Grilled Chicken Sandwich (no mayo); or Hamburger (no mayo).

❖ **STEAK 'N' BAKE.** Try the Steakburger (no mayo) or Three-Way Chili.

❖ **CHICK-FIL-A.** Grilled Chicken Salad (no-oil salad dressing) is a smart choice, as is the Grilled Chicken Sandwich (no mayo).

❖ **TACO BELL.** Order a Soft Taco (chicken); taco, hard-shell (chicken); Fiesta Tostada.

❖ **DAIRY QUEEN.** Try the BBQ Beef Sandwich or Grilled Chicken Fillet Sandwich (no sauce).

❖ **ARBY'S OR RAX.** The Arby's Roast Beef or Chicken Sandwich (no mayo) is okay, as is Arby's Fajita Pita. Or try the Rax Turkey (no mayo) or Roast Beef Sandwich (no sauce).

❖ **PIZZA PLACES.** Order the personal-size cheese pizza, with vegetables if desired (eat three-quarters and save the remaining quarter for a snack). Or if you're sharing a pizza with others, try a thin crust thirteen-inch (medium) cheese pizza, with vegetables if desired (no sausage or pepperoni)—two slices for women, three slices for men.

❖ **SUB SHOPS OR DELIS.** Get a small six-inch sub (turkey or roast beef; no oil or mayo). Subway's Roasted Chicken on whole wheat (no mayo or dressing) is also a good choice. Avoid tuna subs—they're loaded with fat! Deli and grocery stores will usually make you turkey, roast beef, or Jarlsberg Lite sandwiches (ask for three ounces of meat on whole-grain bread).

Appetizers

Many restaurants specialize in appetizers: fried cheese; nachos; fried potato skins loaded with bacon, sour cream, and cheese; fried zucchini and mushrooms; those gigantic onion "blossoms." These are cardiovascular nightmares when you consider that two potato skins or two pieces of fried cheese are basically the fat calories of a whole meal (and should be used as such!). Many restaurants are offering raw vegetable platters, but the dip will negate the value of the veggies. If you indulge, do so very carefully!

EAT-SMART IDEAS: chicken burritos or fajitas; grilled seafood; marinated chicken breast; non-creamed soup.

Breakfast

Breakfast can be a special meal out because most restaurants offer safe and easy choices. If breakfast is later than normal, energize with a snack when you arise, then the later meal. You also may choose to have your larger lunch portions for breakfast and a smaller lunch three to four hours later. Follow these guidelines in ordering:

❖ Order whole wheat toast or grits *unbuttered;* then add one teaspoon of butter, if desired.
❖ Ordering à la carte is usually safer so that you are not tempted by the abundance of food in the "breakfast specials" or buffets.
❖ Be bold and creative in ordering! Rather than accepting French toast with syrup and bacon, ask for it prepared with whole wheat bread, no syrup, and a side of fresh berries or fruit

instead. Some restaurants will substitute cottage cheese or one egg for the meat. Many also serve oatmeal and cereal even though it's not always on the menu. It's a nice carbohydrate with milk and fresh fruit, especially strawberries or blueberries.

❖ Always look for a protein *and* a carbohydrate source. A Danish doesn't do it!

> **EAT-SMART IDEAS:** Eggs scrambled (without fat), or egg substitute, and whole wheat toast or English muffin; French toast (with whole wheat bread) and berries; fresh vegetable and egg-white omelet and toast; whole-grain cereal with skim milk and fruit; Fresh fruit bowl with cottage cheese and whole wheat toast.

Power Lunches

The '80s-style power lunch is dead. According to research done by Market Facts, of Arlington Heights, Illinois, 56 percent of working people wolf down lunch in fifteen minutes or less. Forty-two percent eat lunch at their desk or on the go and get it from the easiest source.

Next time you're face to face with the vending machine, wondering which buttons to push, think of the chart below—and go for the tasty, easy-to-find, low-fat yet high-voltage alternatives to all your favorite "sure-to-burn-out-quick" treats.

EAT-SMART IDEAS: INSTEAD OF...	CHOOSE...
Snickers bar (280 calories/14 g fat/6 g protein)	Crisp apple, mozzarella string cheese (115 calories/ 4 g fat/ 7 g protein)
1.74 oz. bag peanut M & M's (250 cals/13 g fat/5 g pro)	2 whole-wheat Wasa crisp breads with 8 oz. Stonyfield Farm non-fat yogurt (270 cals/1 g fat/12 g pro)
60 Ruffles potato chips (560 cals/35 g fat/7 g pro)	24 Baked Lays potato crisps, 1 oz. part-skim cheddar cheese (300 cals/6 g fat/11 g pro)
16 oz. Coca-Cola Classic, 6 Ritz crackers (299 cals/5 g fat/2 g pro)	Bottle of water; turkey sandwich with 1 slice bread, 1/4 lb. turkey, lettuce, tomato, mustard (214 cals, 5 g fat/24 g protein)

4 cups microwave popcorn, 1 bottle Snapple Iced Tea (240 cals/7 g fat/3 g pro)	4 cups light microwave popcorn, tall Starbucks Frappuccino (248 cals/4 g fat/6 g protein)
1 jelly doughnut (220 cals/9 g fat/4 g pro)	1/2 whole-grain bagel with 2 tbsp light cream cheese, 1 tsp. all fruit jam (141 cals, 4 g fat, 8 g protein)
Wendy's medium Frosty (440 cals/11 g fat/11 g pro)	1/2 cup vanilla yogurt and fresh berries sprinkled with 1/4 cup low-fat granola (205 cals/1 g fat/6 g protein)

Don't get discouraged and think you can't ever eat out. You can have a healthy meal away from home, but you must learn to make good choices. The trick is to learn what you *can* eat, and then think positively. Rather than feeling dismayed about everything you can't order, use your creativity and knowledge to find good things you can.

CHAPTER TWENTY-FIVE

Losing weight without losing energy

When you're overweight, it's easy to forget what it's like to feel energetic. Shaving off excess body weight may not let you slip into your high school jeans, but it can help you live longer—and *feel better*. Healthy weight loss can help prevent high blood pressure, heart disease, cancer, and diabetes—and fight fatigue.

The fatigue that comes from carrying around extra pounds is easy to get used to. Yet imagine carrying around a ten-pound sack of groceries all day! Extra weight on your body tires you in the same way. But losing just ten pounds can make a tremendous difference in your looks, your health, and your energy level.

It can even affect your sleeping—excess fat in the abdomen in particular forces your lungs to work harder while you're asleep. And fatty tissue in the throat area also decreases the size of your airway when you're lying down. Both add up to an energy drain. Losing even a little bit of weight may help your spouse sleep better too: a 1995 study on male snorers found that a seven-pound weight loss cut snoring in half, while a sixteen-pound weight loss eliminated it entirely.

Can the image of the perfect body. Instead of thinking that you have to reach some unattainable—and difficult to maintain—goal, focus on losing just ten pounds. Keep it off for a while and let your body adjust. Then if you want to lose more, you can. In the meantime, you'll feel better!

The Dieting Dilemma

A vast number of Americans begin each year with "Diet!" as the headline of their resolutions. Yet, statistics show that most of those would-be dieters don't make it through the first week.

Why can one person go on a diet, get rid of fat and keep it off easily, while nine others get caught in a never-ending cycle of disappointing diets that lead to despair and defeat? The odds are just that overwhelming—nine to one—that people who've lost weight will gain it back within a year.

Why is it so easy to gain weight and so hard to lose it? Why is it so hard to keep the weight off? The good news on the dieting front is that the secrets to successful weight loss aren't such a mystery any longer. Many of us have embraced the truth that diets never have, and never will, work over the long run. Long-term weight loss success is found in being set free from the dieting mindset and embarking on a lifestyle of health. The solution begins with an honest acknowledgment: weight is not the problem; it is only a symptom. Our eating patterns and perspectives about food are the real problems that need to be dealt with.

Smart weight loss occurs only when you 1) burn more calories than you take in, 2) fan the flame of your metabolism with exercise, and 3) change your perspective about the way you eat and live. Whether you have eight pounds to lose or eighty, don't get started until you are really ready to do what it takes. False starts dilute your commitment and motivation.

I think that the word *diet* is a nasty four-letter word—it implies temporarily being "good" only to be "bad" later. Card-carrying members of the "Diet Generation" have to separate fat from fiction! Use this "blunder checklist" to help you identify the wrong thinking that belongs in the trash heap—right along with those old diet books.

Twenty Weight Loss Blunders

NO. 1: Binge eating before going on a diet.

NO. 2: Fasting, or cutting calories, to lose weight. Cutting too many calories will send the message to your body that you're starving, and your metabolism will slow down to preserve the very fat you are trying to eliminate. Cut no more than 500 to 1000 calories daily.

NO. 3: Expecting to lose more than one to two pounds a week. Any more than this is the loss of body fluids and valuable muscle tissue.

NO. 4: Skipping meals, particularly breakfast. Regular meals, beginning with breakfast, help prevent the "famine-then-feast" syndrome.

NO. 5: Skipping wisely chosen snacks. Smart snacking keeps your metabolism burning high, and your appetite in control.

NO. 6: Substituting coffee, tea, or diet soda for energy-producing meals, snacks, and water.

NO. 7: Going to a salad bar and heaping on cheeses, meats, and pasta mixed with mayonnaise and salad dressing.

NO. 8: Having an "on a diet" or "off a diet" mentality, rather than eating moderately and wisely as a lifestyle.

NO. 9: Thinking of any food as "bad" or "forbidden." Food is simply food; it's the power we let it have over us that is bad.

NO. 10: Neglecting to exercise regularly (at least thirty minutes, three times a week). Regular exercise is key to an activated metabolism.

NO. 11: Losing weight to look good for someone else.

NO. 12: Losing weight thinking that when you shed unwanted pounds, you'll become a wonderful person—forgetting that you already are a wonderful person.

NO. 13: Relying on diet pills, or a shake, or any product that promises to miraculously do the work for you.

NO. 14: Thinking of weight loss as something you have to do, rather than what you choose to do.

NO. 15: Focusing on which foods to avoid, rather than which foods to include.

NO. 16: Buying, preparing, and eating your meals on the run. A frantic, frenzied lifestyle prevents you from enjoying and feeling satisfied with the food you do eat.

NO. 17: Considering losing excess weight as an end in itself, rather than as a means to an end: a healthier, happier, more energetic and productive you!

NO. 18: Believing that all calories are created equal. They aren't; it's fat that makes you fat. Calories consumed as fat are converted into fat on the body more readily than the same number of calories consumed as protein or carbohydrate.

NO. 19: Falling into the trap of substituting all the fat-free foods that are often nothing more than sugary chemical brews.

NO. 20: Failing to take charge the moment you discover you have gained two pounds over your desired weight.

Can you identify with any of these belief systems and habit patterns? If so, it's time to break the diet mentality with a personal nutrition plan that works—for life. You *can* take charge; you *can* feel better, have abundant energy from morning till night, and look more radiant and healthy. You can slip gently into a healthier way of eating, without starving yourself or running yourself ragged. Just make the decision, today, to turn from the dieting path, and take a small step on the road to looking and feeling better. Refuse to sacrifice energy at the altar of improper weight loss.

Why Fad Diets Don't Work

A human baby produces a certain number of fat cells, depending on genetics and how he or she is fed. The baby never loses these cells, and the body can add more if overfed for an extended period of time.

It appears that the more fat cells we have, the hungrier we feel; they are continually signaling the brain to feed them. If we drastically cut our food intake by going on an unbalanced fad or semi-starvation diet, our bodies slip into famine mode. Our metabolism slows down, using fewer calories than usual for the same activities. This is why there are plateaus in dieting (which occur in even healthy, sensible weight loss)—the body is working hard to maintain weight for survival. It is also why weight is regained so quickly when the diet is over. The body reads that the time for feasting is here, and it had better "stock up" fat in the cells for the next famine.

All fad diets are variations on five themes (or is it schemes?) of deception: 1) the high protein, low carbohydrate diet; 2) the high carbohydrate, low protein diet; 3) the semi-starvation diet (cabbage soup diet, grapefruit diet, liquid fasting); 4) the food combining diet (fruit only in the morning, carbohydrate at lunch, protein at dinner, and never carb and protein together; and 5) the "lose-it-while-you-sleep" diet (herbs and supplements). Many of these diets have come back from the seventies like bell bottoms, just under a different name or new packaging. All work, *quickly*, by throwing the body into a state of imbalance, promoting sudden weight loss from dehydration.

When you're on a fad diet, ten percent of your body's fluid weight can be lost in just two weeks—which, depending on your size, can fulfill the sensational "Lose twenty-five pounds in twenty-five days!" promise. After the first two weeks, these diets will continue to promote weight loss, for the short term, by eating away at valuable lean muscle tissue, which weighs more than fat. The waste products from your muscle tissue breakdown will, over time, depress your appetite, so you continue to lose because you are eating less.

Healthy weight loss can help prevent high blood pressure, heart disease, cancer, and diabetes— and fight fatigue.

The tide turns, however, when you "cheat" or stop the diet. Your body's survival mode turns your appetite on high, stockpiling the calories you consume. You don't even have to gorge to regain the weight; your sluggish metabolism will do that for you. And sadly, the weight you gain back is fat, not muscle.

Years of this kind of dieting will leave you in terrible shape. Losing muscle weight only to gain back fat causes you to yo-yo from a larger pear shape to a smaller pear shape, back to a larger pear shape, until you begin to deposit fat in new places—and finally diet yourself into a pumpkin shape!

The only desirable kind of weight to lose is fat, never muscle. This is best accomplished through a "leaning down" process that comes from a balanced intake of nutrients. On an unbalanced fad diet, you *do* lose—you lose your health, your energy, and your money.

The Bottom Line

What it all comes down to is a basic truth about weight control:

If you want to lose weight, there's no magic-bullet remedy that will do it for you. You simply need to eat less and exercise more. To lose pounds and inches, you must expend more calories than you take in—without starving yourself and throwing your body into self-imposed malnutrition. These basic "to do's" never change:

Activate Your Metabolism

Remember, it's not the calories you take in but the calories you burn that count! Our contemporary lifestyles have slowed our metabolic rate down to a snail's pace, resulting in fat being stored rather than burned for energy. This "cocooning" effect is the result of constant stress demands, and not enough energy supply to meet the needs. Our body was created to slow itself down as a protective response, so our erratic, catch-as-catch-can eating patterns keep our metabolism stuck in low gear, storing away every meal we do eat as if it's our last.

As you've read, the key to keeping your metabolism revved up is to use the Energy Edge eat-right prescription: smaller meals, more often, carbohydrates together with lean proteins. And remember, this starts with breakfast. A recent Vanderbilt study showed overweight breakfast skippers who started to eat breakfast lost an average of seventeen pounds in twelve weeks. Not only did adding this most important meal speed up their metabolisms, it had a payoff later on as well: the research showed the breakfast eaters to be less hungry all day long and less impulsive about unhealthy snacking.

Tell Your Metabolism to Take a Hike

Eating to boost your metabolism has another payoff: it energizes you to exercise! Eating smart is only half the battle in your quest for an active metabolism. Regular exercise is also a key to keep your body burning calories at a high rate.

In addition to burning calories while you're running the track or pedaling the stationary bike, exercise gives you an "after-burn"—it boosts up your metabolism so you use up more calories for hours *after* you finish your workout. Exercise also decreases your appetite and gives you a healthy outlet for stress.

Regular aerobic exercise doesn't just speed up your metabolism for successful weight loss, it's also the key to lasting weight maintenance. A study done in Boston over a decade ago showed that weight loss subjects who dieted but did not exercise gained back nearly all their weight, while those who exercised along with dieting, and continued to do so, didn't regain any.

If your schedule and personality allow, try to exercise in the morning. After a night's fast, two-thirds of the calories you burn come from stored fat rather than stored glycogen. Just be sure to break your body out of the fast with breakfast, or at least a quick glass of juice.

Count Fat, Not Calories

Just cutting calories is too broad: what you most need to do is cut *fat* calories. Remember, it's the kind of calories you eat, more than the sheer number, that has the most impact. In other words, 100 calories of butter (1 tbsp.) are more likely to go to your hips than are 100 calories of whole wheat bread (about 2 slices).

Keep the following tips in mind as you practice trimming the fat from your daily diet.

When Grocery Shopping...

❖ Switch from whole milk dairy products to skim or 1 percent milk, buttermilk, and nonfat plain yogurt. Look for fat-free or low-fat cheeses such as ricotta, pot or farmers cheese, skim-milk mozzarella, cottage cheese, and fat-free or "light" cream cheese. Check the label to be sure the dairy product has less than five grams of fat per ounce. You may also want to try some of new soy food versions of dairy. They are loaded with substances that help protect against disease.

❖ At the deli, go for the leanest cuts. Instead of the usual "lunch-eon meats," select sliced turkey or chicken, lean ham, and low-fat cheeses. Limit use of high-fat, high sodium, processed sausages and meats, hot dogs, bacon, and salami.

❖ Leave products made with tropical oils and partially hydro-genated oils at the store. Avoid buying safflower, sunflower, corn, soy, peanut, or cottonseed oil, or products made from them, including margarine and vegetable shortenings.

❖ Use this formula for figuring the fat percentage of calories when assessing whether new food products are as good as they claim: 9 calories per gram of fat x grams of fat, divided by calories per serving. Buy foods that derive less than 25 percent of their calories from fat.

❖ Buy whole-grain and freshly baked breads and rolls. They have more flavor and don't need butter or margarine to taste good.

❖ Use all-fruit jams on breads or toast, rather than fat spreads like butter or margarine.

❖ Keep an abundant supply of fresh fruits and munchy vegeta-bles on hand for snacking. Buy light popcorn and low-fat crackers rather than chips and cookies. Substitute sorbet or frozen juice bars for ice cream.

❖ Try to replace animal protein foods with fish and soy foods.

When Cooking...

❖ Eat more fish and skinless poultry, and less red meat. If you eat red meat, buy lean, and trim well before and after cooking. Cook in a way that diminishes fat, such as grilling, broiling, or roasting on a rack.

❖ Use marinades, flavored vinegars, plain yogurt, or juices when grilling or broiling to tenderize leaner cuts of meat and seal in their moisture and flavor. Mix these marinades with fresh or dried herbs such as basil, oregano, and parsley to add flavor.

❖ Limit protein portions to 5 ounces, precooked. After cooking, the size will resemble the size of a deck of cards. This is the typical lunch portion of fish or chicken served in a restaurant. The typical dinner portion is 9 ounces. Let rice, pastas, potatoes, and vegetables become the centerpiece of your meals.

❖ Use nonstick cooking sprays and skillets. These will enable you to brown meats without grease, and sauté ingredients in stocks and broths rather than fats and oils. If a recipe calls for basting in butter or its "juices," baste instead with tomato or lemon juice.

❖ Skim the fat from soups, stocks, and meat drippings. Refrigerate and remove the hardened surface layer of fat before reheating. As you do, think how that fat would have hardened in your body, and how you are doing yourself a great favor!

Losing just ten pounds can make a tremendous difference in your looks, your health, and your energy level.

❖ Use legumes (dried beans and peas) as a main dish at least twice each week. These meat substitutes can be a high nutrition, low-fat meal. If beans have made you gaseous in the past, try "Beano" (available from your pharmacy or health food store). It's a natural enzyme that works wonders for digestion of beans and other gas-forming foods while your body is becoming more tolerant on its own.

❖ Substitute plain, nonfat yogurt or fat-free ricotta cheese in dips or sauces calling for sour cream or mayo. Also use these as toppings for baked potatoes and chili. And don't forget low-fat, flavorful salsa, a hot topping for anything!

❖ Use two egg whites in place of one whole egg. Egg whites are pure protein; egg yolks are pure fat and cholesterol!

Don't Make Any Food a Forbidden Fruit
Putting our focus on what we shouldn't do and what we shouldn't

eat only sets us up for failure. Our eyes are so fixed on the negative behavior or food that it becomes an obsession—and it's only a matter of time before we fall into it headfirst!

Although you need to get in touch with your true hunger, and not be controlled by anything, feeding your body is about much more than fatness versus thinness. It's caring for your body as something precious. Rather than eating just what you "feel" you need—and being thrilled to lose weight on a half bag of peanut M&M's—eat to bless your body with nutrients that give you energy and fortify your health.

Stick With It

Eating well is a lot like riding a bike. If you fall off, so what? It's no problem to climb back on. No matter how often you fall off, don't lose heart. The more often you try, the better you'll get. And, like bike riding, once you learn to live more healthfully, you'll never forget. Once you start living a life filled with energy, and find you can lose weight, too, why would you ever want to go back to your old patterns of eating?

CHAPTER TWENTY-SIX

High-octane meal plans and recipes

When trying to make a change in your life, or in your behavior, or in your energy levels, you'll make dramatic strides if you'll just begin to keep track of what you do. Although behavioral science remains unclear about why self-monitoring is such a success technique in change, it definitely is.

A great way to begin enacting the Energy Edge way of life is by heightening your awareness of what you are currently doing. For five days, keep track of what you eat and drink, how much you exercise, how much you sleep or nap, how often you take breaks, even how you breathe. Also monitor how you feel at different

The Energy Edge Meal Plan gives you a strategy for eating (and drinking) to fuel your body with the right foods at the right times.

times of your day. Is your energy high or low? How about your moods? How's your alertness and concentration? Feeling productive? When did you last get sick? After you've evaluated your present-day eating and living patterns and have identified your weak spots, you can get on your way toward living on the Energy Edge.

The Energy Edge Meal Plans

The Energy Edge Meal Plan gives you a strategy for eating (and drinking) to fuel your body with the right foods at the right times. The emphasis is not just on what to eat, but how and when. This plan is not designed for weight loss, but for maintaining your body's weight while dramatically boosting your energy. The meal plan for women provides approximately 1500 calories a day; the meal plan for men provides approximately 2000 calories per day. Portions may need to be adjusted for individual caloric needs.

If you are desperately in need of immediate energy, want to stabilize your blood sugar, or are in the midst of high stress, the Quick Energy Meal Plan is for you. This plan is based on eating often, *very* often: every two hours. This may seem difficult, but it is worth the effort. Follow this plan for up to three weeks. By then, you may be energized enough to move into the basic Energy Edge Meal Plan. While some people experience an energy boost right away when they follow the meal plan, it usually takes two to three days for your body chemistry to stabilize—and for you to feel an increase in energy.

❖ QUICK TIP ❖

When you cook, do so in abundance, then freeze properly portioned leftovers in freezer bags, providing quick meals when you need them.

The Quick Energy Boosting Meal Plan

Upon arising—6 oz. unsweetened juice (no citrus)

Breakfast—Within 1/2 hour of rising—7:00 am

Complex carbo:	1 slice of 100% whole wheat bread OR 1/2 whole wheat English muffin OR 1 cup cereal WITH added bran
Protein:	1 oz. low-fat cheese OR 1 egg OR 6 oz. skim milk for cereal
Simple carbo:	1 piece of fresh fruit

1st am snack—9:00 am

Carbo:	5 whole-grain crackers OR 1 large pc. fruit OR 2 rice cakes
Protein:	1 oz. cheese/lean meat OR 1/2 cup yogurt OR 1/4 cup cottage cheese2nd am snack—11:00 am

Repeat AM snack choices OR 1/4 cup Trail Mix (page 50)

Lunch—1:00 pm

Complex carbo:	1 slice of bread OR 1 baked potato OR 5 crackers OR 1/2 whole wheat pita
Protein:	2 oz. cooked poultry, fish, roast beef OR low-fat cheese
Simple carbo:	1 small piece of fresh fruit OR 1 cup noncreamed soup
Healthy munchie:	Raw vegetable salad, if desired
Added fat:	1 tsp. mayonnaise OR 1 tbsp. dressing OR 1 tsp. olive oil

1st afternoon snack—3:00 pm

Repeat earlier snack choices OR 1/2 cup plain yogurt mixed with 1/2 cup fruit OR 1 tbsp. all-fruit jam

2nd afternoon snack   5:00 pm

Repeat earlier snack choices

Dinner—7:00 pm

Complex carbo:	1 cup rice or pasta OR 1 cup starchy vegetable
Protein:	2-3 oz. cooked chicken, turkey, fish, seafood, lean roast beef OR 1/2 cup cooked beans
Simple carbo:	1 cup nonstarchy vegetable OR 1 pc. fresh fruit
Healthy munchie:	Raw vegetable salad, if desired
Added fat:	May use 1 tsp. of margarine/butter or olive oil OR 2 tbsp. sour cream OR 1 tbsp. salad dressing

Night snack

Any "Power Snack" (page 50) OR 3/4 cup cereal with 1/2 cup skim milk

The Energy Edge Meal Plan For Women

Breakfast—Within 1/2 hour of arising

Simple carbo:	1 serving fresh fruit
Complex carbo:	2 slices whole wheat toast OR 1 English muffin/bagel OR 2 homemade low-fat muffins OR 1 1/2 cups cereal (with added bran)
Protein:	1 oz. low-fat cheese or 1/4 cup low-fat cottage cheese OR 1 egg (three times/wk) or 1/4 cup egg substitute OR 1 cup skim milk or nonfat yogurt for cereal

Morning snack

Carbo:	1 lg. fresh fruit OR 5 whole grain crackers OR 2 rice cakes OR 2 Wasa OR 1 slice whole wheat bread
Protein:	1 oz. part-skim or fat-free cheese OR lean meat OR 1 cup nonfat yogurt OR 1/4 cup low-fat cottage cheese

Lunch—(If prone to fatigue after lunch, begin your meal with your fruit or soup)

Simple carbo:	1 pc. fruit OR 1 cup cooked vegetables OR noncreamed soup
Complex carbo:	2 slices bread OR 1 baked potato OR 1 whole wheat pita
Protein:	2-3 oz. cooked poultry, fish, seafood, lean beef or low-fat cheese OR 3/4 cup cooked legumes
Healthy munchies:	Raw vegetables as desired (up to 2 cups) with lemon juice, vinegar, (optional) mustard or no-oil salad dressing
Added fat:	1 tbsp. light mayo OR 1 tsp. olive oil OR 1 tbsp. salad dressing (optional) OR 1 tsp. butter

Afternoon snack—Repeat earlier snack choices OR 1/2 cup Trail Mix (page 50)

Dinner—Begin with 1 pc. of fruit or 1/2 cup mixed fruit OR 1 cup noncreamed soup

Simple carbo:	The above fresh fruit or soup AND 1 cup nonstarchy vegetables
Complex carbo:	1/2 cup rice or pasta OR 1/2 cup starchy vegetables
Protein:	2-3 oz. cooked skinless poultry, seafood, fish, lean beef OR 1 cup cooked legumes
Healthy munchies:	Raw vegetables (up to 2 cups) as desired with lemon juice, vinegar, or no-oil salad dressing
Added fat:	May use 1 tsp. olive or canola oil OR 1 tbsp. salad dressing OR 1 tsp. butter or margarine

Night snack— 3/4 cup cereal with 1/2 cup skim milk or nonfat yogurt

The Energy Edge Meal Plan For Men

Breakfast—Within 1/2 hour of arising

Simple carbo:	1 serving fresh fruit
Complex carbo:	2 slices whole wheat toast OR 1 English muffin/bagel OR 2 homemade low-fat muffins OR 1 1/2 cups cereal (with added bran)
Protein:	2 oz. low-fat cheese or 1/2 cup low-fat cottage cheese OR 2 eggs (only 2 times/wk) or 1/2 cup egg substitute OR 1 1/2 cups skim milk or nonfat yogurt for cereal

Morning snack

Carbo:	1 pc. of fruit AND 5 whole grain crackers OR 2 rice cakes or 2 Wasa OR 1 slice whole wheat bread
Protein:	2 oz. part-skim or fat-free cheese OR lean meat OR 1 cup nonfat yogurt OR 1/2 cup low-fat cottage cheese

Lunch—(If prone to fatigue after lunch, begin your meal with your fruit or soup)

Simple carbo:	Another serving fruit OR 1 cup cooked vegetables OR 1 cup noncreamed soup
Complex carbo:	2 slices bread OR 1 baked potato OR 1 whole wheat pita
Protein:	3-4 oz. cooked poultry, fish, seafood, lean beef, or low-fat cheese OR 1 cup cooked legumes
Healthy munchies:	Raw vegetables as desired (up to 2 cups) with lemon juice, vinegar, (optional) mustard or no-oil salad dressing
Added fat:	1 tbsp. light mayo OR 1 tsp. oil/butter OR 1 tbsp. salad dressing (optional)

Afternoon snack—Repeat earlier snack choices OR 1/2 cup Trail Mix (page 50)

Dinner—Begin with 1 pc. (1/2 cup) fruit OR 1 cup noncreamed soup

Simple carbo:	The above fresh fruit or soup AND 1 cup nonstarchy vegetables
Complex carbo:	1 1/2 cups rice or pasta OR 1 1/2 cups starchy vegetables
Protein:	3 oz. cooked skinless poultry, seafood, fish, lean beef OR 1 cup cooked legumes
Healthy munchies:	Raw vegetables (up to 2 cups) as desired with lemon juice, vinegar, or no-oil salad dressing
Added fat:	May use 1 tsp. olive or canola oil OR 1 tbsp. salad dressing OR 1 tsp. butter

Night snack—1 cup cereal with 1 cup skim milk or nonfat yogurt

The "I-Hate-To-Cook" Guide To Energizing Meals

Too often, in our frenzied way of doing things, something important is compromised: taste, health, or the entire satisfaction of making and enjoying a home-cooked meal. Yet, many interesting and delicious meals can be made in short order.

According to a recent survey by the NPD Group market research firm, most cooks spend sixteen to forty-five minutes preparing dinner. Small wonder that there's a boomlet in convenience foods, recipes that rely on pantry staples, and cookbooks and magazines promising to cut kitchen time. Studies show that people want to made a contribution to the meal they're providing for their families, but they don't want to make the whole thing.

Most people don't really hate to cook. What they hate is the stress of spending more time in the kitchen, preparing food and cleaning it up. Here are some suggestions for beating the last-minute dinnertime blues.

PLAN AHEAD. Set aside fifteen minutes a week with your family to plan dinners. After a couple of weeks, you'll have menus that you can use over and over again.

STREAMLINE SHOPPING. With a week's worth of menus in hand, it's easy to cut back on last-minute trips to the supermarket. Choosing recipes with fewer ingredients will also speed you through the checkout lane.

TAKE SHORTCUTS. Visit the supermarket salad bar for diced or cubed fresh veggies—you can buy exactly the amount you need. Also stock up on bags of precut salad greens from the produce section. Get peeled, freshly cooked shrimp at the seafood counter, grilled chicken breasts from the deli. Instead of cooking a turkey, buy eight ounces of unsliced cooked turkey breast, then dice at home.

KEEP A WELL-STOCKED PANTRY. Besides canned broth, canned tomatoes, and pasta, have a few nonperishables on hand to add interest to those basics: chutneys, dried mushrooms, flavored vinegars, etc.

It's time-savvy to group similar items together and always restock in the same way. Knowing what you have on hand saves you time rummaging through cabinets when cooking and making shopping lists.

USE YOUR FREEZER. If you're grilling two chicken breasts, why not grill twelve and store ten? Besides storing defrost-n-serve meals and leftovers, use the freezer for quick-to-thaw meal makers such as frozen veggies, cooked brown rice, and freezer-to-oven proteins.

USE THE MICROWAVE. Stick frozen chicken breasts in the microwave, cook them at full power for two to three minutes, then slice the still partially frozen chicken into strips. Then throw them into a skillet for stir frying—they'll be thin enough to heat through quickly.

USE SPEEDIER COOKING METHODS. Forget roasting or braising and go with broiling, sautéing, or steaming. And try pressure cooking, particularly for preparing whole grains. When you're most pressed for time, you can cut cooking time by a third. And invest in good sharp knives. You may not even need to haul out the food processor or chopper.

CUT DOWN ON CLEANUP. Try to keep the number of utensils to a minimum and use nonstick pans whenever possible. And the best tip: get someone else to wash the dishes!

DESIGNATE A FALL-BACK RECIPE. Find one recipe you love and tape it on your cupboard door nearest your stove. Keep the ingredients for the recipe on hand at all times so you can make it when time is crunched to the max.

My Quickest Meals

CHEESE QUESADILLAS: Fat-free tortillas sprinkled with shredded part-skim cheddar cheese and drizzled with salsa—folded and browned in nonstick skillet till cheese melts. Serve with apple slices.

BAKED SPAGHETTI: Place cooked angel hair pasta in a sheet pan and top with one jar of Classico Tomato Basil Sauce. Sprinkle with 1 lb. of shredded mozzarella cheese. Bake for 8-10 minutes at 375 degrees or until cheese is browned. Serve with "Salad in a Bag" with a low-fat vinaigrette dressing.

VEGETABLE TORTILLA PIZZA: Brush a large flour tortilla with Classico's Tomato and Basil Sauce, top with your choice of chopped veggies, and sprinkle with grated mozzarella. Bake until lightly browned and crisp (about 5 minutes) at 450 degrees. Serve with baby carrots for a munchie.

GRILLED CHICKEN SANDWICH: Place hot grilled marinated chicken breast (from your freezer!) on whole grain bread or bun with lettuce, tomato, and salsa or Dijon mustard. Serve with raw veggies and fresh fruit.

SMOKED TURKEY AND WHITE BEAN SOUP: Make precooked smoked turkey breast into soup with chicken stock and cannelini beans. Serve with raw veggies and fruit.

QUICK TACO SALAD: Rinse canned black beans and spice with creole seasoning. Sprinkle with shredded part-skim cheddar cheese. Heat and serve over mixed greens with crumbled baked tortilla chips and salsa. Serve with sliced oranges.

EVEN QUICKER GREEK SALAD: Top mixed greens (from a bag) with crumbled feta cheese, sliced cucumber, tomatoes, and peppers. Drizzle with low-fat vinaigrette and serve with toasted petite pita and fresh fruit.

CHEESE BAKED POTATOES: Microwave potatoes for four minutes each, cut open and top with cooked broccoli florets and part-skim cheese. Microwave again until cheese melts. Top with nonfat sour cream. Serve with salad with low-fat vinaigrette dressing.

High-Energy Recipes

On the following pages are menus that incorporate all of my principles for energizing eating. These recipes and menus are assembled from my books *Eat Well-Live Well*, *Food for Life*, and *The Good Life: A Healthy Cookbook (Creation House)*. Each menu is made up of separate recipes that have been designed to form a pleasing whole of contrasting tastes, textures, colors, and nutritional balance. Use them as points of departure, reorganizing the meals as you wish, taking a recipe from one meal and adding to another. Substitute green beans if you don't have asparagus, leave out a spice or herb if you don't have it available. You can use foods on hand to create something new and personally yours.

I have analyzed each recipe for its nutritional value. Besides the calories, carbohydrate, protein, and fat grams, I have included information about sodium and cholesterol for those of you watching these numbers as well. The fat grams are also expressed in terms of the percentage of calories derived from fat in each particular dish. My meals are designed with less than 25 percent of the calories from fat, with the average dish yielding 17 percent. Individual recipes that may be higher in percentage of fat calories are paired with those having low or no fat to balance the whole meal properly.

I have used these profiles to plan balanced meals that give you appropriate levels of nutrients, as well as

If you are in need of immediate energy, want to stabilize your blood sugar, or are in the midst of high stress, the Quick Energy Meal Plan is for you.

plenty of flavor and ease of preparation. Portion sizes may need to be adjusted to fit your own calorie requirements, which will vary according to your age, size, weight, level of activity, and even stress levels. So don't get obsessed with counting every calorie you eat. Instead, focus on eating great foods, prepared in great ways, that will give you great energy!

High-Octane Breakfasts

Orange Vanilla French Toast

4 egg whites, lightly beaten
1/2 tsp. ground cinnamon
1/2 cup skim milk
4 slices whole wheat bread
2 tablespoons frozen, unsweetened orange juice, concentrate, undiluted
4 tablespoons all-fruit jam
1 tsp. vanilla
nonstick cooking spray

Beat together the egg whites, milk, orange juice concentrate, vanilla, and cinnamon. Add the bread slices one at a time, letting the bread absorb the liquid; this may take a few minutes. Coat a skillet with nonstick cooking spray and heat. Gently lift each bread slice with a spatula and place it in the skillet; cook on each side until golden brown. Serve each slice of toast topped with 1 tablespoon all-fruit jam or all-fruit pourable syrup. Freeze the leftovers in individual freezer bags. When ready to use a slice, toast it to thaw and heat. Makes four servings, each giving 1 complex carbohydrate (the bread), 1 ounce protein (the egg whites and milk), and 1 simple carbohydrate (the juice and all-fruit jam).

NUTRITIONAL PROFILE PER SERVING
28 g carbohydrate; 8 g protein; 1.5 g fat; 11% calories from fat;
2 mg cholesterol; 250 mg sodium; 152 calories

❖ QUICK TIP ❖

*Keep two empty shoeboxes in your freezer to store
ready-made meals. Put main-dish portions in one box,
complements to the meal (rice, pastas, vegetables)
in the other box.*

Breakfast Sundae Supreme

1/2 banana, quartered lengthwise
1/4 cup crushed unsweetened pineapple
1/2 cup nonfat ricotta cheese
2 tablespoons Grape-Nuts or low-fat granola
1/4 cup strawberries, sliced
1 tsp. honey or all-fruit pourable syrup

Place the banana quarters star-fashion on a small plate. Scoop ricotta cheese onto the center points. Surround with the other fruit; then sprinkle with cereal. Drizzle with honey or all-fruit syrup. One serving gives 1 complex carbohydrate (cereal), 2 ounces protein (ricotta), and 2 simple carbohydrates (fruit).

NUTRITIONAL PROFILE PER SERVING
42 g carbohydrate; 15 g protein; 1 g fat; 4% calories from fat;
5 mg cholesterol; 111 mg sodium; 224 calories

Hot Apple Cinnamon Oatmeal

2/3 cup old-fashioned oats
1 tsp. vanilla
1 1/2 cups skim milk
1/2 tsp. cinnamon
1/2 cup apple or white grape juice, unsweetened
1/2 tsp. pumpkin pie spice
2 tbsp. raisins, dark or golden

In a small pot, bring the oats, milk and juice to a boil. Cook for 5 minutes, stirring occasionally. Add raisins, vanilla, cinnamon, and pumpkin pie spice. Remove from heat, cover the pot and let the oats sit for 2 to 3 minutes to thicken. This recipe also works well in the microwave. Combine all ingredients and cook for 5 to 6 minutes on high. Makes 2 servings, giving 1 complex carbohydrate (oats), 1 ounce protein (milk), and 1 simple carbohydrate (juice and raisins).

NUTRITIONAL PROFILE PER SERVING
29 g carbohydrate; 11 g protein; 1 g fat; 5% calories from fat;
3 mg cholesterol; 97 mg sodium; 169 calories

Baked Breakfast Apple

1 small Golden Delicious apple, cored
1 tablespoon raisins
2 tablespoons old-fashioned oats
2 tablespoons apple juice
1/4 tsp. cinnamon
1/2 cup nonfat ricotta cheese

Place the apple in a microwavable bowl. Mix together oats, cinnamon, and raisins. Fill the cavity of the cored apple with the mixture. Pour the apple juice over the apple, and cover it with plastic wrap. Microwave on high for 1 minute. Turn the dish around halfway and microwave for 1 minute more. Spoon the ricotta cheese onto a plate, and top it with the apple and the heated juice mixture. Makes 1 serving, giving 1 complex carbohydrate (oats), 2 ounces protein (ricotta), and 1 simple carbohydrate (apple, juice, and raisins).

NUTRITIONAL PROFILE PER SERVING
30 g carbohydrate; 14 g protein; 1 g fat; 6% calories from fat;
23 mg cholesterol; 100 mg sodium; 183 calories

❖ QUICK TIP ❖

Spend one hour each week preparing some of the basics that will make each night's meal a healthy delight with minimum effort. For example, make a batch of tomato sauce for use with pasta or as a topping for meat or pita pizzas.

High-Octane Lunches

Pita Pizzas

1 whole-wheat pita, cut in half into rounds (like a saucer)
2 tbsp. spaghetti sauce
3 oz. or 3/4 cup part-skim or nonfat mozzarella cheese, shredded
1 small apple, cut into wedges

Preheat oven to 375 degrees. Place the two pita circles on a baking sheet. Spread each one with half of the spaghetti sauce and top each with half of the cheese. Bake for 8 to 10 minutes or until cheese is bubbly. Serve with apple wedges. Makes 1 serving, giving 2 complex carbohydrates (pita bread), 2 ounces protein (cheese), and 1 simple carbohydrate (sauce).

NUTRITIONAL PROFILE PER SERVING
37 g carbohydrate; 22 g protein; 12 g fat; 36% calories from fat;
24 mg cholesterol; 570 mg sodium; 344 calories

Smoked Turkey and White Bean Soup

1 tsp. olive oil
2 cloves garlic, minced
1 can (14 oz.) whole tomatoes, drained
2 tbsp. chopped fresh basil (or 2 tsp. dried)
6 cups chicken stock (fat free/low salt)
2 cans (19 oz. each) or 4 cups cooked cannelini or white beans,
drained and rinsed
1 lb. smoked turkey, rough chopped
1/2 tsp. creole seasoning
1 tsp. Mrs. Dash seasoning

Spray a large stockpot with cooking spray. Add olive oil and bring to low heat. Add garlic and cook, stirring, about 1 minute. Add tomatoes and basil; simmer for 5 minutes, crushing the tomatoes with stirring spoon. Pour in chicken stock and simmer over medium heat. Stir in cannelini beans and smoked turkey along with the seasonings. Heat through. Serve with mixed green salad. Makes 5 servings (3 cups each), giving 2 complex carbohydrates (beans), 4 ounces protein (turkey and beans), 1 simple carbohydrate (tomatoes), and added fat (olive oil).

NUTRITIONAL PROFILE PER SERVING
38 g protein; 34 g carbohydrates; 8 g fat; 20% calories form fat;
66 mg cholesterol; 1120 mg sodium; 364 calories

Swiss Stuffed Potatoes

4 baking potatoes (about 5 oz. each)
1/2 cup part-skim or nonfat ricotta cheese
1/4 teaspoon salt
1/4 teaspoon black pepper
6 oz. part-skim or 1 1/2 cups nonfat mozzarella cheese, shredded
paprika
2 cups mixed, chopped seasonal fruit

Preheat oven to 400 degrees. Wash the potatoes and bake for 1 hour until done. Or microwave potatoes by pricking and cooking on high for 8 minutes, turning and microwaving for another 8 minutes. Once cooked, cut the potatoes in half length-wise and scoop out most of the pulp, leaving a 1/4-inch shell. In a bowl, mash the potato pulp with the ricotta cheese, salt, and pepper. Stir in the mozzarella cheese and spoon the mixture into the potato shells. Sprinkle with paprika. Increase the oven temperature to broil; broil the stuffed potato shells for 3 to 5 minutes or until they are heated through and lightly browned on top. Serve each potato with 1/2 cup mixed, chopped fruit. Makes 4 servings of 2 halves each. Each serving gives 1 com-plex carbohydrate (potato), 2 ounces protein (cheese), and 1 simple carbohydrate (fruit).

NUTRITIONAL PROFILE PER SERVING:
28 g carbohydrate; 17 g protein; 9 g fat; 24% calories from fat;
34 mg cholesterol; 513 mg sodium, 339 calories

❖ QUICK TIP ❖

*For extra-quick stir-fry, use frozen bags of
assorted vegetables.*

Terrific Tuna Grill

2 cans (6 1/2 oz. each) solid white tuna, water-packed, drained
1/2 cup carrots, shredded
1 stalk celery, diced
1 apple, diced (1/2 cup)
2 tbsp. light mayonnaise
2 tbsp. orange juice
2 tbsp. plain, nonfat yogurt
1 tsp. Dijon-style mustard
1/2 tsp. creole seasoning
2 plum tomatoes, sliced
8 slices 100% whole-wheat bread
nonstick cooking spray

Combine tuna, carrots, celery, and apple. In a separate bowl stir together mayonnaise, orange juice, yogurt, mustard, and creole seasoning until blended. Pour the mixture over the salad, stirring to coat it. Divide the salad into 4 portions, spreading each portion onto one slice of bread. Top each with 2 slices of tomato and the other slice of bread. Spray a skillet with nonstick cooking spray and heat on medium high. Grill the sandwiches until brown. Makes 4 servings, each giving 2 complex carbohydrates (bread), 3 ounces protein (tuna), and 1 simple carbohydrate (veggies and fruit).

NUTRITIONAL PROFILE PER SERVING
37 g carbohydrate; 28 g protein; 4.7 g fat; 14% calories from fat;
30 mg cholesterol; 567 mg sodium; 300 calories

❖ QUICK TIP ❖

For basic, quick salads, tear romaine lettuce and top with tomato, no-oil Italian dressing, and a sprinkle of grated cheese.

Greek Chicken and Pasta Salad

12 oz. smoked (or roasted) chicken breast
1 recipe of Greek Pasta*
2 cups fresh spinach, washed, stemmed, and snipped
2 cups romaine or red leaf lettuce
1 cup radicchio leaves, torn or extra romaine
4 plum tomatoes, quartered
1/2 cup feta cheese, crumbled
1/4 cup Greek Vinaigrette**
2 tbsp. chopped fresh herbs (cilantro, basil, rosemary, thyme)

Cut chicken breast into chunks; mix with Greek Pasta. Place spinach, romaine, and radicchio on each of four plates; top with pasta salad. Add tomatoes and crumbled feta cheese. Ladle 1 tablespoon of Greek Vinaigrette onto each plate, then sprinkle with herbs. Serves 4, each giving 2 complex carbohydrates (pasta, spinach, lettuce, and radicchio), 4 ounces of protein (chicken and cheese), and 1 simple carbohydrate.

NUTRITIONAL PROFILE PER SERVING
28 g protein; 41 g carbohydrate; 9 g fat; 22% calories from fat;
0 mg cholesterol; 720 mg sodium; 357 calories

*Greek Pasta

4 cups bowtie pasta, cooked and cooled
1 red bell pepper, finely diced
1 green bell pepper, finely diced
1 yellow pepper, finely diced
1/2 red onion, finely minced
2 tbsp. chopped fresh herbs (cilantro, basil, rosemary, thyme)
1 cup Greek Vinaigrette (recipe follows)
1 tsp. creole seasoning

Combine all ingredients. Allow to marinate at least one hour. Makes 4 servings. Each serving gives 2 complex carbohydrates (pasta), and 1 ounce protein.

NUTRITIONAL PROFILE PER SERVING
7 g protein; 35 g carbohydrate; 4 g fat; 18% calories from fat;
0 mg cholesterol; 420 mg sodium; 204 calories

**Greek Vinaigrette

1/4 cup olive oil
1 1/4 cups rice wine vinegar
3/4 cup chicken stock (fat-free/low salt)
1/4 cup Dijon mustard
1/2 cup pepperoncini juice
1 tbsp. minced garlic
1 tbsp. minced shallots
1 tsp. creole seasoning
2 tbsp. chopped fresh herbs (cilantro, basil, rosemary, thyme)
1 tbsp. chopped fresh oregano (or 1 tsp. dried)

In a large bowl, whisk together ingredients. Refrigerate. Makes 24 servings, 2 tablespoons each.

NUTRITIONAL PROFILE PER SERVING
0 g protein; 1 g carbohydrate; 2 g fat; 66% calories from fat;
0 mg cholesterol; 139 mg sodium; 21 calories

Turkey Tortilla Roll

1 10-inch whole-wheat flour tortilla
1 tsp. Dijon-style mustard
2 oz. skinned turkey breast, fully cooked and sliced
1/2 oz. (1 tbsp.) part-skim milk cheddar cheese, grated
1/2 tomato, cut into strips
1/4 cup romaine lettuce, shredded
freshly ground black pepper, if desired
celery and carrot sticks
10 fresh strawberries or other fruit

Spread the tortilla with mustard. Top with the sliced turkey, cheese, tomato, lettuce, and pepper, if desired. Fold in the sides of the tortilla, roll it up burrito-style, and cut it in half. Serve with celery, carrot sticks, and fresh fruit. Makes 1 serving, giving 1 complex carbohydrate (tortilla), 3 ounces protein (turkey and cheese), and 1 simple carbohydrate (fruit).

NUTRITIONAL PROFILE PER SERVING
31 g carbohydrate; 25 g protein; 7.9 g fat; 24% calories from fat;
49 mg cholesterol; 194 mg sodium; 296 calories

Quick Mexican Chili

1 lb. ground turkey
1 small onion, diced
1 small green pepper
1 can (15 1/2 oz.) tomato sauce
1 can (15 1/2 oz.) crushed tomatoes
1 can (15 1/2 oz.) kidney beans, rinsed
2 tsp. chili powder
1 tsp. garlic powder
1/2 tsp. creole seasoning
1 1/2 cups brown rice, cooked

Crumble the ground turkey into a hard plastic colander. Microwave the turkey on high for 3 minutes; stir and break it apart. Add the onion and the green pepper. Microwave another 3 to 4 minutes until the turkey is browned. Spoon the meat and vegetables into a saucepan and add the remaining ingredients. Cook the mixture over medium-high heat until it boils. Simmer uncovered for 10 more minutes, stirring to prevent it from burning. Serve over 1/4 cup cooked brown rice in a large soup bowl. Freeze the remaining servings in individual freezer bags for later use.

Makes 6 servings (1 1/2 cups each), giving 1 complex carbohydrate (rice), 3 ounces protein (turkey and beans), and 1 simple carbohydrate (veggies).

NUTRITIONAL PROFILE PER SERVING:
32 g carbohydrate; 25 g protein, 1 g fat; 4% calories from fat; 47 mg cholesterol; 742 mg sodium; 237 calories

❖ QUICK TIP ❖

Substitute plain, nonfat yogurt or fat-free ricotta cheese in dips and sauces calling for sour cream or mayonnaise—there are so many sauces and so little time!

Vegetable Tortilla Pizza

2 fajita-sized, fat-free tortillas
2/3 cup fat-free mozzarella/Parmesan cheese blend, divided
(2 parts mozzarella, 1 part Parmesan)
1/4 cup Classico Tomato & Basil Sauce
1 tbsp. chopped fresh herbs (cilantro, basil, rosemary, thyme), divided
6 strips red bell pepper
6 strips green bell pepper
6 strips yellow bell pepper
3 broccoli florets
1/4 small red onion, diced

Preheat oven to 450 degrees. Lay one tortilla on round wire mesh pan. Sprinkle it with 2 tablespoons cheese blend; top with remaining tortilla. Brush the top of tortilla with Tomato & Basil Sauce and sprinkle with 1/2 tablespoon herbs. Lay peppers, broccoli, and onions on top of sauce. Sprinkle with the remaining cheese blend. Bake until lightly browned and crisp, about 5 minutes. Sprinkle with remaining herbs. Makes 1 serving, giving 2 complex carbohydrates (tortillas), 4 ounces of protein (cheese blend), 1 simple carbohydrate (tomato sauce).

NUTRITIONAL PROFILE PER SERVING
36 g protein; 48 g carbohydrate; 10 g fat; 21% calories from fat;
64 mg cholesterol; 700 mg sodium; 426 calories

❖ QUICK TIP ❖

Keep raw veggies marinating in no-oil Italian dressing for a quick salad. Add a small can of tuna to make a main dish and cooked pasta to make a whole meal.

High-Octane Dinners

Shrimp Creole
(3 OUNCES PROTEIN AND 1 COMPLEX CARBOHYDRATE)

Steamed Broccoli
(2 SIMPLE CARBOHYDRATES)

Caesar Salad
(YOUR HEALTHY MUNCHIE AND AN ADDED FAT)

Shrimp Creole

white wine Worcestershire sauce
1 lb. fresh medium shrimp
nonstick cooking spray
2 tsp. olive oil
2 cloves garlic, finely chopped
1 small red onion, finely chopped
1/2 teaspoon creole seasoning
2 cups tomato puree, canned
1/2 cups chicken stock, defatted
2 plum tomatoes, cut lengthwise into strips
2 cups brown rice, cooked
1 lemon wedge
sprinkle of fresh chopped herbs (such as basil or thyme)
2 cups broccoli, steamed

Marinate the shrimp in Worcestershire sauce for 1 hour. Spray nonstick skillet with nonstick cooking spray; heat with 2 teaspoons of olive oil. Add garlic and onions and sauté until they are softened and transparent. Season shrimp with creole seasoning and sauté quickly in the hot pan. Add tomato puree and chicken stock, heating through. Add tomato strips at the end of cooking. Mound 1/2 cup rice in the center of each of four plates; spoon 1/4 of shrimp and sauce over each rice mound. Garnish with a lemon wedge and sprinkle with the chopped herbs. Serve with the steamed broccoli. Makes 4 servings.

NUTRITIONAL PROFILE PER SERVING
38 g carbohydrate; 23 g protein; 4 g fat; 14% calories from fat;
66 mg cholesterol; 357 mg sodium; 279 calories

Caesar Salad

4 cups romaine lettuce, washed and torn
1 clove minced garlic
1 1/2 tbsp. olive oil
1/2 tsp. dry mustard
1 tsp. Worcestershire sauce
1/8 tsp. coarse black pepper
1/8 tsp. salt (optional)
1 coddled egg*
juice of 1 lemon
1/4 cup Parmesan cheese, grated
croutons (from 2 slices whole-wheat bread sprinkled with garlic powder and toasted until brown)

Rub the bottom and sides of a large salad bowl with the garlic; leave the garlic in the bowl. Add the oil, the mustard, the Worcestershire sauce, and the spices; beat together with a fork or wire whisk. Add the chilled romaine lettuce; toss well. Crack the coddled egg over the salad; add the lemon juice and toss until the lettuce is well covered. Top with the Parmesan cheese and croutons. Toss well and enjoy! Makes 6 servings.

*Coddle an egg by immersing the egg in its shell in boiling water for 30 seconds. This makes it safe to eat.

NUTRITIONAL PROFILE PER SERVING
6 g carbohydrates; 4 g protein; 5 g fat; 51% calories from fat; 39 mg cholesterol; 152 mg sodium; 81 calories

❖ QUICK TIP ❖

*Be sure to go shopping after you've eaten.
Do not go to the grocery store with your blood
sugars low and your appetite out of control.*

Black Bean Soup over Rice
(2 OUNCES PROTEIN AND 2 COMPLEX CARBOHYDRATES)

Spinach and Apple Salad
(1 SIMPLE CARBOHYDRATE)

Black Bean Soup over Rice

nonstick cooking spray
2 tsp. olive oil
2 cloves garlic, finely chopped
1 small red onion, diced
2 cups chicken stock, defatted
4 cups cooked black beans (if canned, rinse and drain)
1 tsp. creole seasoning
1 tsp. ground cumin
2 cups brown rice, cooked
3 limes, halved
1 cilantro leaf (optional)

Spray a nonstick pan with a nonstick cooking spray. Heat the olive oil in the pan. Add the onion and the garlic; sauté until translucent. Add the chicken stock, 2 1/2 cups of the cooked black beans, and the creole seasoning. Bring the mixture to a gentle boil and cook until the amount is reduced by a third; puree in a blender or a food processor until smooth. You may refrigerate this now for serving later. Then reheat the bean puree; if necessary, thin the puree with additional chicken stock to make it smooth. When serving, place cup of the cooked brown rice in each of 6 bowls. Top with 1/4 cup of the reserved whole black beans. Add 1 cup heated bean puree. Squeeze 1/2 lime over each bowl. Garnish with a cilantro leaf if desired. Makes 6 servings.

NUTRITIONAL PROFILE PER SERVING
47 g carbohydrate; 12 g protein; 3 g fat; 12% calories from fat;
0 mg cholesterol; 367 mg sodium; 261 calories

Spinach and Apple Salad

2 tbsp. canola oil
1 1/2 tsp. basil
1 tsp. onion powder
1/2 tsp. salt (optional)
1/8 tsp. pepper
3/4 cup apple juice
2 tbsp. apple cider vinegar
1/2 cup orange segments
4 cups spinach, torn in pieces
2 cups apple, thinly sliced

In a small bowl prepare the dressing by combining the oil, basil, onion powder, salt, and pepper; set aside for 10 minutes to allow the flavors to blend. Stir in the apple juice and vinegar. In a large bowl, combine the spinach, apple, and oranges. Toss with 1/2 cup dressing; serve immediately. Refrigerate the remaining dressing for other salads or a marinade. Makes 6 servings.

NUTRITIONAL PROFILE PER SERVING
12 g carbohydrate; 1 g protein; 2 g fat; 26% calories from fat; 0 mg cholesterol; 30 mg sodium; 69 calories

❖ QUICK TIP ❖

Make a list of what foods you plan to buy—and stick to the plan. Let grocery shopping be a time to look for foods that benefit your body.

Snapper with Tomato and Feta Cheese
(4 OUNCES PROTEIN AND 1/2 SIMPLE CARBOHYDRATE)

Corn on the Cob
(1 COMPLEX CARBOHYDRATE)

Cabbage Slaw
(YOUR HEALTHY MUNCHIE AND 1/2 SIMPLE CARBOHYDRATE)

Snapper with Tomato and Feta Cheese

2 ripe tomatoes, sliced
2 cloves garlic, finely minced
1 lb. red snapper fillets (1/2-inch thick)
1 tsp. dried basil
1 lemon, thinly sliced
1/2 tsp. dried oregano
1/3 cup feta cheese, crumbled

Arrange the tomato slices on the bottom of a 9-inch glass pie dish. Sprinkle the garlic over the tomatoes and arrange the fish over the top. Sprinkle the basil over the fish. Place the lemon slices on top; sprinkle with the oregano and the crumbled feta cheese. If possible, let the fish sit for about 30 minutes. Cover the fish with vented plastic wrap and microwave on high for 4 1/2 to 5 minutes. Let it stand for 5 minutes. Makes 4 servings.

NUTRITIONAL PROFILE PER SERVING
7 g carbohydrate; 27 g protein; 6 g fat; 28% calories from fat;
60 mg cholesterol; 318 mg sodium; 190 calories

Cabbage Slaw

3 cups shredded cabbage
1 cup shredded red cabbage
1 cup shredded carrot
1/4 cup finely chopped onion
1/4 cup rice wine vinegar
1/4 cup unsweetened pineapple juice
1 tbsp. Dijon-style mustard
1/8 tsp. salt
1/8 tsp. pepper

Combine the cabbages, carrot, and onion in a medium bowl; toss gently. Combine the vinegar with the remaining ingredients and stir well. Add to the cabbage mixture and toss gently. Cover and chill at least 1 hour. Makes 8 servings (1/2 cup each).

NUTRITIONAL PROFILE PER SERVING
5 g carbohydrate; 1 g protein; 2 g fat; 43% calories from fat;
0 mg cholesterol; 124 mg sodium; 42 calories

❖ QUICK TIP ❖

Resist the temptation to feed others the very foods you are choosing to avoid. Don't feed your friends and loved ones energy-robbing, health-robbing foods.

Marvelous Meat Loaf
(3 OUNCES PROTEIN AND 1 COMPLEX CARBOHYDRATE)

Corn on the Cob
(1 COMPLEX CARBOHYDRATE)

Colorful Green Beans
(1 SIMPLE CARBOHYDRATE)

Romaine Salad
(YOUR HEALTHY MUNCHIE)

Marvelous Meat Loaf

2 lbs. ground round or ground turkey
2 cups old-fashioned oats
3/4 cup minced onion
1/4 green pepper, minced
2 eggs, slightly beaten
1/2 tsp. salt
1/2 tsp. pepper
1 tbsp. Worcestershire sauce
1 tsp. dry mustard
1/4 cup skim milk
3/4 cup tomato sauce

In large bowl, mix together all ingredients except 1/2 cup of the tomato sauce. Shape meat into 2 loaves and place in loaf pans sprayed with cooking spray. Spread the additional 1/2 cup tomato sauce on top. Bake in 400 degree oven for 40 minutes. Makes 10 servings.

NUTRITIONAL PROFILE PER SERVING
11 g carbohydrate; 22 g protein; 9 g fat; 25% calories from fat;
98 mg cholesterol; 257 mg sodium; 213 calories

Colorful Green Beans

1 lb. green beans
1/2 cup chopped onion
1/2 tsp. salt (optional)
1/4 tsp. pepper
2 medium tomatoes, peeled and cut into 8 wedges
1 tsp. olive oil
1/2 cup chopped celery

Remove strings from beans; wash and cut diagonally into 2-inch pieces. Heat oil in skillet, add onion and celery to skillet, and sauté until tender; add beans, salt, and pepper. Cover and simmer 10 minutes, stirring occasionally. Add tomato; cover and cook an additional 5 minutes. Makes 4 servings.

NUTRITIONAL PROFILE PER SERVING
9 g carbohydrate; 2 g protein; 1 g fat; 17% calories from fat;
0 mg cholesterol; 4 mg sodium; 53 calories

❖ QUICK TIP ❖

Don't starve yourself on the day of a big party or meal. You will throw off your metabolism. Eat small, evenly spaced meals throughout the day, which will keep your metabolism and appetite in better control.

Oven Baked Chicken
(3 OUNCES PROTEIN)

Peas Rosemary
(1 COMPLEX CARBOHYDRATE)

Carrot Salad à la Difference
(1 SIMPLE CARBOHYDRATE)

Oven-Baked Chicken

2 egg whites, lightly beaten
2 cups Nutri-Grain Golden Wheat cereal, crushed
1/4 tsp. pepper
6 chicken half-breasts, deboned and skinned
1 tbsp. water
1/4 tsp. garlic powder
1/4 tsp. seasoned salt (optional)

Mix together egg and water in shallow dish; set aside. Combine crushed cereal and spices. Dip chicken in egg mixture, then dredge in cereal mixture, coating well. Arrange in baking pan coated with cooking spray. Bake, uncovered, at 350 degrees for 45 minutes, or until tender. It tastes like fried chicken! Yields 6 servings.

NUTRITIONAL PROFILE PER SERVING
7 g carbohydrate; 27 g protein; 4 g fat; 21% calories from fat;
108 mg cholesterol; 123 mg sodium; 176 calories

Peas Rosemary

1 pkg. frozen peas, cooked and drained
2 tsp. olive oil
2 cloves minced garlic
1/4 cup chopped onion
1/4 tsp. pepper
1 tsp. rosemary
1/4 tsp. salt (optional)

Sauté garlic and onion in oil until tender. Add rosemary, salt, and pepper; continue to sauté one more minute. Toss with peas. Makes 4 servings.

NUTRITIONAL PROFILE PER SERVING
12 g carbohydrate; 4 g protein; 2 g fat; 23% calories from fat;
0 mg cholesterol; 95 mg sodium; 83 calories

Carrot Salad à la Difference

1 lb. coarsely grated carrots
2 medium apples, grated
1 cup firm, plain, nonfat yogurt
1/2 cup crushed unsweetened pineapple
1/2 cup raisins

Combine all ingredients and chill. Makes 12 1-cup servings.

NUTRITIONAL PROFILE PER SERVING
14 g carbohydrate; 2 g protein; 0 g fat; 0% calories from fat;
0 g cholesterol; 28 mg sodium; 62 calories

❖ QUICK TIP ❖

Use legumes (dried beans and peas) as a main dish. These meat substitutes make a high nutrition, low-fat meal; try them at least twice a week.

Spaghetti Pie
(2 OUNCES PROTEIN, 1 COMPLEX AND 1 SIMPLE CARBOHYDRATE)

Marinated Veggies**
Fresh Fruit Salad

Spaghetti Pie

6 oz. vermicelli or whole-wheat pasta
2 tsp. olive oil
1/3 cup grated Parmesan cheese
2 egg whites, well beaten
1/2 lb. ground turkey*
1/2 cup chopped onion
1/4 cup chopped green pepper
8 oz. can stewed tomatoes
6 oz. can tomato paste
3/4 tsp. dried oregano
1/4 tsp. salt (optional)
1/2 tsp. garlic powder
1 cup part-skim ricotta cheese
1/2 cup shredded mozzarella cheese

Cook pasta according to package directions; drain. Stir olive oil and Parmesan cheese into hot pasta. Add egg whites, stirring well. Spoon mixture into a 10-inch pie plate. Use a spoon to shape the spaghetti into a pie shell. Microwave uncovered on high 3 minutes or until set. Set aside. Crumble turkey in a colander, stir in onion and green pepper. Cover with plastic wrap and microwave on high 5 to 6 minutes, stirring every 2 minutes. Let drain well. Put into a bowl and stir in tomatoes, tomato paste, and seasonings. Cover and microwave on high 3 1/2 to 4 minutes, stirring once. Set aside. Spread ricotta evenly over pie shell. Top with meat sauce. Cover with plastic wrap and microwave on high 6 to 6 1/2 minutes; sprinkle with mozzarella cheese. Microwave uncovered on high 30 seconds, or until cheese melts. Makes 6 servings.

*May substitute ground round; drain well after cooking
**Variety of raw veggies marinated in no-oil Italian dressing, sprinkled with Parmesan cheese

NUTRITIONAL PROFILE PER SERVING
21 g carbohydrate; 23 g protein; 8 g fat; 29% calories from fat;
46 mg cholesterol; 349 mg sodium; 248 calories

Sicilian Chicken and Pasta
(3 OUNCES PROTEIN, 1 COMPLEX AND 1 SIMPLE CARBOHYDRATE)

Mixed Green Salad
(HEALTHY MUNCHIE)

Sicilian Chicken and Pasta

4 boneless, skinless chicken breasts
2 tablespoons cornstarch
1/2 tsp. creole seasoning
1/4 tsp. Tabasco sauce
1/2 tsp. dried basil
2 cloves minced garlic
1/2 tsp. dried oregano
1/4 cup grated Parmesan cheese
2 cans (15 1/2 ounces) Italian-style tomatoes
1 small package of angel hair pasta (8 ounces)

Preheat the oven to 425 degrees. Sprinkle the chicken with the seasoning, and pat it with the herbs. Place the chicken in a baking dish, and cover it with foil. Bake for 15 minutes. While the chicken is baking, pour the canned tomatoes into a medium saucepan and add the cornstarch, Tabasco sauce, and the garlic. Cook the mixture until it is thickened, about 5 minutes. After 15 minutes, remove the chicken from the oven, pouring off any liquid from the pan. Pour the heated sauce over the chicken and sprinkle the grated cheese on top. Place the pan back in the oven and cook, uncovered, for ten more minutes. Cook the pasta according to the package directions. Drain and place it on a platter. Top the pasta with the chicken and the sauce. Makes four servings, each giving 1 complex carbohydrate (pasta), 3 ounces protein (chicken and cheese), and 1 simple carbohydrate (tomatoes).

NUTRITIONAL PROFILE PER SERVING
27 g carbohydrate; 25 g protein; 9 g fat; 20% calories from fat;
50 mg cholesterol; 878 mg sodium; 396 calories

Pollo Pasta Primavera
(4 OUNCES PROTEIN, 2 COMPLEX AND 2 SIMPLE CARBOHYDRATES)

Mixed Green Salad
(HEALTHY MUNCHIE)

Pollo Pasta Primavera

4 oz. dry bowtie pasta
2 tsp. extra virgin olive oil
2 cloves minced garlic
1/2 medium red onion, chopped
1 tsp. dried chopped basil
1 tsp. dried chopped oregano
1 tbsp. dried chopped parsley
1 bunch broccoli, cut into florets, blanched
1 cup baby carrots, blanched
1 head cauliflower, cut into florets, blanched
1/2 cup frozen green peas, thawed
1/2 cup mushroom, chopped
12 oz. chicken breast, poached and chopped
1 cup chicken stock (fat-free/low salt)
1/2 cup skim milk
2/3 cup shredded, part-skim cheddar or mozzarella cheese
kosher salt and cracked black pepper to taste

In a large saucepan, cook bowtie pasta in salted water. Drain. Spray a large non-stick pan with cooking spray. Add olive oil and heat over medium-high heat. Lightly sauté garlic and red onion; add herbs and continue to sauté for 30 seconds. Add vegetables and chicken breast; lightly sauté and then add chicken stock and milk. Let cook for another 1 to 2 minutes until liquid reduces slightly. Add cheese to pan with pasta. Toss to heat. Sprinkle with additional grated Parmesan to serve. Makes four servings. Each serving gives 4 ounces protein (chicken and cheese), 2 complex carbohydrates (pasta), 2 simple carbohydrates (vegetables).

NUTRITIONAL PROFILE PER SERVING
52 g carbohydrate; 33 g protein; 9 g fat; 19% calories from fat;
72 mg cholesterol; 775 mg sodium; 421 calories

Your Grocery

Your grocery list should include "real foods" rather than highly processed packaged food. For example, real orange juice or frozen concentrate is far superior to fortified orange-flavored drink. Think "Mother Nature" when you shop. Your grocery store is crammed full of healthful foods, and you don't have to shop at a health food store to get them.

Pam Smith's Energy Edge Grocery List

GRAINS AND BREADS
Brown rice:
❏ Instant
❏ Long-grain
❏ Short-grain
❏ Wild rice
❏ Arborio rice
❏ Cornmeal
❏ Couscous

Tortillas, flour:
❏ Mission
❏ Buena Vida fat-free
❏ whole-wheat bagels
❏ 100% whole-wheat bread *("whole" is the first word of the ingredients)*
❏ whole-wheat English muffins
❏ whole-wheat hamburger buns

whole-wheat or artichoke pasta:
❏ Angel hair
❏ Elbows
❏ Flat
❏ Lasagna
❏ Orzo
❏ Penne
❏ Spaghetti
❏ Rotini (spirals)

❏ whole-wheat pastry flour
❏ whole-wheat pita bread

CEREALS *(whole grain and less than 5 grams of added sugar):*
❏ All Bran With Extra Fiber
❏ Cheerios
❏ Familia Müesli
❏ Granola
❏ Grape-Nuts
❏ Grits
❏ Kashi
❏ Kellogg's Just Right
❏ Kellogg's Low-Fat Granola
❏ Kellogg's Nutri-Grain Almond Raisin
❏ Kellogg's Raisin Squares
❏ Nabisco Shredded Wheat
❏ Ralston Müesli
❏ Post Bran Flakes
❏ Wheatena

Oats:
❏ Old-fashioned
❏ Quick-cooking

Puffed cereals:
❏ Rice
❏ Wheat
❏ Shredded Wheat 'N Bran

Unprocessed bran:
❏ Oat
❏ Wheat

CRACKERS
Crispbread:
❏ Kavli
❏ Wasa
❏ Crispy cakes
❏ Health Valley graham crackers
❏ Harvest Crisps 5-Grain *(not all whole grain, but good for variety)*
❏ Mr. Phipps Rice Cakes:
❏ Plain
❏ Quaker Banana Nut
❏ Ry Krisp

DAIRY
❏ Butter
❏ Light butter

Cheese: *(low-fat — fewer than 5 grams of fat per ounce):*

Cheddar:
- Kraft Fat-Free
- Kraft Natural Reduced Fat
- Cottage cheese *(1% or nonfat)*

Cream cheese:
- Philadelphia Light (tub)
- Philadelphia Free
- Farmer's
- Jarlsberg Lite

Mozzarella:
- Nonfat
- Part-skim
- String cheese

Nonrefrigerated:
- Laughing Cow Light
- Parmesan

Ricotta:
- Nonfat
- Skim milk

- Sun-Ni Armenian String
- Egg substitute
- Eggs
- Milk (skim or 1%)
- Nonfat sour cream
- Nonfat plain yogurt
- Stonyfield Farm yogurt

CANNED GOODS
- **Chicken broth:**
- Swanson's
- Natural Goodness

- Evaporated skim milk
- Hearts of Palm

Soups:
- Healthy Choice

- Pritikin
- Progresso:
- Hearty Black Bean
- Lentil

Tomatoes:
- Paste
- Sauce
- Stewed
- Whole

CONDIMENTS
- Honey

Hot pepper sauce:
- Pickapeppa sauce
- Shriracha Chili Sauce
- Jamaican Hell Fire
- Tabasco

Mayonnaise:
- Light
- Miracle Whip Light

Mustard:
- Dijon
- Spicy hot

- Pepperoncini peppers

Salad dressing:
- Bernstein's Reduced Calorie
- Good Seasons
- Kraft Free
- Jardine's fat-free Garlic
- Vinaigrette
- Pritikin

- Soy sauce (low sodium)
- Salsa or picante sauce

Spices and herbs:
- Allspice
- Basil
- Black pepper

- Cayenne
- Celery seed
- Chili powder
- Cinnamon
- Creole seasoning
- Curry
- Dill weed
- Five spice
- Garlic powder
- Ginger
- Mrs. Dash Original Blend
- Mrs. Dash Garlic and Herb Seasoning
- Mustard
- Nutmeg
- Oregano
- Onion powder
- Paprika
- Parsley
- Pepper, cracked
- Rosemary
- Saffron
- Salt
- Thyme

Fresh herbs:
- Basil
- Chives
- Cilantro
- Ginger
- Parsley
- Rosemary
- Thyme

- Vanilla extract

Vinegars:
- Balsamic
- Cider
- Red wine
- Rice wine
- Tarragon
- White wine

❑ Worcestershire sauce

FRUITS
Fresh fruits:
❑ Apples
❑ Apricots
❑ Bananas
❑ Berries
❑ Cherries
❑ Dates *(unsweetened, pitted)*
❑ Grapefruit
❑ Grapes
❑ Kiwi
❑ Lemons
❑ Limes
❑ Mango
❑ Melon
❑ Nectarines
❑ Oranges
❑ Papaya
❑ Peaches
❑ Pears
❑ Pineapple
❑ Plantains
❑ Plums

Dried fruits:
❑ Apricots
❑ Peaches
❑ Pineapple
❑ Raisins *(dark and golden)*
❑ Mixed

VEGETABLES
❑ Asparagus
❑ Beets
❑ Bell peppers
❑ Broccoli
❑ Brussels sprouts
❑ Cabbage
❑ Carrots
❑ Cauliflower
❑ Celery
❑ Corn
❑ Cucumbers
❑ Eggplant
❑ Garlic
❑ Green beans
❑ Greens
❑ Hot peppers
❑ Kale
❑ Mushrooms
❑ Okra
❑ Onions
❑ Peas
❑ Red Potatoes
❑ Radicchio
❑ Romaine lettuce
❑ Salad greens
❑ Shallots
❑ Simply Potatoes hash browns
❑ Spinach
❑ Squash *(yellow, crookneck)*
❑ Sugar snap peas *(frozen)*
❑ Sun-dried tomatoes
❑ Sweet potatoes
❑ Tomatoes
❑ Whote potatoes
❑ Zucchini

BEANS AND MEATS
Beans and peas:
❑ Black
❑ Chickpeas/ garbanzo beans
❑ Cannelini
❑ Kidney
❑ Lentils
❑ Navy
❑ Pinto
❑ Split peas

Beef (lean):
❑ Deli-sliced
❑ Ground round
❑ London broil
❑ Round steak

Fish and seafood:
❑ Clams
❑ Cod
❑ Grouper
❑ Mussels
❑ Salmon
❑ Scallops
❑ Shrimp
❑ Snapper
❑ Swordfish
❑ Tuna

Lamb:
❑ Leg
❑ Loin chops

Pork:
❑ Canadian bacon
❑ Center cut chops
❑ Tenderloin

POULTRY
Chicken:
❑ Boneless breasts
❑ Legs/thighs
❑ Whole fryer

Turkey:
❑ Bacon
❑ Breast
❑ Ground
❑ Deli-sliced
❑ Whole

Veal:
❑ Chops
❑ Cutlets
❑ Ground

Water-packed cans:
❑ Chicken
❑ Salmon
❑ Tuna
❑ Charlie's Lunch Kit

MISCELLANEOUS

All-fruit spreads and pourable fruit:
- ❑ Knudsen
- ❑ Polaner
- ❑ Smucker's Simply Fruit
- ❑ Welch's Totally Fruit

- ❑ Baking powder
- ❑ Baking soda

Bean dips:
- ❑ Jardine's
- ❑ Guiltless Gourmet

- ❑ Bread crumbs

Cooking oils:
- ❑ Canola
- ❑ Olive

- ❑ Cornstarch

Fruit Juices *(unsweetened):*
- ❑ Apple
- ❑ Cranberry-apple
- ❑ White grape
- ❑ Orange

- ❑ Nonstick cooking spray

Nuts/seeds *(dry-roasted, unsalted):*
- ❑ Peanuts
- ❑ Sunflower kernels
- ❑ Pecans
- ❑ Walnuts

Pasta sauce:
- ❑ Pritikin
- ❑ Classico Tomato and Basil
- ❑ Ragú Chunky Gardenstyle

- ❑ Peanut butter *(natural)*
- ❑ Phyllo dough

Popcorn:
- ❑ Orville Redenbacher's Natural
- ❑ Light or Smart Pop microwave pocorn
- ❑ Plain kernels

Tortilla chips:
- ❑ Baked Tostitos
- ❑ Guiltless Gourmet

- ❑ Water *(spring or sparkling)*

Wine:
- ❑ Dealcoholized
- ❑ Red
- ❑ White

NOTES AND OTHER ITEMS

_____

_____

_____

_____

_____

_____

_____

_____

_____

_____

_____

_____

_____

_____

PART SIX

Energy for living
and loving

CHAPTER TWENTY-SEVEN

The power of spirituality

A s vital as meeting your physical needs is to maintaining the Energy Edge, it is also important to identify the needs of your soul and to begin nourishing them in effective ways. In addition to the energizers we've already discussed, there are "Power Points for the Soul" that are every bit as crucial to your vitality.

The scientific and medical fields are beginning to identify one incredible current of energy and healing: spiritual connection. Studies from around the world are emerging with suggestions that humanity has been created "wired for God"—with medical evidence that prayer and other specifically religious practices can help significantly to heal the ravages of stress, fatigue, and illness.

The latest revelations about spirituality and wellness emphasize the vitality of three powerful components of religious experience: 1) personal faith, 2) religious practice, and 3) prayer. One such study, conducted at Duke University Medical Center, revealed that religious practice—prayer, faith in God, Bible reading—was a powerful tool in the fight against illness and stress. Another showed that regular prayer can work to slow a person's heart and breathing rates, lower blood pressure, and slow brain waves, all without drugs or surgery.

Relaxation techniques, such as meditation, have also been shown to have a positive physiological effect, but without significant enhancement in emotional well-being. But when these techniques are combined with prayer, many subjects report a significant drop in feelings of anxiety and stress.

Studies have also revealed a powerful impact on health through prayer, even from a distance. Patients receiving prayer from another part of the country—even if they don't know they are being prayed for—have experienced health benefits that groups not being prayed for have not.

A physician often quoted in discussions about faith and wellness is Dr. Jeffrey S. Levin of Eastern Virginia Medical School. In a review of medical research on the effect of religious faith on the outcomes of such conditions as heart disease, cancer, tuberculosis, and such, he reported that of twenty-seven studies in which patients had some religious connection, twenty-two showed a significant effect on the subjects' disease state.

More Than A Body

I believe that we humans are three-parted beings: body, soul, and spirit—and that through the body and soul, our spirit interacts with the physical world. And I believe that all three parts—body, soul, and spirit—need to be nourished. Caring for the whole being means that we do special things to develop and maintain the inherent potential and health of our physical, emotional, and spiritual components.

I first came to this belief when I was twenty-four. At this point, my life had all of the trappings of success—but I felt empty and without purpose. My relationships weren't working; I was very tired. Although I had been raised with religious tradition, that was all I had known: religion, not personal connection with my Creator.

From this very low place, I looked up and came into a relationship with a living God who could impact every part of my life. That relationship and connection changed my life and why I was living it. My message of wellness took on a higher significance. It was now focused on caring for the magnificently created human being, on helping people walk in the fullness of all they were created to be. I became convinced that striving for wellness without addressing spiritual and emotional health is a futile exercise—we are a sum of our parts, and soul needs cannot be separated from physical ones. Living well—physically, emotionally, and spiritually—continues to be my message today.

And life continues to be hard—even harder than when I was twenty-four. I'm balancing even more roles and responsibilities, often feeling overwhelmed and torn by the opportunities I'm called upon—and expected—to fulfill. It's a battle. I have commitments to my husband, daughters, parents, extended family, friends, church, and profession. My need to spiritually connect and nourish my soul has become even more urgent to me as a choice for energized living. I have come to realize that this choice is really a daily one for who or what I'm allowing to take control of me—and my life.

Unleashing Your Soul Power
The Power of Letting Go

I read a story recently that describes well these day-by-day choices I must make. It's a story about a fellow named Harry, and it sounded all too familiar to me! One afternoon, Harry had gone mountain climbing. All in all, things were going very well. Then suddenly, the path he was walking on gave way, taking Harry with it. With flailing arms, Harry managed to grab a small branch on the side of the mountain. Holding on for dear life, he screamed, "Help! Help! Is anybody up there?"

Miraculously, the clouds parted, and a beam of light illuminated Harry as he hung tenuously from the branch. A voice—clearly the voice of God—spoke directly to Harry and said, "Yes, Harry, I am here, and I am God. Harry, I will save you. I am all that is good, all that is true, all that is life, and all that has meaning. Let go, Harry; I will save you. Trust in me; just let go."

Harry thought hard about this. Then with a sudden burst of conviction, he looked up the mountain and shouted, "Is anybody *else* up there?"

How often have you been in Harry's position? I find myself there every day, sometimes every moment of each day! I find ways to hold on tighter and tighter to what I know won't support me, rather than letting go and being lifted—rescued—by the arms of God.

For me, letting go moves me from a closed fist to an open-handed attitude toward life. It allows me to live free of the self-made obstructions that litter my path. To let go of what I am tightly holding onto is a process of relinquishing the belief that I can control or manipulate things, situations, or people to make me happy. It is releasing the responsibility of controlling others, allowing them instead to be responsible for their own choices.

Try as I might, I can't control the traffic. What I can control is my choice of when I leave for my destination, and the route I take.

Try as I might, I can't control the choices of my teenage daughters. I can help them to see the consequences of their actions (and enforce them!), and I can help them to grow in their decision-making skills. I can teach them my chosen values by living a life based on those values. And, while I can "make" them do certain things, I can't make them BE a certain way. It's not my job to control them, or anyone else. Controlling won't rescue me from feeling uncomfortable with the inevitable fact that I'm not in charge of the universe.

The energy requirement to hold onto things that I was never meant to control wears on my soul, my mind, *and* my body. The body "wear" shows up in strong physical messages: headaches, illness, fatigue. These messages are voices telling me, warning me, that I have been diverted from a spiritual path. These tangents manifest as physical and emotional "dis-eases."

The bottom line: I have come to realize that I have been given, spiritually, all the peace, love, and power that I could ever need. What I *do* need is to remove the blockades to this peace—anything that dams the powerful river of life running through my spirit, soul, and body. My daily time-outs to connect with God are quiet times of reading and still times of prayer, asking for and receiving strength and direction in my daily choices. I emerge refreshed, with inspired insights and fresh promise.

Like many people, I have a personal definition of what being connected "spiritually" means. My personal religious orientation is that of the traditional Christian faith, and my use of the term "spiritual" is rooted in the Bible and historic Old and New Testament theology. I don't believe that God is a disconnected higher power that I am struggling to reach up to. I believe that God, in his love, has reached down to humanity; he empowers me by living within me. By inviting his Spirit to dwell within my spirit, my life is linked with the unlimited love and power of the divine.

> *The scientific and medical fields are beginning to identify one incredible current of energy and healing: spiritual connection.*

Choosing to let go and live rescued by God is my path to living a life of spiritual connection and significance. Rather than trying in all of my human power to make things work, I now know, deep in my soul, that I will see change through prayer, not by attempting to control situations. I pray about things I'm concerned about, asking for guidance and strength, rather than focusing on results. I ask for a heavenly perspective about specific problems, an ability to see with clear vision. And because giving up control over the events and details of my life has been a very important result of spiritually connecting with God, I pray for more growth in that area.

The Power of Gratitude

Expressing gratitude for my life exactly as it is has also been a huge breakthrough for me, enabling me to live in the NOW, rather than waiting until everything is perfect. I remember as a child being reminded that I should be grateful for all the good things I had in my life. I learned to say grace, say my bedtime prayers, and to be thankful for loving parents, plenty of food, a warm bed, a big family, good health, and all the other things I took for granted. Whenever I'd erupt with a tirade about how miserable and unfair life was, and that I never got anything I wanted, I was usually encouraged to "count my blessings." What I *didn't* have seemed to cloud my vision of what I *did* have.

Yes, I was a kid then. As an adult, I have come to place high value on having an "attitude of gratitude." I've learned about the power that comes through giving thanks and rejoicing in all things. But now and again, the little girl inside me rises up and starts to whine about the way things are—or are not. At those times, I really need my dad to send me to my room with a pencil and paper to make a list of all the things I have to be grateful for!

Interestingly, there is both spiritual and scientific wisdom behind gratefulness; it is imperative to our energy and well-being that we be thankful for what we have. The wisdom behind this is that our mind is a magnet; we gravitate toward what we think about most. If I continually grouse that nothing ever works for me, that there is never enough time, that nobody cares for me, that only bad things come my way, then I will attract more of the same. Because my eyes are only on my lack, I will overlook opportunity, refuse offers of help, and continue to propel myself into emotional and spiritual bankruptcy. If my inner landscape convinces me that I miss out and go without, I will create an external life for myself according to that belief system.

Looking at the good things doesn't come naturally. If there are ten things right and one thing wrong, we tend to pay attention to what is wrong. When we get eleven questions right on a math test, we focus on the nine that we missed. When we have a toothache, we don't notice that the rest of us feels great. We call this being "realistic." But I have observed that if a person consistently concentrates on what he doesn't have, he will get less and less of what he wants. Alternatively, the people who are continually rejoicing in what life gives them lead active and fulfilling lives. Those who have the most beautiful lives are those who value life highly.

I'm not suggesting that the answer to life's problems comes through a Pollyanna-like denial of the things that trouble us; rather, I believe that true joy transcends circumstances. An attitude of gratitude is born deep within our souls and flows from our spiritual connection. I believe that the world has been given an abundance of peace, love, and joy by our Creator. When I don't see those things in my everyday life, I must ask what is blocking my view. Have my problems become my priorities? Are the obstacles in my life all I can see? My vision becomes distorted when I look at life only in terms of my expectations or others' standards.

When it comes to becoming more physically, emotionally, and spiritually healthy, attitude is everything. How can we make positive changes in our lifestyle if we view them as dampers on our fun and freedom? How can we feel better if all we do is whine?

The Transcendent Spirit

I know that spiritually I have been given an incredible gift—spiritual eyes to see with 20/20 vision. When I can view the world through the eyes of my Creator, it makes all the difference in my mood, my attitude—and my energy.

At some point in our lives, we all experience feelings and circumstances that challenge us, sometimes beyond what we think we can handle. Evil in the world is real, and human nature is capable of many ugly things. Tragic circumstances can change our lives in a heartbeat, with seemingly no explanation. And it is these very difficult, baffling challenges that the spirit can transcend.

I know that I can get on my feet only by getting on my knees. My connection with God can be made in the beauty of nature, through the power of music, in the quietness of church or a garden, through the reaching out of my heart to another's. I believe that coming before my Creator with a genuine willingness to receive what he has planned for me, with faith that he loves me beyond measure, is the single most important step I can take in a day. The result of that spiritual connection is renewed strength and energy to live my life on life's terms.

Connecting spiritually nourishes the soul the same way that food and water nourish the body. With a powerhouse of strength within, unlimited resources can be tapped that allow us to soar!

CHAPTER TWENTY-EIGHT

The power of reflection

Sometimes even when you're eating for energy, sleeping well, and exercising regularly—when you're bravely fending off the energy vandalizers and overcoming the neutralizers—you are still exhausted. Chances are there are other factors—such as overwhelming worry, grief, fear, or anger—that may be sapping your energy. While some of your external circumstances are beyond your control, you may be able to release the blockades that are log jamming your energy flow by carefully examining your responses to those circumstances. Honest, courageous personal reflection is a crucial link in the energy chain.

Face Your Feelings

Internalizing emotions like hurt, anger, or shame can result in a dramatic drain on your personal energy. But facing and embracing your feelings allows you to experience emotions that might normally be bottled up or stuffed down with food, alcohol, or drugs.

You were created with feelings that you can't ignore. They don't just "go away" because you deny them. If repressed, feelings linger and grow stronger, eventually becoming a driving force in your life. But your feelings don't have to control you; they do not have to dictate or control your behavior. Just because you're angry doesn't mean that you have to scream and hurt someone, nor does it mean that you are "unspiritual."

All feelings are legitimate; there is nothing good or bad about any of them. They are all part of who we humans were created to be. Emotions produce energy (E-motion = Energy in motion), and if we don't release that energy, we must work hard to keep it in. And feelings packed down inside can come out "sideways" through physical ailments: headaches, joint and muscle pain, insomnia. Instead of crying, we get headaches. Instead of saying we don't want to go someplace with someone, we get stomach cramps. Instead of saying no to another work project, we push ourselves to exhaustion and develop fatigue or high blood pressure—or we overeat to "reward" ourselves for our labors.

Our bodies react whether we like it or not. The unreleased energy robs us of our well-being by causing increased tension, anxiety, or depression. The fact is, the feelings we don't express must be repressed, causing us to be depressed, and opening the door to becoming oppressed.

Picture the emotional you as a teacup in the center of your soul. Every unexpressed emotion gets poured into the teacup. Day after day you allow the unexpressed and the unidentified to drip into the cup until it is filled to the brim. Then, at some bizarre moment, maybe when the coat hangers won't separate properly, the whole teacup spills out, emptying in a torrent of rage. You really aren't that angry about the coat hangers, but heaven help the coat hangers, your closet, and any poor soul who happens to be in the house. Feelings that aren't expressed legitimately will ultimately be expressed some way, somehow.

To prevent emotions from building up internal barriers to your energy flow, it is vital to allow yourself to feel whatever feelings are inside, fighting the desire to judge them as good or bad. The feelings are simply a readout on where you are in life. Once you've identified them, you can choose to express them in a positive, proactive way.

You can release the feelings in a number of positive ways: create something with your hands, sing, talk, write, exercise, pray. Give yourself permission to feel your emotions and process them.

Write Your Way To Health

The most effective—and freeing—step I took in this area was to begin keeping a journal. In the privacy of my journal's pages, I can frankly say whatever I am feeling.

I had been encouraged to keep a journal for quite a while, but I always protested "That's not for me!" I didn't feel that I had the time, patience—or the privacy. What if someone got hold of it?

A loving friend challenged me to look honestly at my protests, asking if they were really excuses. Out of respect for her guidance, I began to write. I found ten extra minutes in my day, and I embarked on a miraculous journey to a new kind of freedom.

My system had always been to deal with emotions in a "Scarlett O'Hara" way: "I don't have time to think about that today, I'll deal with it tomorrow." But tomorrow became today when I began journaling. I found that by looking at my life's happenings, I could get in touch with how I *felt* about what was occurring. I discovered that under my "Nice and Busy" smile, there was often hurt and anger.

> *Honest, courageous personal reflection is a crucial link in the energy chain.*

Slowly my self-consciousness began to fade, and I was able to write out more and more of the feelings and thoughts that were flooding my soul and spirit—and draining my energy reserves. By turning those feelings within, I was forming a brick wall around my heart—a wall that was separating me from love, peace, and joy. Through journaling I came to know the reality of words penned by wise King Solomon: "A heart at peace gives life to the body." (Proverbs 14:30)

One very powerful function of my journaling is to help me to identify the many roles I have in my life, and where I am emotionally, spiritually, physically, and relationally—overall and in each unique role. This was how I started journaling—with a blank piece of paper before me, assessing if I was "empty" or "full" in these different arenas of life. You might want to try the same exercises I did when I started putting pen to paper.

WHERE AM I?

SPIRITUALLY, I AM:
connected |_____|_____|_____|_____| in a vacuum

EMOTIONALLY, I AM:
stable |_____|_____|_____|_____| confused

PHYSICALLY, I AM:
strong and well |_____|_____|_____|_____| sick and tired

RELATIONALLY, I AM:
connected |_____|_____|_____|_____| distant

By taking a close look at my "soul fuel" gauge, I could go beyond all I was doing and look at *how* I was doing. This was difficult for me; my answer to "How are you?" had always been "Fine." A great teacher, Richard Lord, once declared that that word means: Feeling Insecure Neurotic and Emotional. How true that was for me!

Once a week in my withdrawal and quiet time, I continue to ask myself these same questions. They jump start my journaling process—and keep me honest!

If you need a jump start as well, these practical tips from my experience may help.

Journaling Tips
THE JOURNAL. I've used an inexpensive spiral-bound notebook at times, and I've used my portable computer. The important thing is to provide yourself with a designated place to record your feelings and reflections. This will be your personal storehouse and place for exploration. If your journal is not portable, keep a small notebook with you for jotting down people, places, or things that

impact you in some way during the day. You can examine your feelings about them on paper at your regular journaling time.

WHERE TO JOURNAL. Choose a place in your house that has a particular ambiance for you—somewhere to "go to" when you write. If this room, desk, table, corner, bed, or sitting area can also accommodate small objects to stir your memory and creativity, all the better. You may want to keep a box of old pictures, trinkets, and mementos in your writing area to help get your reflective juices flowing. If you feel particularly dry, unfeeling, or "wordless" at journaling time, look at an old picture. Remember what you were doing, what you were wearing, how you felt. Write about that—or draw a picture of your feelings.

WHEN TO JOURNAL. If possible, choose a consistent time of day for your writing. It will depend on your circumstances and can be changed or extended as you go. Just choosing the time—the best time—helps to establish a sense of purpose and value from the beginning. Choose a time of day that best suits who you are. Not a morning person? You may do best journaling on your lunch break, or before you go to sleep.

> *Internalizing emotions like hurt, anger, or shame can result in a dramatic drain on your personal energy.*

Some of my clients choose one morning a week to write. It's their day. I write most every day for about fifteen minutes. Because I look at journaling as a gift of time to myself, I feel cheated when I miss a day for some reason. Once a week, I carve out more time to write about things that require more thought and reflection.

WHAT TO JOURNAL. What do I write about? I start every journal day with *Yesterday, I....* Yes, I often start with what has happened to me, but I don't stop there. I write about how I *feel* about what has happened—or what might happen in the future.

You can write about your fears, inadequacies, regrets, joys, hopes, and discoveries. When you feel happy, write it down. When you feel sad or angry or rejected, tell your journal. Let your journal help you identify what you're feeling. The act of writing forces you to name vague, free-floating feelings. Believe me, there is enormous power in calling a spade a spade. Once you name how you feel about something, you begin to take power over it. It is no longer a faceless attacker.

It may be difficult for you to just pull your feelings about a situation out of the air. To facilitate feeling-identification, you may benefit by making a list of strong emotion-words: RAGE, REJECTION, JEALOUSY, JOY, FEAR, LOVE. Choose one, then write quickly (without censoring yourself) whatever things, events, people, fragments are called up by that word. Don't worry about grammar, the bizarre, the ridiculous.

You may find that using word pictures can better help you to name your feelings and trace their origin. For example, Carolyn writes, *"I feel like life is an incredibly blue skyed, sunny Autumn day—and I'm in the middle of a forest clearing filled with beautiful fallen leaves. The leaves are vivid colors, of all shapes and sizes— much like the things and the people in my life. The wind is swirling the leaves all around me, and it smells wonderful! The sun is shining and warming me. I love my life!"*

But on another day, just a week later, she writes, *"I feel trapped, suffocated, as if I can't get air. Like I'm stuck under an overturned innertube with flailing legs and arms holding me down—my face is pushed into the slime of the lake's bottom. The mud and weeds are so thick, I can't breathe. I'm too weak to fight through the people."*

By identifying and naming your feelings, you are giving yourself the power to choose how best to process them. Remember, feeling an emotion is *not* a problem. It is what you do with a feeling that takes you toward or away from health and wholeness. As you start to write about a feeling, you can start to let go of it. As you look at it on paper, you can gain a new perspective about the situation that may have caused the feeling in the first place. Why did a certain person or situation trigger such a feeling? Did it remind you of something in your childhood? Did it scratch a memory? Did it make you feel ashamed or inadequate? Is there tension with another person that you need to discuss? These and similar questions can be answered only in a still, quiet time.

It may be enough to feel the emotions and acknowledge them. Whatever the case, don't cling to unhealthy feelings. Letting go of them opens up space within you for joy, freedom, health—and energy. Your journal can be a powerful tool on your journey to living on the Energy Edge.

CHAPTER TWENTY-NINE

The power of vision

risis is often the wake-up call that tells us it's time to change—or else. For you, it may be something as simple as an expensive suit that no longer fits, screaming at you to get in shape. It may be a doctor instructing you to change your eating habits—or else go on medication for diabetes, hypertension, or elevated cholesterol. It may be that you are picking up every cold, flu, and virus you're exposed to—and you're sick and tired of being sick and tired.

The desire to change is foundational to living on the Energy Edge. But that desire must become a *passion* if successful lifestyle upgrades are to hold fast over the long term.

It is impossible to be passionate, for long, about a list of rules. So don't focus on the behavior you're trying to avoid; instead, look at what you want to obtain. You are destined to hit whatever you have your eyes on!

Living On Purpose

I greatly admire people who live life on purpose—with a deep-seated personal mission. Nothing sustains energy over the long haul like knowing *why* we're here, why we're upgrading our lifestyle, and what we're ultimately trying to accomplish. When life becomes a race and our bodies become machines, we need to ask ourselves, "What do I want? What are my dreams? Why am I here?"

Being energized by our life's purpose is one of the keys to staying motivated to take care of ourselves. An Old Testament proverb says, "A man without vision casts off restraints." Without vision, or understanding our destination, we have no way to focus on goals and directions. We are easily distracted—our energy is neutralized or vandalized—and we flounder through life. In contrast, having a vision—a clear sense of our purpose and dreams—delivers energy to our whole lifestyle.

The question about our desires and dreams is not to be confused with goal identification. It's not a "to do" list; rather, it's an uncovering of our vision for what we want in our life next month, next year, in five years.

How about you? Do you have a dream? Do you know what you're living life for? Without a personal vision, it will be difficult for you to treat yourself with respect and take care of your body, mind, and spirit. After all, the whole reason to eat well, drink water, exercise, reflect, and relate is to produce the energy to live meaningfully and purposefully. Without vision, you may as well eat, drink, and be merry—for tomorrow you may die. If you don't feel valuable or purposeful, taking care of yourself will seem unimportant. It will be easy to get caught in destructive lifestyle traps. If you think you are worthless, you will treat yourself accordingly.

I believe that none of us is a mistake; we have not been created by chance. We are each unique, with a valuable and vital purpose. We deserve to be treated well. If you believe this, you will make positive choices for self-care.

Embracing Your Personal Vision

If you can identify the WHY of living on the Energy Edge, then the WHAT won't be so difficult. Clarifying your personal vision gives you something to live for, to look forward to. And anticipation brings with it hope—a terrific energy booster.

To find directions to your personal destination, you first need to know where you are. Think about it: you're in a foreign country, looking for the inn where you plan to stay overnight. You call for directions and the first question you are asked is, "Where are you now?" Knowing precisely where you're coming from will determine your success in getting to where you want to go.

Many have been successful in their quest to identify their personal direction and vision with the following exercises:

Write a character sketch of yourself from a different perspective:

1. You've just been chosen for the star of "This is Your Life." Pretend you're the editor who's writing your bio.
2. Imagine your mate writing home about you for the first time. How would you be described?
3. Think of a turning point in your life, a time when you were at a fork in the road and you made a difficult but definite choice. Now imagine what your life would be like, and where you would be today, if you had traveled down the other road. Start with "What if I had...."
4. Imagine a typical day in your life five, ten, or twenty years from now. What would it be like? How would you be spending it?
5. Spend time answering these questions:

❖ "When in high school, I valued _____; today I value _____."
❖ "If I weren't doing what I do now, I would be doing _____."
❖ "Although I've chosen the right career, the things that would make me feel more fulfilled and happy are _____."
❖ "If I could be anyone, I would be _____."
❖ "_____ is the person I admire most, because _____."
❖ "The things I like most about myself are _____."
❖ "The things I dislike most about myself are _____."
❖ "The things in my lifestyle I would most like to see changed are _____."

❖ "The accomplishments in life I am most proud of are _____."
❖ "I regret not having done _____."
❖ "Some ways I help others are _____."
❖ "Ways I plan to help others are _____."
❖ "The person who influences me the most is _____."

These questions can help you look back at where you've been, consider where you are now, and set the course for where you want to go. Life assessment is the first vital step in answering the question, "What is my life about?" This is a right-brain activity, creatively dreaming without boundaries or "I can'ts" in place.

I urge you to write out your answers to the questions because writing forces your left brain into action, doing what it does best: intellectualizing and scrutinizing, giving your dreams critical evaluation. Seeing them on paper gives you a firm direction, makes them official, and provides you with the inspiration and motivation to stay the course.

Now ponder these questions:

❖ "I am passionate about _____."
❖ "If I didn't have to worry about money, I would work
   at _____."
❖ "I believe I was put on this earth to_____."
❖ "I will be remembered by future generations for _____."
❖ Imagine being on your deathbed, and a reporter asks you to
   reflect on your life—not whether you've been "good or bad,"
   but what you've done that brought you or others fulfillment.
   What do you still want to do?

Tapping Into The Passion

As you've read *The Energy Edge*, what have you learned? What has most struck a chord, inspiring you to make positive changes? Maybe it's a practical energizer: you realize you need to drink water, you need to choose a better place for lunch than KFC, or you need to sleep more, and sleep better. Or maybe it's that you need to worry less, and nurture your spiritual life more.

Before you turn this last page, and resolve "to do" a whole list of new things, take a few moments to write down the specific things that you want to experience in your life. Only after identifying these desires should you determine what action steps are necessary to obtain them. Again, if you can determine your destination, you can better determine the steps you need to take to get there. You may want to make a list that looks something like this:

❖ *I want to live a life FILLED with energy.*
❖ *I want to be fit; I want a body that works for me.*
❖ *I want to be well; I want to an immune system that protects me from illness and disease.*
❖ *I want to provide the framework for a healthy attitude about food for my children.*

If you want to live a life filled with energy, you must identify the action steps you need to employ to enjoy an energized lifestyle. If you want to live with a stronger immune system, what are the action steps that will allow you to get well and stay well?

One last point to remember: it's your day-to-day lifestyle choices that count most for health and wellness—not what you eat or drink at a ball game or on your birthday. One day, even a week, of less-than-great choices will not send your body head-first into disease or nutrient deficiency. What is important is getting started with the energy and excitement of a new way of living! It's progress, not perfection, that counts. You may start with eating breakfast, for the first time since you were five years old. You may try drinking the water your body is so thirsty for. Or, you may start placing more value on the power of a well-tended soul.

Whatever you choose as your first step, the rewards will come quickly: terrific energy, great moods, superior concentration, alertness, a better memory, getting well. Ultimately, our energy has everything to do with how alive we feel, and what we're living for. May you live the life of your dreams; may your days be ever vibrant with the Energy Edge!

Books and Tapes
BY PAMELA M. SMITH, R.D.

The Good Life—A Healthy Cookbook

A wonderful feast of Pam's most savory recipes. This cookbook offers complete meals for breakfast, lunch, and dinner, plus scrumptious desserts and power snack ideas. Cooking techniques and plate design are presented easily and practically. Food that is good for you tastes great! For the novice or gourmet cook, this book is designed for everyone to enjoy—and it's beautiful! It's a deluxe hardback edition with full-color photography.

Eat Well—Live Well

A *bestseller*, this is Pam's nutrition guidebook for healthy, productive living. This large, hardback edition presents "The Ten Commandments of Good Nutrition" in detail, along with directions for menu planning, grocery shopping, and dining out—from fast food to gourmet. The large cookbook section contains innovative, time-saving recipes. Meal plans for weight loss and weight management are included.

The Seven Secrets to Living the Good Life
A VIDEO AND AUDIO TAPE SERIES

In this dynamic four-tape series (audio or video), you will learn how to fit healthy living into your busy schedule, turbo-charge your metabolism and your immune system, seal all the "energy leaks" in your body, and recharge and refuel while you lean down. Pam demonstrates her healthy and delicious cooking techniques and gives easy tips for traveling and dining out healthfully. Available in: 4–tape video series or 4–tape audio series.

Food for Life

More than a nutrition guide and cookbook, *Food for Life* shows how to eat smart and walk in abundant life. It presents Pam's secrets for staying fit, fueled, and free—helping you to explore your relationship with food and yourself. You will discover how to choose the best food, manage weight, and develop a proper perspective for feeding yourself emotionally and spiritually. Meal plans, recipes, and specific action steps are included. Available in: deluxe hardback edition or paperback edition.

Food for Life: A-Day-at-a-Time

This thirty-day devotional guide will equip and empower you to break free from the food trap—forever!

Come Cook with Me

This is the kid's cookbook! A wonderful way to teach children nutrition through the basics of healthy cooking. Great for picky eaters! Includes kid-proven recipes, how to set a table, and some great lessons on manners. Handwritten and fun.

Alive and Well in the Fast Lane

A lighthearted and informative nutritional guidebook for the whole family—in a fun, handwritten, and illustrated format. Includes tips for healthy eating on the run.

The Food Trap Seminar—Book and Tape Album

Hear Pam present a live seminar asking the question, "Is the

Refrigerator Light the Light of your Life?" Informative and enlightening, this four-tape audiocassette series and book reveals case studies and personal insights into the physical, emotional, and spiritual aspects of food dependencies. Learn how to break free and live free in all areas of life.

Healthy Expectations

A practical guide filled with sound advice on preparing a healthy body for a healthy baby. Pam gives proven strategies for overcoming morning sickness, assuring ideal weight gain, and achieving boundless energy and peak stamina—even while pregnant.

For more information on Pamela Smith's books, tapes, speaking, and seminars/workshops, please write or call:

LifeLine
Press

One Massachusetts Avenue, NW
Suite 600
Washington, DC 20001
800-219-4747

Visit Pam's website at www.pamsmith.com

Index

Recipes